P9-DBK-006

AMERICAN
WARRIOR

AMERICAN WARRIOR

THE TRUE STORY OF A LEGENDARY RANGER

GARY O'NEAL
WITH DAVID FISHER

THOMAS DUNNE BOOKS
ST. MARTIN'S PRESS
NEW YORK

Note to Readers: The names of a few individuals depicted in this book have been changed.

THOMAS DUNNE BOOKS.
An imprint of St. Martin's Press.

Design by Omar Chapa

www.thomasdunnebooks.com
www.stmartins.com

Library of Congress Cataloging-in-Publication Data

O'Neal, Gary.
American warrior : the true story of a legendary Ranger / Gary O'Neal with David Fisher.—First edition.
p. cm
ISBN 978-1-250-00432-1 (hardcover)
ISBN 978-1-250-02275-2 (e-book)
1. O'Neal, Gary. 2. United States. Army. Ranger Regiment, 75th—Biography. 3. United States. Army—Commando troops—Biography. 4. United States. Army—Warrant officers—Biography. 5. Oglala Sioux Tribe of the Pine Ridge Reservation, South Dakota—Biography. 6. Vietnam War, 1961–1975—Personal narratives, American. 7. Vietnam War, 1961–1975—Jungle warfare. 8. Military assistance, American—Nicaragua—History—20th century. 9. Nicaragua—History—1937–1979. 10. United States. Army—Commando troops—Training of. 11. Special forces (Military science)—United States—Biography. I. Fisher, David, 1946– II. Title. III. Title: True story of a legendary Ranger.
UA34.R36O64 2013
355.0092—dc23
[B]

2013003723

St. Martin's Press books may be purchased for educational, business, or promotional use. For information on bulk purchases, please contact Macmillan Corporate and Premium Sales Department at 1-800-221-7945 extension 5442 or write specialmarkets@macmillan.com.

First Edition: May 2013

10 9 8 7 6 5 4 3 2 1

I would like to dedicate this book to those people who trained me, to those people I trained, and all of those brave men and women who have sacrificed all in defense of *America's freedoms.*

Especially to the woman who put things right in my life and who enabled me to come home, Jo D. McEwan, with my love and appreciation.

FOREWORD

After reading this chronicle of escapades, and having known Gary O'Neal and his legend for quite some time now, I can honestly say that perhaps one of the hardest things in life to be is Gary O'Neal. Only to be superseded by being his friend or in most cases his commander.

To some people he is a myth, like the illustrious Corporal Steiner in the Willie Heinrich novel about German soldiers on the Eastern Front in World War II, *The Cross of Iron.* He's that wild man who always seems to survive, often with physical injuries and always with a slightly greater irreverence for command. To others he is the person they hear, fear, and tell tales about, yet they don't really know him or do they really want to.

Now consider this . . . of the citizens in the United States, only 1 percent voluntarily joins the armed forces, for whatever reason. Of that number only 1 percent joins the ranks of the Special Operations community. The top 1 percent of that group makes it in the ranks of the super soldiers in the Joint Special Operations Command (JSOC). Then there are the individuals like Gary O'Neal.

As far as history, O'Neal is the first former member of the Army Golden Knights Parachute Team to gain entry into the Ranger Hall of Fame. Then again he's been a first for many things, so don't even get me started. All kidding aside, O'Neal is one fine piece of work. He's an inspiration to many, and he just won't quit, although I hear that he's been slowing down some lately.

He could be the biblical "Caska" of this generation; doomed by Jesus to wander the earth aimlessly, always as a soldier, until the Second Coming, but for certain he is the Quintessential American Warrior: Airborne, Ranger, Special Forces, bloodied in combat at the age of fifteen, with a blood line that begins with the Lakota Sioux Indian tribe and a heraldry that includes the lodge poles of Black Elk, Red Cloud, Crazy Horse, and Sitting Bull.

Since Maryland was settled in the colonial times of the seventeen hundreds, a member of the O'Neal clan has taken up arms and fought for this country in every conflict, almost timely, like rites of passage. The O'Neal clan merged with the Lakota Sioux when Gary's father returned well decorated from World War II and married into the South Dakota tribe. That made O'Neal a mixed blood to the elders of the tribe. These same elders removed that stigma and welcomed him as a warrior after he proved his spirit in the performance of the sun dance.

To really know O'Neal is to recognize that the only thing he lacks in life is a formal education and probably for the best. He certainly would have intimidated his officers and commanders even more if he would have quoted Shakespeare or any of the great philosophers in Latin or Greek, while debriefing a combat operation or teaching a class on silent killing. One simple axiom has guided his life: If it sounds stupid but it works then it isn't stupid . . . especially if it will get you out of a jam or save lives in combat.

From his childhood to his teens, through his young adult and adult life O'Neal has lived only one way, the hard way, in the face of danger, full speed ahead. He has always and forever pushed himself to the edge, pegging the torque on his pitch to the red line. A few times he's gone over the edge, but he has always made it back, not always in one piece. Above all he has never failed to Charlie Mike—"continue the mission"—and never has he failed a comrade in battle.

This book is his story. It is easy to read but don't you dare attempt any of his antics at home or in training, at least, not without his supervision or his blessing. The era of combat he has survived spans forty years and takes place on every continent in the known world. Many talk the talk but only Gary O'Neal has walked the walk around the world.

President John F. Kennedy. The father of the Green Berets, once said, "The time has come to pass the torch to a new generation." It is my hope that O'Neal's life, his story, and this book serves as a legacy and primer that motivates the next generation of Americans to "Ranger Up" and take on the enemies of this great nation. Anything, anytime, anywhere; O'Neal wouldn't want it any other way.

Gary O'Neal's commitment to life and for the rest of his life is to do just that; teach those who want to learn, talk to those who will listen, and for the few who dare, push them to their outer limits where, who dares, wins. He will guide them to follow in his footsteps, *sua sponte,* so they can blaze their own trail, then, like all good Rangers . . . Lead the Way!

John K. Sinlaub
Major General, U.S. Army (Ret.)

PREFACE

MEMORIAL DAY 2010 AT ARLINGTON NATIONAL CEMETERY IN WASHINGTON, D.C., was a beautiful, sunny day. A nice young lady was standing at the front gate, and as each person entered, she handed them two roses. There was a big box right next to her, and she was reaching down and taking the roses out of that box. Two at a time. When she handed me my two roses, I stopped there and I smiled and I said politely, "Excuse me, ma'm, but you'd better give me that whole box. I got a lot of friends here."

PROLOGUE

OCTOBER 1978, NICARAGUA

I had lost all comprehension of time. I could have been hanging up there in that barn for two days or two weeks. They had tied my hands behind my back and then they lifted me up and slipped the rope over a hook. Then they dropped me down. Both my shoulders were yanked right out of their sockets, my shoulder blades pressed down on my lungs. It didn't matter. I was beyond the physical pain anyway. They asked me all kinds of questions about different people; but I didn't believe their intention was to get information, they wanted to torture me. This was punishment. Nothing more. This was their vengeance for what Somoza's army had done to them. Their desire was to make me suffer—and they did. They took me to extremes.

Sometimes people would come into the barn and beat up on me. They figured I was never leaving that barn, so they didn't take care to hide their faces. I saw them all, I knew what they looked like. I remembered.

I went in and out of consciousness. I focused on the techniques I'd been teaching people about how to resist interrogation. Rather than trying to resist the pain, I accepted it, absorbed it, and controlled it. I knew that the most important thing I could do was keep the pain from cluttering my mind. If I allowed the pain to become so intense that I couldn't focus on anything else, I was done. With my shoulders collapsed I couldn't breathe very well, I could only take short breaths, but I was still able to release some of the pain through my breathing. I could imagine it, encapsulate it, and project it out.

They beat me regularly. If I didn't answer their questions they would hit me, butt stroke me with the back of their AKs, slap me, and smack my shins with boards. If I did mumble some kind of made-up answer, they still hit me. They were enjoying this, and they wanted to keep me alive as long as possible. When the pain got too intense, I forced myself to focus on positive images rather than dwelling on it. This was the one time all those breathing exercises I had been doing through the years really paid off. When I could, I let my spirit soar free and away, as I had been taught by the elders. I projected myself outside of my body, leaving that pain behind me. I tried to be somewhere else. I looked into the fire, just as I had done growing up on my grandfather's farm.

The truth is I was grateful when I lost consciousness.

No matter how much training you have to prepare for that moment, there are some things that pain you so deeply that the human mind can't absorb it. The mind is merciful that way. There are things you see that are beyond understanding, so that you're never sure what's real and what's imagination. I never allow my mind to stay too long on the things that I saw happen in that barn. There are images that come and go; when I let my guard down there are flashes of things that may or may not be real. I try to block it all out, but sometimes in the night, they still sneak through.

My family was murdered in that barn. I woke up and there was my wife lying in a pool of blood, there were my kids lying in a pool of blood. They were being hit and kicked, my wife was being molested, my kids were screaming for me to help them. I lost consciousness.

Before I did, I swore vengeance on all of them.

CHAPTER ONE

> Although there was no legal compulsion to the performance of military duty; yet every man of full age and size was expected to do his full share of public service. If he did not do so, he was "hated out as a coward." Even the want of any article of war equipments, such as ammunition, a sharp flint, a priming wire, a scalping-knife or tomahawk, was thought highly disgraceful. A man who, without a reasonable cause, failed to go on a scout or campaign, when it came to his turn, met with an expression of indignation in the countenances of his neighbors, and epithets of dishonor were fastened on him without mercy.
>
> The Great West, *by Henry Howe (1851)*

I have sat on the mountaintop and seen the eagles soar. I sat on that same small staked-out piece of land where Sitting Bull and Black Elk, Red Cloud, and other great chiefs had sat long before me and looked outside to find themselves. I sat there all alone for four days and four nights, and I said my prayers and sang my songs and asked the elders to guide me to a peaceful place. For a time, my spirit flew with those eagles, but when they went to nest, it came home to me.

When I came down from the mountain, only I knew what I'd left behind.

I know who I am. I know what I've done. I know who I did it for. I don't pretend to be anything but what I am. I'm a soldier; I'm a warrior. I am an American fighting man. For the last half century, wherever American soldiers were fighting an enemy, some piece of me was there. If I wasn't there myself, someone I'd fought alongside or trained to kill silently or taught to survive was there. It didn't matter if it was a jungle, a forest, a field, or a desert, if Americans were on the ground, some part of me was there. I've got plenty of wounds to prove it, although sometimes I think the deepest ones are those you can't see.

My reputation is pretty direct. At Fort Bragg it has always been possible to find experts in almost every kind of warfare: shooting any type of weapon, all the martial arts, surviving on the land, there is always someone there who can teach the best way to do it. When my name was mentioned there, people would respond, "If you want to know about combat, go see O'Neal. He'll teach you how to kill."

Every man is born with the skills of a warrior, but it is the circumstances of his life that put him on that path. When you have to fight to survive, you fight; and if you do survive, then you remember those lessons. The fighting makes you a different person, a harder, tougher person. Then you continue the journey by training your heart, your mind, your body, and your soul to be better prepared for the next time. The next time always comes.

Fighting fills my soul. I've spent my life walking the path of the warrior. I've got nine bullet holes in me, and I've been left for dead twice. I've been cut and stabbed more times than I can count. I have served my country, and I killed the enemies of my country. I killed a lot of them, more than I ever counted. That was my job. It was what I was trained to do, and so I did it to the very best of my ability. I did whatever I needed to do to survive; I didn't think about it, I didn't worry about it, I just did it. I used whatever weapon I could find. I killed the enemy from a long distance, and I looked him right in the face from a few inches away and I killed him.

I got damn good at it.

The O'Neals settled in Maryland in the 1700s, and since then an ancestor of mine has served in every war in our history. My direct ancestor Nathaniel Thurber was a guerrilla fighter in the Massachusetts Line in the Revolutionary War. My fifth great-grandfather John O'Neal signed the Oath of Allegiance and served with the Maryland Militia during the Revolution alongside his son, Peter O'Neal. My fourth great-granduncle Solomon Sparks was a member of Captain John Boyd's "Rangeing Company" from Pennsylvania and was named captain of a company of Pennsylvania Riflemen during the War of 1812.

My great-great-granduncle Emanuel O'Neal was with General Sheridan during the Shenandoah Valley Campaign in the Civil War and is believed to have been present for Robert E. Lee's surrender at Appomattox Court House.

Three weeks after the Japanese bombed Pearl Harbor my grandparents signed the papers that let my father, Chester David O'Neal, enlist in the army, even though he was a minor. He fought with the 88th Infantry Division, the Blue Devils, for the whole Italian campaign. He won a Bronze Star with service stars during his nearly four years in the army. Sometimes he talked about it, but whatever happened to him he carried with him for the rest of his life. After the war he came home to South Dakota and met a young Sioux woman. That was my mother. The Sioux were a nation of fighting men. I'm sure there was blood spilled for the Indian nation on that side of my heritage.

I never knew my mother. Never knew one thing about her. By the time I was old enough to remember, she was gone. I never knew her name, never even saw a picture of her. There's a name on my birth certificate but no other record anywhere of a woman with that name having lived. In fact, until I was about ten years old I believed my stepmother was my natural mother. That all changed when I caught my stepmother in a car with another man, a friend of my father's. I warned her that if it ever happened again I would tell my father, so she set out to poison his mind against me. It got real rough between my dad and me. By the time I told him the truth he had me down as a liar and a troublemaker. The man knocked me around and then threw me out of the house. That was easier for him than knowing the truth about his wife. I was twelve years old.

I went to stay at the home of one of my few friends. His mother was a beautiful, kind lady who was hurting for me. She sat me down and told me that everybody in the town knew what happened and that I was welcome to stay in their house as long as I wanted. It was all beyond my understanding. I asked her why my mother hated me so bad.

Then she told me, "Gary, she's not your mother. She's your stepmother. Your mother is not here anymore. You need to talk with your dad about that."

I guess on some level I had always known that, but I was relieved to hear it. What I couldn't understand was why nobody had told me that before. I never found out what happened between my mother and my father; even after he divorced my stepmother and we healed that wound between us, he never would talk about it. He carried all those answers with him into the ground. The most he would ever tell me was that I had native blood in me and I came from the Pine Ridge area in South Dakota.

I didn't need him to tell me that. I could feel it in me when the wind blew. I could sense the presence of danger, I could always move swiftly and silently, and it was easy for me to make friends with the spirits.

I came up hard. I lived for a time with my dad and my stepmother in Pretty Prairie, which is outside Nickerson, Kansas. Farm country. Mostly I got passed around to relatives in Colorado, Nebraska, Utah, and South Dakota. Supposedly they were all my uncles, but who knows. I didn't stay with any of them too long. Maybe because I moved a lot, I never made serious friends; I definitely was an outcast. Seemed like I was always having problems in school and getting into fights. A lot of the white kids didn't like me 'cause I was Indian, and the Indians didn't like me 'cause I was white. If somebody said something derogatory to me I'd hit him. I didn't care where I was, in the classroom, on the playground, in the hallway, I hit him. I had no tolerance for those remarks. I didn't win a lot of those fights, but I never quit trying. I'd get knocked down, but I'd get right up again and go at it. Nobody could keep me down. Sometimes people would just quit because they got tired of hitting me. They could beat me, but they couldn't hurt me. I already was filled up with pain. I would never give them that satisfaction.

I was never afraid of getting hurt, never afraid of pain. There was nothing I wouldn't do, especially if somebody told me it couldn't be done. For me, that was a direct challenge. So I was always doing things like jumping out of the barn onto a horse or riding the bucking bull out of the barn. I would jump my bike off a ridge, dive off the bridge, climb a sheer cliff. I would never admit there was something I couldn't do. I broke both my arms once by trying to do a three-sixty on a swing set. When I went over the top it flung me straight out, and I flew with my arms outstretched like Superman. When I landed I broke 'em both, and then I went through the rest of the school day without complaining.

I stayed the longest with my grandparents on their ranch in western Kansas, mostly because they let me be. It was a big operation, probably 16,000 acres, and they farmed wheat and maize and raised cattle and horses. I loved it there; that was the only place in my life where I wasn't confined by other people's boundaries. I was on my own, mostly with the animals, and I got along with animals far better than with people. Most animals weren't afraid of me; I could approach them, even wild animals, without difficulty. I could ride horses no one else could ride, and when I walked into the barn the cows would follow me. Whatever it was about me they sensed, it made them feel safe.

I searched to find my roots. I was drawn to the Native American reservation, trying with no success to find any information about my mother. As a result I embraced the Indian traditions. They seemed to make sense to me. Once I went up to Sturgis, South Dakota, where they had a vision quest going on. You needed to be invited to participate; it's an honor, and I hadn't earned it. I was just a spectator. I sat and watched the ceremonies, and even then I envied the people chosen to go up the mountain. I was sitting with several other people around a campfire, drinking tea, when an elder came up to me and handed me a feather from an immature golden eagle. "Carry it with you," he told me. "Where you are going, you will need this."

That was all he said. It made no sense, he didn't know me at all, but it seemed like he had seen a vision or my aura and knew that I would need this. To receive an eagle feather from an elder was a great honor, one that I knew I hadn't done anything to earn. It meant that he respected me as a warrior. From that day I carried that feather with me everywhere that I went. I wrapped it in a red cloth and kept it in my whole baggage, which is what I called the little kit I kept with me.

Between my dad and my grandfather I learned the skills that would make the difference in my life. By the time I was six years old I could survive in the woods; I knew how to hunt and fish, make a fire and cook what I caught, and build a shelter.

My father was a genius with his hands. He could make or repair just about anything; he could fabricate or repair machine parts. He actually built his own tractors. I used to sit and watch him for hours beating on the anvil, patiently shaping white-hot steel to fit his needs. He taught me the practical things a man should know: how to drive a car or a tractor, how to weld, how to build a motor or fix an engine. I bought my own first car, a '47 Pontiac, off a junkyard for ten dollars when I was ten years old and fixed it up by myself. It was a flathead six, and I painted it red right out of a paint can. I wanted people to know I was coming. By the time I was twelve I could barely see over the steering wheel, but I was driving my grandparents to church on Sunday, and a couple of years later, I was racing stripped-down hot rods on a quarter-mile dirt track.

It was my grandfather who taught me respect for the land and all living things on it. He taught me how to live off the land. He taught me how to plant and harvest, how to track, trap, and hunt food animals. He taught me how to be in the woods without fear and to recognize the signs, and how to move without leaving my mark. He taught me that there was more around me than I could see with my eyes and that my most valuable tool was my mind.

Later, in the jungles of my life, I would use all of this to track my enemy, find him, and kill him.

I grew up comfortable with guns and knives. My dad kept all types of weapons in the house. He had a Thompson machine gun he'd carried with him in the war and brought home; he had a German Luger; he had Japanese swords and British knives. I can't remember a time when I wasn't comfortable carrying a weapon. When I was six or seven years old, I would take my grandfather's .22 long rifle and go out hunting. As I got older I got myself a 12-gauge. I'd spend hours in the woods by myself, but as I was taught by both my grandfather and my father, I never killed anything I wasn't going to eat. That was a rule we lived by. When I killed an animal or a fish, I always said my little prayer thanking them for helping me survive and wishing them a good journey.

It was from my mother that I got my spiritual side. It was always in me. I had a place where I would go when I was troubled or needed my peace. At the south end of the ranch there was a big cottonwood tree surrounded by willows, and I would ride my pony down there. It was my place, a secret place no one else ever visited. When I felt the need, I would go down there and gather willow saplings and build a fire and sit back and look into it. The native peoples call this a vision quest, although I did not know that at the time. Later we would describe it as Ranger TV. As I looked into that fire I could let my imagination loose and go anywhere in the universe. I would spend days hidden in the willows, staring into the fire and opening my mind. Eventually I would be visited by all the elders.

A lot of kids struggle to have imaginary friends, but this was more than that. These people were my teachers. They would teach me about fire, about weapons, and animals. They taught me about nature. I never questioned any of it. I accepted it and I absorbed it. It would be a long time before I understood that these were the spirit guides that were giving me access to my subconscious being, teaching me how to use all of my senses, all of my mental capabilities.

I didn't realize this type of intense experience wasn't that common—it was real to me, and I just assumed everyone else would understand it. When I told my stepmother about these elders, though, she thought I was crazy and wanted to take me to a child psychologist. My grandmother accepted it as the product of my imagination. Tell me about it, she said, tell your grandfather about it, but don't tell anybody else. They won't understand, and it'll just make everything worse for you.

When I looked into the fire I had visions. I saw things. Mostly it was combat. It was battles, battles from the past and, while I couldn't know it then, battles I would fight in the future. Not so many years later these visions would save my life more than once. I didn't see the details; it wasn't on that type of conscious level. Instead it would be the sense of the moment. I would be in a situation and I would know what I was going to find. I would stare at a map and see the enemy. I would come to a clearing and know what was on the other side. I didn't have to think about it on any conscious level; the knowledge was already there. The only thing I had to learn was to accept it.

I was wandering. After that fight with my father I had no destination in life; I didn't seem to have any purpose. I was just moving through the days, dealing with whatever happened today without any thought about tomorrow. I stopped going to school, and it seemed like nobody even noticed. I didn't really care much about anything or anybody. If people got in my way, I pushed them out of my way. I wasn't ever a mean person, I never intended to hurt people, but there's no question I could have gone that way.

I didn't know it, but I was ready to be molded. It was a question of what came along first.

When I was fifteen I'd gone to stay at my older cousin Butch's house in Kansas. The only thing it had to offer was that it wasn't my house. I just wanted to be gone from anywhere near my stepmother. One day I saw that Butch had left all his identity papers lying around, including his birth certificate. I picked it all up and left. I had no plan to use it, but it was there and I took it. It wasn't too much later that I first began thinking about enlisting.

We were a patriotic family even before I understood what that meant. The people from my part of the world had always believed in doing their duty. At that time this country was in the middle of the Vietnam War, and even with the draft the army was desperate for volunteers. It seemed like a good place to have an adventure. All I knew about the army was what I'd seen in John Wayne movies and the little my father told me. I knew we were fighting in Vietnam, I'd seen it on the new TV we'd gotten, but Vietnam, wherever that was, seemed awfully far away from western Kansas. I never really thought about the possibility of getting hurt or killed. I knew that wasn't going to happen to me. Legally, I was still too young to enlist, but Butch O'Neal wasn't. I decided to go up and talk to the recruiter.

I was waiting in the lobby to go upstairs when the elevator doors opened and standing right in front of me was about the most impressive sight I had ever seen. It was a large man wearing an absolutely perfect-fitting tan army-dress uniform, several rows of medals laid out neatly on his chest, spit-shined jump boots laced up his calves, and he was holding a green beret in his hands. I looked at him in awe, in absolute awe, and asked, "What army are you in?"

The answer didn't matter to me. Whatever army it was, that's the one I wanted to be in.

He told me, "I'm in the Special Forces."

I didn't even know what that meant, but I said to him, "I want to be like you." This turned out to be the recruiter. Everything about him was absolutely in order. Spit and polish. When he asked me my name, I told him what my papers said, "Butch O'Neal." It was that easy to become somebody else.

We sat down and talked. He had served in three wars, World War II, Korea, and Vietnam, and he was retiring, so they'd assigned him to recruiting duty. His job was to visit high schools and talk about the military as a career. When I asked him how I could get to be like him, he told me that the Green Berets were an elite force. I would have to enlist in the army and eventually volunteer for Ranger training, and if I made it through Ranger School I could apply to Special Forces.

I signed up. I raised my right hand and swore that I, Butch O'Neal, would defend the Constitution. I was fifteen years old and alone in the world. I had completely separated myself from my family and they didn't know where I was. The army sent me to Fort Benning, Georgia, for my basic training.

I fit in. For the first time in my life, I finally fit in somewhere. I was accepted by the people around me for the skills that I had. They were teaching me, not criticizing me. I had never before felt like I was a part of something important. It just came to me naturally. From the first day I felt that I belonged there. Everything about it was comfortable for me—the uniform, holding a weapon, walking through the day, sleeping in the woods at night. Everything. Those things we were taught in training were the things I had always been doing. They gave us baby guns to shoot, and I just knocked down the targets. Our PT—physical training—was mostly running; on the farm it had been quicker for me to herd the cows by running around them than to saddle a horse, bring in the cattle, then cool down and feed the horse, so I could run through the morning and afternoon without even breathing hard. The training was easy for me. I wanted to shoot, I wanted to throw grenades, I wanted to learn how to read maps and track the enemy. I wanted to learn everything. This was my school.

I'd lie in my bunk at night waiting for the morning to come to get it started all over again. They made me an assistant squad leader, a responsibility I took very seriously. No one had ever given me authority before, or pretty much even trusted me. I pushed my guys, and when it was necessary, like up the hills on long hikes, I pulled them. Maybe because I had never been part of a team, that feeling of having people depend on me, and having people I could depend on, really affected me. This was just about the first time that I had a purpose in my life. The army was the perfect place for me.

Even the daily bullshit didn't bother me. I knew it wasn't aimed at me. While I had self-discipline, most of the people I was with did not. Most of them had come off the street and did not want to be there. They had to have somebody smoke their ass to put them in a position mentally to be trainable. That meant shaking up their minds by coming down hard on them for the petty shit. Our senior drill instructor was pretty good at figuring out who needed to be disciplined. He recognized that I had embraced the program and never focused on me. We all had to do our normal squad details, but I was used to working hard, so it made no difference to me. I did what they told me to do when they told me to do it, and I never had a problem. I made hospital corners on my bed, I memorized the serial number of my weapon and my RA—regular army—number, so I never got harassed.

We knew we all were going to Vietnam. There was no doubt about that. In 1967 the war was escalating and eating up troops, and we were the next meal. Several of our trainers, mostly E-7s and E-8s, had been over there and would tell us a little about it. You'd better learn this stuff, they told us. Almost all of you are going to be in combat, and the enemy is smart and well trained, and if you don't learn it you are going to die. Our senior DI said, "I learned the hard way, you don't need to do that. Listen to me, do what I tell you, and you may come back alive. Don't listen to me, then God help you."

None of that scared me. I had no grand thoughts about the meaning of life. I figured, if I lived, I lived; if I died . . . I didn't intend to die. I bought into the training. I still accepted the notion that if you were well trained, if you did things the right way and listened to your commanding officers, you would survive. Like it was a game and if you played by the rules you'd come out a winner.

I was fifteen years old. Back then, I didn't know how the world worked.

When I finished my basic training and my advanced individual training, which was learning how to be an infantryman, a frontline fighter, I applied and was accepted for Airborne training. There was never a doubt in my mind that I would apply for that. All of the elite units in the army are Airborne. That was their main delivery system.

If you wanted to be a Ranger, if you wanted to be Special Forces, you started by going to jump school.

I knew how to parachute. From the time I was old enough I had been skydiving. My grandmother had paid me seventy-five cents an hour for working on the farm, and I used that money to put gas in my car and go skydiving. I was always fascinated by flight. I could lie on the ground and watch the birds flying for hours. I jumped off bridges because I loved those few seconds of being totally free in the air, and I wanted to go higher and make that sensation of free falling last a little longer. Years later I would become a member of the army's Golden Knights, the greatest competitive parachuting team in the world, make jumps to test survival gear from as high as 38,000 feet, and even become the first person to parachute into Stonehenge in England, but when I began jumping in the early 1960s skydiving wasn't organized at all. There were no rules, no safety regulations. It was all outlaw—just find somebody to take you up in a plane and jump out. I bought my first parachute for twenty-six dollars in an army-navy store, an old air force bail-out chute. On my reserve chute's rucksack I carried a big-ass altimeter that had come out of an airplane. It didn't look so good, but it did the job. Though sometimes when I was falling it would bounce on up and crack me in the face.

I admit it, first jump I made, I definitely was afraid. That's the only sane way to be, but the way I was shaped, fear was a challenge to be overcome, not anything to be backed away from. I never let fear dictate my actions. Instead, I met my fears head-on. That first time I had three hours of instruction, and then we went up about 4,000 feet in a little Cessna 180, a tail-dragger. I thought I was ready for it, but when the door opened and I heard that *whoooosssshhh* of air for an instant I began to reconsider. I was committed, though, and attached to a static line. I closed my eyes and went out of that airplane and experienced the greatest few seconds of my life. There wasn't much for me to do. My chute popped open automatically and I floated down. That day I made three static line jumps and then went up free-fall, meaning I pulled the rip cord when I was ready. Racing through the air hypnotizes you; you're up in the sky doing whatever you want to do, gravity isn't a barrier, so you flip, you stand up, you sail on the wind, flying like a bird, and the feeling is that you can just float above the earth forever. There's no sensation of falling, because there are no stationary objects to measure yourself against. Only when you get lower does your depth perception kick in. As soon as you get down, the only thing you want to do is get back up there.

By the time I went to jump school, I'd already made probably a hundred jumps. In training we worked our asses off on those swing landing trainers, jumping out of a thirty-four-foot tower, then running around in formation. I never bothered to learn the names of the other people there, because they kept disappearing. I'd wake up in the morning and the guy in next bunk was gone. Nobody ever said a word about it; it was as if they never existed.

When I graduated they assigned me to the 173rd Airborne Infantry. "The Herd," which is what it is called, is a highly decorated brigade, known for being a hellacious fighting unit. Some people say Bob Hope put that nickname on us because we were "the herd of animals." The 173rd was activated in World War I and became the first major command deployed to Vietnam. Basically, the Herd was sent wherever the heaviest fighting in country was taking place. One thing you knew for sure, if you were assigned to the 173rd you were going to see combat. By the time I got there, they had been kicking ass for almost three years. Their mission was pretty straightforward: Search and destroy. Go out there in the boonies and find Charlie and kill him.

We landed at Tan Son Nhut Air Base outside Saigon. The first thing that hit me when I got off that plane in Vietnam was the overwhelming humidity and the putrid smell of burning shit. No one who served there will ever forget the heat or the stink. By the time I took three steps on the tarmac I was dripping with sweat. I literally could see the heat rising in rippling waves from the concrete runway. I thought, *I'm back in Georgia,* but it was much worse than that. No matter where you went, the humidity hung on you like a wool coat in August. It rotted away your clothes and clogged up your weapons. One of the first things we were told was to throw away our underwear and prize dry socks, 'cause if you wore underwear you were eventually going to get a painful rash, and if you didn't keep your feet dry they were going to rot. There was never any escape from the heat and humidity. The thing I learned right away, and never forgot, was that whatever I had to deal with, my enemy had to deal with it, too.

By the time I hit the ground, I'd gotten used to being Butch O'Neal. I was sixteen years old and I looked it, but all us grunts were kids and we all looked young, so nobody ever wondered about it. I couldn't tell anybody the truth because they would have booted me right home, while all I wanted to do was get into the mix. There was an irony to that. Most of the people I met were trying to get out of the army; I had to lie my way in.

It took about three weeks for us to get processed. I remember during that time they gave us a little book about Vietnam. Most people just tossed it in their footlocker, but I read it carefully, because I wanted to know what kind of creatures were out there waiting for me. It had all the information about our enemy: the NVA, North Vietnamese Army, seasoned troops who moved and fought like a regular army; and the VC, Vietcong, guerrilla fighters that too often lived in the villages as farmers during the day and became killers at night. It also discussed the animals and insects that lived in the jungles, including tigers, elephants, wild boar, monkeys, snakes, and the biggest fucking bugs you have ever seen in your life. Just the pictures were scary. Everything was big, big spiders, scorpions, creepy crawlers, big and ugly. They had all kinds of eyes and legs and stingers. According to this book only certain snakes and insects were dangerous, but none of them looked especially friendly.

Hanging over everything, even more than the heat, was the fear of battle. Like every other soldier who has ever gone to war, I was wondering how I would react in combat. I definitely knew that I was going to be in combat. There was no question about that; that's what we were there for. While I was real excited, I also was anxious to experience it, and I was scared. Everybody was scared; if you weren't scared in that situation there was something wrong with you. We had landed in a war zone; we knew that some of the people getting off that plane were going to die. In fact, as I got off that cargo plane I had seen flag-draped coffins on a conveyer belt being loaded onto another plane for the flight home. Nobody was paying special attention to them. I was a little shook by the fact that everybody was treating a conveyer belt of coffins like something normal.

The fear was natural. The ability to control it was personal. No matter how bravely anybody talked, nobody knew how well or how poorly they would respond until they were in it. We talked about it, and when we weren't talking about it we were thinking about it. We just wanted to get it over with. We wanted to know. We were "cherries," the new guys. The waiting for it to come was really hard. The people who had been there awhile kept telling us to stop worrying about it, that worrying didn't do anybody any good. There was no way to prepare for being in combat because there is nothing to compare it to; the live fire exercises we'd done in training were about as realistic as pictures of food in magazines were filling. The combat veterans I spoke with admitted to their own fears but tried to be reassuring. When it comes, it comes, that's when you'll find out. You'll do fine. That's what they said, you'll do fine.

From brigade headquarters I got on a bird and was flown to the battalion. When I got there, the company I was assigned to was out in the field. I just stored all my belongings in the supply conex, which was basically a steel shed, took my rucksack and my weapon, and got on a helicopter. About forty minutes later they dropped me off into my new world. I had left civilization. In just a few hours I'd been transported from a massive military base to a company in the middle of the jungle, and finally assigned to my squad.

I reported for duty just like I had been taught—and the first thing I did was throw away everything that I'd been taught. We had never fought this kind of war before, and it had taken the army some time to adapt to it. The Vietnam War wasn't anything like those set-piece battles that we had fought in World War II or even Korea, wars that could be plotted on maps and you could measure progress by how much territory you gained. This was an unending series of small ambushes and skirmishes. It was a war with no front lines against an enemy that seemed to be able to strike and vanish into the earth. The only land that mattered was the strategic points, the heights from which you could observe enemy movements, or those places where the jungle trails came together, and even that was only temporary. When our first large force got there, we didn't understand this type of warfare at all; we tried to make the North Vietnamese and the Vietcong fight our war. Too many people died before we finally figured out that wasn't going to work, and that's when we began to learn from our enemy. This war wasn't about gaining and protecting territory. About the only thing that would really make a difference was the attrition rate—how many enemy did we kill?

At Fort Benning we were still being trained to fight World War II, so my real training began when I got to my squad. I was exhausted, but I didn't sleep much that first night. I'd spent nights in the woods before, but never anything like this. The night was dark and peaceful. It was much too dark to see anything at all, and nobody lit anything out in the open, so I just lay there and listened, with my weapon right next to me. I had no idea how many people were around me, but I felt alone. In the jungle you learn really quick to rely on your senses, the regular five senses plus the additional ones you didn't even know you had. That first night the sounds were all new to me. There wasn't any of that comfortable crickets chirping. I heard people stumbling around, making noise while trying to be quiet, and I heard the jungle. I heard the tops of the trees moving, I heard a few animals, I heard the breeze easing through. I didn't know what was normal, so I couldn't know what was different, so I just hunched up and paid attention to everything going on around me. I figured if there was a problem I'd find out quick enough.

The important thing was to grab hold of your imagination and keep it tight. I had the sense that if I let it go, the night would be even more difficult. I knew that the enemy was out there somewhere, and I knew that he was comfortable in the night. I had spent most of my life moving, I had rarely waited for anything; so staying still, waiting, was hard for me. I had been warned about the shadows, that eventually if you stared at a shadow long enough it would begin to resemble a person and it would move. That was your imagination playing with your mind. I had been taught when I was a kid, camping out at night back in Kansas, that you were supposed to look at a position, then take your eyes off it and scan all around, then go back to it fresh to see if there had been any changes. That was the way to determine if it was really moving. I had been warned about that, but it didn't make a difference. At night, shadows moved. So too often for us to get comfortable, somebody would fire a burst, giving away his position and making everybody else respond.

For security at night we put out two-man advance observation posts, and several squads would set up ambushes. The thunder of a claymore mine exploding is the best possible early warning system. The next few days I started going out on patrol, searching for any sign of the enemy, hoping for contact while wary of it. That was when I began to get to know the real Vietnam. There were several different types of landscape; we moved through open fields and rice paddies, we walked around villages, and we disappeared into the jungle. We walked up and down hills and on the sides of mountains. We walked alongside streams and occasionally on a path. Generally, though, we tried to stay off the paths because that's where most ambushes were set up. Usually we cut our way through fields; sometimes the grass was so high that if you didn't keep focused on the man directly in front of you, the grass would close up behind him and you could lose him in three steps. Or we followed animal tracks; if the animals had used that path and not gotten blown up, we knew it wasn't booby-trapped.

I spent more than three years basically living in those jungles, and there wasn't one day I felt truly comfortable. In different areas of that part of the world we worked in triple-canopy jungle, meaning there was no difference between and night and day. The jungle was claustrophobic; it seemed like it was always closing in on you. Eventually I would learn how to use the jungle to my advantage. It wasn't my "friend"—the jungle doesn't make friends. Even the NVA and the Vietcong didn't like being in the jungle. Still, I understood it and respected its power. There were times when we were on an ambush that I would stand hidden a foot off a path, literally one foot, and the enemy would pass by me and not see me or sense me. I would wait, and wait, and wait, as a patrol passed, and then in one motion I would grab the rear guard, yank him off the path, and kill him instantly and silently. The enemy would never see him again, never know what happened to him; as far as they were concerned the jungle just swallowed him up.

That was later. In my first days in country, when we were on patrol with the 173rd, we were always on alert. The anticipation was worse than the fear. Where the fuck were they? We never knew what was around the bend or waiting at the edge of the jungle. Everybody was trying hard to be as quiet as possible, but with as many as two hundred people on patrol, that was never very quiet. A line company is about as quiet as a herd of elephants. Equipment would bang, people would cough or curse—there was always some human sound that I knew would give us away if the enemy was listening. The enemy *was* listening, of course, but there was nothing I could do about it.

Those first few weeks we didn't have any contact. A couple of times I heard rounds being fired somewhere in the distance, but as I was learning, it was very difficult to determine where one or two gunshots were coming from. Sounds just bounced around the terrain. They echoed off the trees; they were muffled by the grass; they traveled down the streams. We heard them, we tightened up, we kept going. Other platoons made contact and inflicted some damage, took some light casualties. We'd listen to their stories, and it was impossible not to wonder, Why not us?

About my fifth week with the company, we were going up a hill. My squad was walking point for the company, meaning we were out in front. I was third in the line behind our squad leader and the radio guy, and I was thinking . . .

There was movement in the bushes off to our left, and we fired them up. It was the first time I'd seen the enemy, and he was a shadow running through the tall grass. We started moving fast in the direction they were running. That's when they opened up on us from our flank. They had been waiting for us. We strolled into their ambush.

I hit the ground. The noise . . . the noise . . . our officers were shouting commands, the sergeants were screaming, some people went down and were screaming for help. Bullets were flying all around me, zipping through the leaves and hitting tree branches, sending leaves flying off the vines. I was just trying to stay as low as possible. Somewhere to my right I heard the thumping of grenades exploding, *onetwothree, boomboomboom,* then sporadically.

It was nothing like I had anticipated. There was no pace to it at all, no rhythm. There was no break at all in the firing; the intensity of it overwhelmed me. My natural response was to try to make sense of it, but that was impossible. There was nothing in my life to compare it to. I was stunned. I pissed my pants.

My mind was racing, warp 10, but the battle was warp 20. Once I got behind, there was no way to catch up to it. You have to be in it. Once the wave has passed over you, you're behind it forever. I was trying to figure it out; the mistake I made was that I was thinking what to do rather than responding and doing it. The speed of thought is so much slower than what you need to be doing. Thinking gets you killed; responding, reacting, keeps you alive. You see something, you respond. No pausing, no thinking, no analyzing, you respond. A snake is coming at you, you kill it.

In those first few seconds I was frozen with fear, too scared to remember my training. I hadn't fired a round; I didn't know where to shoot. After those first few seconds I started seeing what the people around me were doing, and I began doing the same thing. The guys next to me were wheelin' and dealin', and I did what they did. I followed my leaders. We started concentrating our fire in the direction the bullets were coming from. It wasn't any type of target shooting, it was just blasting, trying to create overwhelming firepower. Most times you never knew if you hit anybody. I was young and dumb and lucky.

During a firefight there is no such thing as time. It goes on until it ends. While you're in the middle of it, you have no past and no future; it is that moment and nothing else. Everything you are, everything you know, every experience you have ever had, you have to bring into that moment. Then when you survive that moment you get to the next moment. You exist totally in each moment, as if you are wrapped in some type of blanket that shields anything but the present. You have to completely block out everything else—your feelings, your senses, everything that is not directly focused on that one moment. Every step you take forward, you have to forget about that step behind you; it's nonexistent. Strange as it sounds, after the first shock I forgot to be scared. I wasn't feeling any emotion; I wasn't thinking about what could happen. I let my training take over. I just kept firing, firing, firing. Instinctive shooting. Target, front sight, squeeze. Twenty rounds, change the magazine, keep firing.

I looked up, and the gunships had showed up on station and were blasting away at the enemy. It could have been five minutes, it could have been forty-five minutes, I had no idea. My mind had separated completely from my body. Those Hueys had brought hell with them. They opened up and tore a hole in the jungle all around us. The enemy was gone; killed or just gone. I lay there, the battle ringing in my ears, covered with my own sweat and piss. Gradually, sounds of life began filtering into my consciousness. People were moving around tentatively, trying to make sure that no enemy had survived that fusillade. I rolled over onto my back. I wasn't ready to stand up. For the first time I felt my weapon in my hands. It was burning hot. A little smoke was rising from it. I could smell the battle, the smoky scent of spent ammunition, all around me.

A sergeant leaned over. "You okay?" I gave him a thumbs-up and sat up. I heard a few seconds of laughter, which was so bizarre; later I'd understand that it was a way of expressing relief, a sound of life. We had one serious casualty, no deaths. A bunch of people had been nicked by shrapnel, but nothing that would even take them off patrol. Gradually, like the sounds, my emotions began filtering into my body. That's when the fear really hit me. I started shaking. The emotions became overwhelming. Not only wasn't I dead, I had never felt more alive.

When I stood up I had to take a few seconds to regain myself, just let all my parts settle into position. I couldn't stop looking around; I wasn't convinced the enemy was gone. He was, though, and he left some of his people behind. I didn't see any complete bodies, just a few scattered body parts. I didn't connect them in my mind to living beings; I didn't have any feelings about them, just curiosity. I'd never seen anything at all like the carnage after a battle.

What was really strange was that I couldn't remember what I'd done during the battle. I tried, but I couldn't remember any of the details. Other people told me what I'd done, that I'd been right next to them and that I'd done my part, but much as I wanted to remember it, it wasn't there.

As we saddled up and moved out, there was one thing I understood completely. I was a totally different person than I had been just a little while earlier, and those changes would affect me for the rest of my life. I was still anxious, but I felt like I had finally been baptized. I'd been in the mix, and I'd survived it. I felt something else, too. I was exhilarated, and I could hardly wait to get back into it. I'd had my first dose and I wanted more.

I got my fill. After that we were in the mix all the time. There was no place in that country where you could just relax. Even when we went back to battalion to take a little break we could get hit by rockets and mortars. We were in the middle of a civil war. The enemy was always around us and looked just like the people who were fighting alongside us, and since we couldn't look into their souls we never could be sure who to trust. So we had to live on the edge all the time.

The enemy was an outstanding soldier. He was smart, he was brave, and he was determined. The enemy had several advantages over us. His people were seasoned troops. They had been fighting consistently since long before World War II; they had fought the Chinese, the Japanese, and the French, and they had developed guerrilla techniques that took us too long to learn. The enemy also had excellent equipment. The Russian AK-47, which was his primary weapon, was superior to the M-16 we were using. Early in the war, especially, the M-16 got people killed. It would get jammed too easily, leaving people without the means to defend themselves. Everybody there knew it, and complained, but the people who could have done something back home didn't seem to pay attention. The AK-47 was prized by Americans. If you could pick one off the ground you did, and you used it.

The enemy was the home team. They knew the terrain. They had built the Ho Chi Minh Trail, the supply route from the North down into the South, which ran into Laos and Cambodia. They knew the safest places to cross rivers, they knew the best places to hide, and they knew how to live off the countryside. They would carry supplies from the north by animal, by bicycle, and when necessary on their backs. In many places they had the cooperation if not the support of the locals.

Most of my first tour I lived at a company base camp. We set up a firebase in the Central Highlands. That was a static position; the enemy knew we were there and constantly probed for our weaknesses. The camp was ringed by concertina wire—barbed wire that would entangle anybody trying to get through—sandbagged bunkers, trip wires, claymore mines, some booby traps, forward observation posts, and patrols waiting in ambush. We took turns going out on patrol or being in the observation posts at night. I never minded. I liked being out there.

We'd change the location every night. We'd move out beyond the perimeter right after dark; sometimes it was so dark we'd have to keep a hand on the shoulder of the man in front of us so we wouldn't get separated. After we settled down into a position we'd wait, but then we'd move again just in case somebody had been watching us. Once we got settled for the night we'd put out claymores around our position, making sure we left ourselves an exit corridor. A claymore mine can do some serious damage, and knowing they were there provided comfort.

One of the first lessons we learned was to make damn sure after an ambush or firefight that every enemy soldier on the ground was dead. I learned that lesson when we were searching for bodies after blowing a claymore. We always searched bodies for any intelligence they might be carrying. A guy who should have known better put his foot under the shoulder of a dink and rolled him over. *Boom!* The dink had a pistol in his hand and put a round through my guy's hip. What I used to do to make sure that dead was really dead was tape an aluminum bag filled with CS powder—that's the riot control gas that makes your eyes tear and causes you to cough—around the mine, and then I'd put a white phosphorus grenade in front of that. When we blew the claymore it spread the CS and ignited the white phosphorus. Willy Peter, we called it. That shit was going to burn as long as it got oxygen, so if it got on your skin it was going to keep burning until it got smothered. Anybody hit in the kill zone was going to be gasping for air and screaming for mercy. One thing guaranteed, they definitely were not going to be lying still. That was the end of that problem.

While there were people who never got used to being out in the boonies at night, right away I was as comfortable as I ever got with it. I wasn't exactly comfortable, but I liked it. It stirred something in me. Being in the night somehow seemed natural to me. When you are vulnerable like that, you can either fight it or embrace it. I made friends with it, in the Indian way. I lay there and I tried to make myself part of nature.

That wasn't easy. Any movement could jeopardize the lives of the whole team. It meant training my mind to ignore all the normal behaviors I'd been doing my whole life. I had to be absolutely still, silent. It meant not slapping the bugs and mosquitoes, not scratching those itches; it meant ignoring my bodily functions. To be undetected when we were out there, we couldn't do anything to change the environment—its sounds, its smells, or its appearance. If we did have to move, like crawling out of a position, each movement had to be slow and precise; it had to flow rather than being abrupt. Doing this forced me to draw on a self-discipline that I never knew I had.

It also forced me to expand my senses. We grow up being told we have five major senses, but in those first few months in Vietnam I discovered two more, at least. One is instinctive feeling. Or maybe a gut feeling. When people say that they "sensed danger," this is the sense they are talking about. I always referred to it as my spirit talking to me. It's the feeling that tells you not to walk through a door or, in Vietnam, not to walk down that path because there is danger. It's the combination of all your conscious and subconscious knowledge and experience coming together to send you a message. It isn't easily defined, but I guarantee that paying attention to it saved my life several times in several countries.

The seventh sense is your mind. People don't generally think of the mind as a sense organ, because it isn't part of our physical being, like our eyes, ears, nose, skin, and tongue, but as I learned, it may well be the most important sense organ. The mind not only provides access to information about our environment, it actually interprets that information and enhances all of our other capabilities. In a life-and-death situation, like combat, your mind takes control. It isn't your brain—the last thing you want to do in combat is think. It is your mind that is running all the machinery of survival. Your body is just transportation for your mind and your spirit. It's the mind that enables a little woman to pick up a 3,000-pound car that has trapped her child; it's the mind that allows you to survive a wound that should have killed you; it's the mind that warns you not to jump off a path when you're ambushed because the enemy has booby-trapped the ditch. It was my mind that enabled me to lie still in an ambush position for hours, focusing on the situation without allowing any distractions to bother me.

I didn't talk about any of this stuff. I didn't care if anybody believed me or agreed with me; I wasn't interested in attracting any attention. For me it was real, and I paid it respect. What got a lot of people shook in Vietnam was the randomness of death or injury. People dealt with that in a lot of different ways. I carried my eagle feather with me in my kit every time I went outside the perimeter, and I also performed a ceremony before going out on a mission. I'd light a little fire and say my prayers for the safety of my team and the success of the mission, and I'd ask that if we did have to mix it up we would be given the guidance to survive. I'd watch as the smoke from that fire carried my prayers up to the Creator.

Then we'd go out hunting.

I'd been lost living in America, and in Vietnam I got found. War was what I was good at. It made me a whole person. Like other people fighting over there, I became addicted to the high of being at risk. Almost right from the start I started taking every opportunity to fight, and in Vietnam there was no shortage of opportunity. We didn't have to look for danger; it would find us. I don't know for sure when I killed my first enemy soldier, but I suspect it was the first time they attacked our firebase.

Firebases were definitely vulnerable. Basically, we were targets. A firebase is a fixed location protected by a limited number of troops, although we were never outside the range of air and artillery support. We would go out and set up a firebase and live there for several weeks, sometimes as long as a month. Then we would pack up and leave. While we were there the enemy was constantly probing us. Suddenly they'd drop a mortar shell on us, or a sniper would take a shot. It was just harassment, just enough to keep us aware. Only on occasion would they actually attempt a full assault. There were a lot of times when the word got passed that they were coming that night, and we'd increase security and wait all night, but they wouldn't attack. When they finally did come, they were relentless and it was intense.

There was little warning. If we were lucky one of them would hit a trip wire and send up a flare. Then they would open up on us with as much firepower as they could generate. The first thing that they would try to do was blow a hole through the concertina wire so they could get inside the perimeter. We'd immediately light up the night with flares and get on the phone to the command post, letting them know we were under attack. Within minutes the artillery fired the first marking round; after that they walked it in dangerously close. For me, there was an instant of terror, then I'd settle into doing my job. The anticipation usually wore on me worse than the combat. By this time I had been under fire several times. I knew what I was supposed to do. While my first time in combat the battle had raced by me, now I was able to slow it down a little. We had four platoons, and each of them had responsibility for a certain segment of our perimeter, and each person in the platoon had an assigned fire point within that segment. We were capable of sending out a rapid ring of fire.

This was the first time I had seen the enemy up close. A mix of NVA regulars and VC, they were wearing uniforms and helmets. They were charging, they were blasting. I just kept firing. There was nothing else I could do. There was no strategy, no aiming, no thinking. Fire twenty rounds on full automatic, drop the magazine, load up, keep firing. Just fire, reload, fire, reload, keep shooting, don't stop. At that moment the enemy was not human, not people, he was just a target that had to be destroyed before he could get to me. See, squeeze; see, squeeze.

They just kept coming. Our artillery was moving closer and closer to our position. Sometimes it seemed impossible anybody could survive the firepower we were putting on them, but they kept coming. Bullets were winging all around me; there was a lot of shit just bouncing around. A round hit the sandbag in front of me, a couple of inches from where my weapon was resting. I thought they had got inside the wire and were coming up on us from behind. Later we figured out that a round had ricocheted off somebody's helmet and bounced back.

It lasted until it was over, ending as abruptly as it had started. When they were gone we took a deep breath, resupplied with ammunition as quick as possible, then sat in our positions waiting for them to come back. Eventually the sun came up.

In that early light I saw the remains of several enemy soldiers caught up in the wire in weird positions. Nobody reacted much to it. We had some wounded who needed to be evacuated, and I believe we had two KIA. We didn't have time to spend talking about the attack; we had too much work to get done. Charlie was coming back. There was no boasting or bravado or analysis. Maybe I felt a little bit of pride in myself—I had done my duty—but if I did, I know I didn't show it. We were professionals, even people like me who were learning our craft, and professionals did their job without the expression of undue emotion.

We had to clean our weapons and check our radios to make sure everything was still functional. We had to replace the concertina wire. We had to get more ammunition and fill the gaps in our positions left by our KIA and wounded. As much as possible we stayed away from the bodies and the wounded; there was nothing we could do for them except make sure the wounded got the care they needed and the bodies of our dead were treated with respect. There were people assigned to take care of the wounded; that wasn't my job. About all I could do was hope they made it. The choppers came in at first light with more ammunition and collected our dead and wounded.

I knew I must have hit some NVA, and I didn't even give it a thought. My hope was that I'd killed them, as many of them as possible, but there was no way of knowing. I didn't think of them as human beings. At that point they were not human, and this had nothing at all to do with humanity. It wasn't about virtue or morality, there wasn't any bigger point; it was kill or be killed. It was get through the night alive. I didn't hate them, that wasn't in the equation. I killed a number of people during my career, and I don't have any regrets. None. I never hurt one person who wasn't trying to kill me. So I looked at the bodies hanging in the wire mostly with curiosity, like I was looking at a freak show or an accident, but without any emotion at all.

Looking back, maybe what was most surprising was how quickly we were able to accept scenes like this as our normal life. We shed the rules of conventional civilization and lived by our own. Even the rules that governed the military got bent and eventually broken. From time to time we would have replacement officers coming in and trying to impose some sort of military structure, but that rarely lasted very long. This wasn't the place for it.

My life was pretty spare. Combat became the routine. That first year I spent at least eight months in a combat environment. I lived out in the boonies, I went out on patrol, set ambushes, killed my enemy. I rarely even thought of what was going on back in the States. This was my home. I'd get an occasional letter from my half brother, and my grandmother would send me packages, but home was fading fast for me. There wasn't anything there I was holding on to. There was nothing there I needed or wanted.

If it's possible to be all alone in the middle of a massive war machine I was alone, and it wasn't bothering me at all. It enabled me to discover resources inside myself that in the noise of a normal life probably would have remained hidden. When I looked into the fires I could see myself catching up to those things I had been chasing my whole life. I wasn't there yet, but in some ways it was beginning to make some sense. My shell was getting harder every day, but my spirit was beginning to soar.

I didn't form any close relationships in Vietnam—if people were there they were there, if they were not they were not. A lot of times I only knew people by their nickname; I couldn't even tell you their real last name. I didn't really get to know the people I was with. It wasn't like the movies in which everybody bonded. I wasn't interested in knowing much about anybody else and didn't want anybody asking me many questions. In earlier wars a group of guys lived together and fought together as they marched across Europe or Korea, but that wasn't the way it was in a line company in Vietnam. People were always coming and going. It'd be a little bit different later, when I joined the Rangers, but in the Herd I was Butch, or kid, or to an officer looking at my name on my uniform, just O'Neal.

I celebrated my sixteenth and seventeenth birthdays with the Herd, but as time went on I realized I didn't belong there. The army is a vast society with its own status and structure. There are line companies, massive units that fight the biggest battles and do the grinding work of war. Most draftees end up in line companies. Then there are the elite outfits, the smaller, highly trained Special Forces who perform the most difficult and most dangerous missions. These are units like the Rangers, the army's Green Berets, and the navy's SEALs, all-volunteer units comprised of the best combatants in the military. Many more people wash out in training for these units than ever get to serve in them. These are the one-percenters. America's elite warriors. After spending just a few weeks clomping around in that jungle with two hundred other guys I knew that I wanted to be part of that group.

What I didn't know yet was how to get there. That would begin when the army discovered Butch O'Neal.

CHAPTER TWO

> Live life so completely that when death comes to you, like a thief in the night, there will be nothing left for him to steal.
>
> Anonymous

Butch O'Neal got killed by paperwork. My cousin got drafted, and when they ran his Social Security number they discovered he had already been serving in the 173rd for more than two years. I guess he was surprised to know that. I was in my hooch one afternoon when two MPs from battalion headquarters showed up and told me to gather up my stuff. They told me I was under arrest, that I had committed a federal offense, and put me on a bird back to Saigon. Man, I didn't know what was going on. I was wondering if they were taking me to Leavenworth and locking me up in prison.

From Saigon I was sent to Fort Ord, California, where I was discharged for enlisting under a false identity. One day I was in the boonies watching out for the VC; three days later I was in California watching out for hippies. It was an abrupt cultural shift.

I was given an honorable discharge, but I was also prohibited from reenlisting. I could get back into the army only if there was a national emergency or if I was drafted. Butch O'Neal ceased to exist, except for the real Butch O'Neal. I knew by then that I needed to solve the mystery of my mother. There was too big a hole in my being. I was drawn to South Dakota and started spending time on the reservations at Standing Rock, Rosebud, and Pine Ridge. There was no knowledge of my mother, or if there was it wasn't something that the native people would talk to me about.

The military had dumped me on the world without any preparation or tools to deal with civilian life, and like so many other people, then and now, I carried the war back to America with me. I missed being in it; I missed the camaraderie and the intensity of living life in a combat zone. As strange as it sounds, I missed the freedom of the military. As long as we did our jobs, the officers pretty much had left us alone there. We lived by our own rules; back home I had to follow different rules. It was harder for me. I kept on the move for a time. Those first few months I spent a lot of time partying and drinking. I had nothing else to do. I wasn't getting drunk every day, it wasn't that type of drinking, but it was steady. During that time I spent several months working on the line assembling farm equipment at Krause Plow. I hated that job, but I showed up on time for work almost every morning, and I did my job without complaining. I knew that my future wasn't going to be at Krause Plow, so that made it okay for the present. People kept telling me that I should go back to school, get my high school diploma, and then take advantage of the GI Bill, but I just couldn't see myself in high school. Those people could never understand what I'd seen and done. It was really strange—after being in Nam for more than two years, I couldn't have survived in high school. I don't know exactly what would have happened, but it definitely would have happened.

I did fall in love for the first time in my life. At least I thought it was love. Emotionally I was still a kid, still a teenager, but with the experiences of a grown man. That can be a confusing mix. In Nam women were always a topic of conversation. I listened a lot more than I talked, and there were moments when I wished hard that I'd had a girlfriend writing to me. This was a very pretty American high school girl, and after what I had seen in Nam she was what I needed. Maybe the thing I liked best about her was that she loved me back without making any demands on me. She loved me for being me. In my whole life I hadn't had too many women put their arms around me and mean it. So when she got pregnant it was easy to get married. I was eighteen years old, and lost.

I had left the real warriors back there, and I knew it; I just didn't know what to do about it. The only peace I found was on the reservations. I made some friends there, people who would become my guides years later, in particular a Lakota medicine chief named Looks for Buffalo. We have called each other brothers for many years. During these months we spent many long days together. I had endless questions about the ways of the native people.

I watched all the ceremonies; they wouldn't let me participate. I wasn't one of them, and I hadn't done anything to earn that right. I'd sit there listening to the drums, feeling the vibrations. As Looks for Buffalo explained to me, the native people believe that our heartbeat is the same heartbeat as Mother Earth's, that the magma at the center of the earth pulsates in the same rhythm as our hearts. There is no other living thing on earth that has that same heartbeat.

The ceremonies were a technique for getting into harmony with the earth. Once you had done that you knew when the tides were coming in—even if you were nowhere near water—and when the moon was rising and how the weather would change. There are so many stories of the native peoples accurately predicting events by moon cycles, like, *This is going to happen in three moons.*

I would listen and try to understand, not only with my mind but also with my soul. I wanted to be able to feel it as well as know it. I wanted to know how to be in tune with the land. I also wanted to know as much as I could about the great fighting skills of the Sioux. The Sioux were among the best warriors in history; as much attention as they paid to the Creator, they also mastered the war skills necessary to kill their enemies. I was always asking questions about their weapons; I wanted to know how they used their bows and arrows and knives and lances. I wanted to know about the traps they laid for their enemy and their methods of killing.

It was that bringing together of the spirit and warrior skills that made the Sioux the most feared warriors of the Plains. That's what I was looking to find in myself.

In 1969 I might have been the only young person in America desperate to get back into the army. Hundreds of brave young Americans were being killed in Southeast Asia every week. It wasn't like I thought I could make the difference, but there definitely was something pulling at me to get back there. I didn't know if it was some missing part of me that needed to be found, or something extra in me that made me want to serve. I'd had the chance to walk away from it, but I couldn't. It was where I belonged.

My aunt, who was on the draft board in Vernal, Utah, used her influence to get my number pulled up. Nobody complained about somebody jumping ahead in that line. I left my pregnant wife and went back into the army. Since my service record as Butch O'Neal had been annulled, I had to go through basic and advanced training again. I went to Fort Leonard Wood, in Missouri. The whole thing was silly, a waste of time; I had more combat experience than almost all of my instructors, but I didn't complain. They were all wearing patches I knew real well, the 101st, the 1st Cav, and naturally the Herd. I wasn't looking to cause any problems. I just wanted to get back to the war. The instructors pretty much left me alone; they spent their time messing with the deadheads, trying to turn them into soldiers.

After finishing basic and advanced training I went to jump school at Fort Benning for the second time. During zero week, which is time spent waiting for the rest of the class to show up, I took my rig and went out skydiving. Some of the black hats, the instructors from the school, were there, and we jumped together. We got to talking, and they asked me what committee I was going to be on, meaning my teaching assignment at the school. "I'm going to start jump school next Monday," I said.

None of those people believed me until they showed up at work Monday morning and saw my smiling face standing in the ranks. They gave me a little harassment, they played their little games with me, but mostly they left me alone. By that time I knew which units over there were doing the real interesting fighting, and I had decided that I wanted to be a LRRP—pronounced "Lurp." The LRRPs, long-range reconnaissance patrols, which eventually would be assigned to Ranger companies, originally were attached to infantry companies. These were the people who got dropped down into enemy territory in small teams and stayed there for several days at a time observing, reporting, and when necessary fighting. They lived in the middle of the mix. No forces in Vietnam had more close-up contact with the enemy than the LRRPs.

I had volunteered to go back to the infantry, back to the rice paddies, figuring that was my clearest path to Ranger School and eventually SF, Special Forces. When we got off the plane, this time at Cam Ranh Bay, everybody started complaining about the heat. Except me. I took in three breaths of that stinking air, that unforgettable aroma of burning shit, and I knew I was back in my element. Almost as soon as I got there I could feel my senses start magnifying again. I was like a dull knife that was just getting sharpened. I was anxious to start slicing and dicing. I had some serious payback to deliver—but the army in its wisdom decided that instead of being in the field I should be a truck driver. I couldn't believe it. I was back in country supposedly for the first time, and they put me in the Airborne Express, driving a truck.

I felt trapped inside the cabs of those trucks. It was a dangerous job. We were running supply convoys through the An Khe Pass, which was a treacherous run. We expected to get hit. It was like driving a stagecoach through Indian territory. After a while you'd see the VC behind every rock. We carried some serious firepower with us. We took burned-out armored personnel carriers, took off their tracks, dropped steel over the windshield and slots, and set them down inside 5-ton dump trucks. We loaded them up with Quad .50s, Quad 60s, four machine guns tied together, M-79s and Mark 19s, grenade launchers, and called them our gunships. Depending on the size of the convoy we would have two or three of these gunships spaced between supply trucks. Trust me, they wreaked some havoc when we opened up. So we weren't exactly like sitting ducks, we were more like armed and pissed-off ducks, but for me it still was boring as hell. My job was to sit there keeping my foot on the accelerator. I felt like I was meant to be on foot. I couldn't understand it; I wanted to be in the thick of it, and the army was doing everything possible to keep me out of it.

I got lucky. In some ways the military is like a giant corporation, except for the fact people are trying to kill you. There is probably as much politics, favoritism, and bureaucracy involved in moving up the ranks as there is in any corporate structure. There are a lot of faceless people making the decisions that will affect your entire career. So sometimes to progress you need to have somebody with clout looking out for you: your elder, your so-called rabbi. Mine was Sergeant Major Marvin Wells, Pappy Wells. One of the most fortunate occurrences of my life was that he found me.

First thing he did was save my career. We were in the An Khe Pass when the truck directly in front of me got hit. It got lifted right off the ground. A second later the second truck in front of me got hit. I didn't hesitate. I knew who got it next. I dived right out of the cab. We took considerable fire, and then our gunships opened up on the hills. We brought down some thunder on their heads. When it was done we started saddling up, but I'd had it, I'd fucking had it. The convoy commander told me to get back into my truck, and I told him, "No, sir. I am not driving a truck anymore. I'll go infantry, I'll go back into the jungles, I do not care, but I am not driving a truck in combat. I will not do it."

He told me I was under arrest and put me in the rear of another vehicle. When we got back to camp they brought me into brigade headquarters. This lieutenant wanted to court-martial me for disobeying a direct order in combat. I didn't know what the penalty for that was, but I knew it wasn't good. Fourth Battalion Sergeant Major Pappy Wells listened to this officer, then said to me, "Okay, now I want to hear your story."

I told him everything. I told him about being in country before and needing to come back, I told him what I'd done, and I told him I couldn't drive a truck anymore. "I'll do anything else," I told him. "I'll go infantry, I'll go Special Forces. You go ahead and do whatever you want to do, hang me, shoot me, but I am not driving a truck anymore."

He went into his office for a little while. When he came out he pointed toward the landing zone. "Bag and baggage, get on that helicopter."

I told him no, I wasn't doing that without a parachute. I'd heard stories about people who broke the rules getting dropped out of helicopters over the South China Sea. That was not going to happen to me.

Pappy grabbed hold of my neck with one iron hand and shoved

me back against the wall. "Young man," he said, "I will kill you right here if you don't get bag and baggage on that helicopter." I grabbed my rucksack and my weapon and got on that ship. He followed me a couple of minutes later and got on board, never saying one word. When we landed at 4th Battalion base camp, Pappy Wells began changing my life.

John Wayne would've played Pappy Wells in the movie, and been lucky to do so. I loved the man. Pappy was a rock. He was hardcore, the best type of individual the military is capable of producing. He was the first person in my military career that I got real close to, and in a lot of ways he became a father figure to me.

It was pretty obvious that when he looked at me he saw his young self. Like he had been, I was good raw material that needed molding. Pappy had joined the army during World War II. He literally joined; when he was about fifteen years old he bought himself an old uniform, put it on, and got in line. He spent almost two years fighting in Europe before they found out he wasn't in the army. So when I told him my story he got it. Pappy Wells became a paratrooper the same way; he didn't bother going to jump school, he just asked a lot of questions and then made his very first jump out of an airplane into combat. In fact, his nickname for me was Mr. Airborne.

After World War II he served in Korea, then all the little fights in the 1950s, and became one of the first so-called advisers in Vietnam. Basically his advice to the South Vietnamese was "Watch how I shoot dinks." Pappy was one of those career soldiers that really ran the army. Everybody respected him and depended on him, the officers, NCOs, first sergeants, and enlisted men. Everybody. If something needed doing, it was Pappy Wells and the men just like him who got it done. He took care of his troops. Beans or bullets, it didn't matter, if we needed it he made sure we got it.

The first thing he did was get me out of that fucking truck. In that environment one time or another everybody in the Central Highlands came under fire—truck drivers, cooks, supply, we were all combatants—but according to regulations only infantrymen were eligible for a Combat Infantryman's Badge, which was an honor. So the 173rd had set up a two-week school for people to get an official 11 Bravo MOS, military occupational specialty. Infantry. Moving targets. They could continue doing the same jobs they were doing but earn the right to receive that CIB. Pappy Wells spoke with 173rd Command Sergeant Major "Preacher" Hodge and got me officially transferred to Headquarters Company, 4th Battalion. Pappy's command. As soon as I got there he sent me to that Infantry School, and I got my 11 Bravo.

When I got back Pappy moved me from the line company to a recon platoon, or hawk platoon. Basically, we were the human advance warning system. Our job was to provide security for the battalion. We'd patrol around the base camp, setting up ambushes and trying to find the enemy. The joke was that when they started shooting at us, we knew we'd found them. Those hawk missions allowed me to practice and perfect my warrior skills, but I wasn't there too long before I ended up in a body bag.

One afternoon the entire company, three platoons for a total of about eighty people, was out searching for an enemy base camp. We were in the A Shau Valley, which was way up in the north on the Laotian border. An important segment of the Ho Chi Minh Trail ran right through it. A lot of hard fighting took place in that area. We knew they were there, they'd been harassing us for a few days, but we just couldn't find them. If you know what you're doing it's not too difficult to stay hidden in the jungle. Our platoon was walking point for the company, and my eight-man squad was on point for the platoon. Most people hated being out in front; it made them feel real hinky. That wasn't us.

There were some outstanding men in this squad, and we were just aching to find the NVA. Instead, they found us. Same difference.

We were moving single file on a jungle trail covered by pretty thick growth, so it was like we were in permanent twilight. Every once in a while a beam of light would cut through the canopy like God was shining a spotlight. In other parts of the country you really had to be watching out for booby traps, but we were using the same trails they were using, so that wasn't usually a problem. We'd been humping since early in the morning, and eventually we reached the end of this section of the trail. It wasn't like stepping out into the open, but suddenly the jungle canopy got a lot less thick. Instead of staying in a single-file line, we were able to spread out a little into more like a V-formation. We were skirting around the side of a rocky hill when we crossed the perimeter of an NVA base camp. We just didn't know it.

They watched us coming, and they waited completely silent as our point squad walked past them. Then when the main body of the platoon had walked into the kill zone they opened up on us. Surviving the first few seconds of an ambush is mostly luck; it depends almost entirely on where you are. We were separated from the main body by the enemy, out on our own little island of land. I dived onto the ground behind a few rocks and started firing. It wasn't much protection, but there wasn't much else. Our squad formed a defensive position like we had been trained to do. They hit us with an avalanche of fire—AK-47s, machine guns, grenades. It was immediately apparent we'd stumbled on a company-sized force. We'd found what we had been looking for, and we were paying for it. We'd stirred the hornet's nest, and they definitely were stinging.

We were in their house. They had us outmanned and outgunned. They had the higher ground and better intelligence. They had been watching us; they probably had a pretty good idea of our size and the disposition of our force. They even had the advantage of the terrain.

The jungle canopy made it tough for the gunships and fast movers—the helicopters and the jet fighters—to make visual contact and put fire on their positions. We had discipline, courage, and artillery.

These were definitely experienced troops, and their attack was well planned and executed with precision. They knew they had to hit us hard, then move out fast. It wouldn't take too long for the birds to bring in more troops and bring down the wrath from the sky on them. I could see them downrange moving around, moving toward our defensive position. They were coming. I had gotten good at combat. I wasn't afraid, I wasn't anything. I was able to block out every emotion, every thought, except what was happening in front of me. It was a transformation to a different realm of existence. It was a level of intensity I have not felt in any other circumstance. I was slinging bullets, tossing grenades, laying down a blanket of fire in an arc when I got hit for the first time.

I never saw it coming. One thing about being a combat soldier, if you're in it long enough you begin to think that maybe you're one of the lucky ones; at least until the instant you aren't. I took a round in my left elbow, through my left elbow actually. It felt more like being hit with a hammer, then jabbed with a big needle, and it knocked me back. In the movies and books characters get "insulted" when they get wounded, like how could it happen to them. That's total bullshit. The fact is it hurt like hell. I looked down at my arm and I was dripping some blood, but it wasn't too bad. The adrenaline that was flowing though my body probably dampened a lot of the pain. There was a horde coming to kill me, I didn't have time to focus on a hole in my arm. I kept firing. I was having some problems holding my weapon because the wound was somehow affecting the nerves in the back of my hand, but I supported it in the crook of my elbow and managed to stay in the battle.

I was also cursing those motherfuckers, yelling at them loud as I could. It wasn't only that I was angry that I had exposed myself and been hit. In a battle you have to keep your mouth open to prevent damage to your hearing and maybe your brain. Those concussions will shake you up good. It turned out I was very fortunate my mouth was wide open—'cause the second bullet ripped right through my jaw. Doctors said later that if my mouth had been shut it might have taken off my whole lower jaw. This one did enough damage; it almost cut my tongue in half and blew out my back teeth. I was spitting out blood and pieces of teeth. I was still fighting, but it was getting tougher. My blood was running down my throat and choking me.

I tried to stay in the fight, but I was bleeding out. Eventually I lost consciousness. I don't have any idea how long the battle lasted or exactly what happened to me. Next thing I remember I was lying on a stretcher getting medevaced out. My wounds were wrapped up, and I was hooked up to a plasma line. That helicopter was a very big target, and as we lifted off we started getting hit. I could hear the *pt-pt-pt-pt* of bullets ripping through the sides. Then I got hit again. A round went right through the bottom of my foot. I had no idea how that happened, where it came from, but I couldn't believe it. Then the rounds coming up hit the blade, and we started rotating wildly and going down. That pilot did a great job getting us back on the ground, but I was all shot up.

I was fading in and out. I remember getting carried off the downed slick, and I remember them pumping me full of morphine. I remember thinking, *Get me the fuck out of here; give me a fucking break,* and for the first time in my life considering the possibility that I was going to die. It wasn't any deep fear, and I didn't see any white lights, but I didn't want to die right there. I thought that would be a real waste. Then I passed out.

In my memory, when I finally regained consciousness two guys were carrying me, getting ready to put me in a body bag. The battle was over, and our people were picking over the carnage on the battlefield. We had about thirty people killed and wounded. As they were putting me in the bag I woke up, and they dropped me on the ground. I definitely can remember the feeling, but I can't tell you that this actually happened. That's the strange thing, I remember it, but I don't know if it's true or not. I was pumped full of painkillers, and I know what that can do to you.

I woke up in a field hospital, like a MASH unit. They fixed me as best they could, and within days I was on my way home. I went through Okinawa to the Letterman Army Medical Center at the Presidio in San Francisco. In addition to being shot three times, I also had some small pieces of shrapnel from a grenade. I was messed up pretty good. There were some great doctors there. I was fortunate; I had a Japanese American doctor who specialized in bone reconstruction and plastic surgery, and he took real good care of me. My jaw healed up, and I had some dental work, but it would always give me problems. My elbow and foot were both clean wounds, and they healed nicely. That doctor also taught me how to play chess. He'd come up to my room and we'd sit and talk for hours while we played that game. Sometimes we'd talk about the future. He had his future mapped out; he was planning to become a plastic surgeon in San Francisco when he got out. All this training he was getting in the army was going to be beneficial. I admitted that I'd never thought too much about the future; mine was pretty much a day-to-day life. I spent about four months in the hospital. I had a lot of time to think about what I really wanted to do with the rest of my life, and I realized I was already doing it. I loved the military, and I didn't see any reason to do anything else. I was an American warrior. That's what made me happy. I just needed to find every means possible to be the best at it.

The army officially awarded me a Purple Heart, but I refused to accept it. I was young, and I took a lot of pride in doing my job without being injured. I wasn't going to wear a medal that showed that the enemy hit his target. At that time getting a medal for failing at my job made no sense to me.

When I got all healed and they were getting ready to release me from the hospital, I went in front of the medical board. Basically, they told me they would change my MOS and I could go anywhere in the free world. They were giving me a choice. I'd done my duty, they said, I didn't have to go back there. If I wanted I could get assigned to an embassy staff in Germany, Ireland, Japan, even the Caribbean.

I told them thank you, but that I needed to go back to the 173rd. That was all I knew in the military, and I knew my future started there. So in mid-1969 I went back to the 4th Battalion, back to Pappy Wells.

Pappy had my back. He definitely knew how the system worked and the people who made it work. Again, just like in every other profession, your personal connections mattered. Once I got back over there I took a short-term reenlist for "present-duty station," which meant my classification went from draftee to RA, regular army. That made me eligible to move forward to the Rangers. To prepare me for that, Pappy gave me a Special Forces education. He gave me all the manuals—unconventional warfare operations, the FM-2175 patrolling manual, weapons, map reading, compass readings, everything I needed to know. I studied them hard. For the first time in life I had a purpose as a student.

There was one last thing that Pappy had to take care of before I could go to the Rangers. One day when I came back in from a patrol, they told me the sergeant major wanted to see me. I went over to his office, and there was a pile of military paperwork on his desk. "You know what this is?" he asked.

"No idea, Sergeant Major," I told him.

"This was your life," he said, pointing to the pile. He had all my records from my days being Butch O'Neal, my 201 file, my finance records, medical records, everything that could have held me up. Then he took the whole pile and tossed it in the burn barrel. "That's it," he said. "Go ahead." I didn't know it yet, but he had already laid the groundwork for me. He sent me on up to Echo Company, 20th LRRPs—Charlie Rangers. At that time Charlie Rangers was assigned to II Corps, one of the five corps that Vietnam was divided into, making E Company the eyes and ears of II Corps territory. When I was assigned there in 1969 the LRRPs had just been designated Rangers, although many of us had never been through Rangers training. That made E Company the largest LRRP company in Vietnam. We had more people and the most territory to cover. In addition to Vietnam we also had Laos and Cambodia, even though officially we were never there.

There were no other units in Vietnam like the LRRPs. In fact, you probably had to go back to the American Revolution and the Civil War to find small units fighting a guerrilla war in enemy territory. The big problem was that when we went into Vietnam we were not prepared to fight a guerrilla war. We were still training troops to fight big, static battles like in World War II and Korea. I believe that if we'd turned the combat responsibility over early to Special Forces–type units and kept the big army out of the fight, the outcome might have been completely different. A big if.

There were some people who figured out right away that to fight this enemy we needed to put small, highly mobile reaction forces on the ground. After the Herd first got there in 1965 Commanding General Ellis W. Williamson realized "small units could get out and get information much better than large search-and-destroy type operations." He called them Delta Teams. Colonel David Hackworth of the 327th Airborne Infantry's 1st Battalion helped organize two volunteer platoons that they called Tiger Forces. One of Hackworth's subordinates called his recon teams Hatchet Teams and gave them hatchets to carry. There's a story that after they used those hatchets to cut off some enemy heads and ears, the army made them drop that name, which is when they first got called LRRPs.

General William Westmoreland made them official in 1966 by ordering "that a comprehensive Long Range Patrol program" be developed in South Vietnam, which he defined as "a specially trained unit organized and equipped for the special purpose of functioning as an information gathering agency responsive to the intelligence requirements of the tactical commander. These patrols consist of specially trained personnel capable of performing reconnaissance, surveillance and target acquisition within the dispatching unit's area of interest." Like I said, track 'em, find 'em, and kill 'em.

There were only thirteen independently operating LRRP units in the whole country. There was no central command and control structure; we were only responsible to whatever command issued our orders. The army never figured out where we properly belonged. The fact that we didn't fit anywhere made some people in the higher echelon a little anxious. We were sort of like rogue units operating outside of normal accountability. We were taking elite personnel out of their units, and very few knew exactly what we were doing.

When I showed up at Charlie Rangers, one of the first people I met was David Dolby, who was already a legend and a Congressional Medal of Honor recipient. He had just come out of the field with his six-man Double Deuce team and asked me who I was and what I was doing there. I was coming to join Charlie Company, I told him. Pappy Wells had sent me up. My orders hadn't been cut yet, but I'd come on up to look around. "Okay," he said. "If this is where you want to be, come with me tomorrow."

I went on two missions with him. David Dolby was an amazing soldier. In demeanor and attitude he was a lot like Pappy. We snuck in and looked at the enemy. We were too far from support to initiate action, so instead we sent back intel, then delivered armored rain upon their heads. I went back to the 173rd and got my orders, and by the time I got back to Charlie Rangers, David had moved to November Company, 173rd. He'd left a spot for me on his Double Deuce team, though.

E Company was based out of An Khe and Pleiku, but we went wherever Special Forces needed us. This was where I finally found the opportunity to put all my knowledge and all my ability to good use. While officially I was assigned to Double Deuce, the truth was Charlie Rangers was pretty informal, so I'd go out with any team that needed me.

These guys were hardcore. This wasn't run anything at all like the regular army. There was basically only one rule, do whatever you had to do to survive. Most of the time there was nobody looking over our shoulders, nobody telling us what to do or how to do it, no one giving us any bullshit about uniforms or military procedure. We lived for the mission, and when we lived through that one, we got ready for the next one. It was as a LRRP that I truly learned how to walk the path of the warrior. The more time I spent in the field, the more time any of us spent in the field, the farther away we got from any type of normal behavior. To survive out there in the jungle, fighting an enemy who understood the environment, we went native.

It's a story that hasn't been told very well. There were generally six people on a team, but at times I went out with as few as three people, and other times missions were "heavy," meaning that more than one team was assigned to them. A recon team was made up of a team leader, the assistant team leader, an RTO—radiotelephone operator—the assistant RTO, a scout, and slack, or rear security. Walking point and rear security were very much the same, but rear security burned up a lot more energy because he was walking backward controlling the area behind the team, while also making sure the team left no evidence of its presence—no footprints, no tall grass pushed over, no litter on the ground. A lot of our Kit Carson scouts, which is what we called them, were Vietnamese. At times they were even Chieu Hois, NVA soldiers who had defected or gotten captured and turned. They had to keep their identities completely secret because some of them had family up in the North who could have been punished for them working with us. It wasn't easy to put our lives in the hands of these people; they had to prove themselves before anybody'd risk going out with them. Naturally it reminded me of the Native American scouts who had worked with the cavalry. The Chieu Hois proved to be extremely loyal people, who were exceptional at their jobs.

I learned more about survival and operating in enemy territory from the indigs than I did by listening to our people. For almost two years I worked with a Kit Carson scout who had been sent down from the North by the NVA as part of a large group assigned to infiltrate into the South and assassinate the president of South Vietnam. The North Vietnamese were holding his family hostage. By the time his team got down to Saigon there were only four of them left, and all of them got captured. The North Vietnamese figured they were all dead.

I was really cautious with him when he first got assigned to my team, but eventually I understood that he was on a vendetta, he wanted revenge. He was a committed warrior. He taught me how to track. We would alternate at point and slack and I learned a lot from him. We were always together. On one mission my five-man team got discovered, and they were in heavy pursuit of us for two days; a company or better was chasing us, and we were getting in and out of firefights trying to evade them long enough to get to an exfil point and get flown out of there. Finally, late on the second day of this shit, they had us pinned down. We were in another good firefight, and they were trying get around our flank. Bullets were flying everywhere. Admittedly, it was not a good situation. I always wanted to stay and fight, but there were times when our best possible strategy was simply to run like hell. The problem for us was that the people trying to kill us were between us and the next scheduled pickup location.

By this time my scout was speaking decent English, and he knew how I felt about all this. He had taken on my attitude, and I had learned his skills. So in the middle of this fight he looked at me and smiled and said, "I'm tired, Big O. Fuck these sons of a bitches, let's go kill them all." Then that little fucker stood up and charged these guys. I couldn't believe it, it was just like in the John Wayne movies. I watched him in awe for a few seconds, and then I thought, *Fuck it, man, if we're gonna die let's at least take as many of them as we can with us.* So I stood up and bolted right after him, and the rest of the team was right with me. We charged into their line, screaming and yelling and firing everything we had like we were crazy. I guess we were. We were throwing grenades, causing an unbelievable ruckus. I guess we shocked them, because we broke through their line, and then we kept humping. We didn't stop for hours. During those two days every one of us got hit by some shrapnel and had some flesh wounds, but incredibly nobody got seriously hurt.

Him telling me "Let's go kill them all" and charging was the most courageous thing I saw in Vietnam. There are people who know me who describe me as "that crazy fucker who charged right into the NVA line," and I tell them that wasn't me, he was the one I was following. I tried to put him in for a medal, but our company commander didn't like handing out medals, mostly because he was never in combat so he couldn't get one, and he especially didn't like awarding medals to the Vietnamese.

I lost track of this scout when I left Vietnam. It was hard to keep up with these people because we knew them mostly by their nicknames; they were defectors, so they didn't want anybody knowing their real names. The last I heard he had been captured by the NVA, but I wasn't sure that was true. If he was captured they probably killed him. Anyway, I never saw him again.

Our jobs on the team were determined by our skills. Rank had no meaning at all in the LRRPs. Although most of our people were E-5s, E-6s, and above, nobody wore any rank and nobody cared. Most of the time I was there, for example, people just assumed I was an NCO because I was an assistant team leader and then a team leader, but in fact I was just a PFC. That didn't matter to anybody as long as I could keep them alive. When my lieutenant found that out, he immediately put me in for corporal, and I finally made E-5, but most of the time I was there I was a private.

While each person had his own responsibility, we also had to have all the necessary team skills, ranging from using the radio to stopping bleeding. Each member of the team was capable of using almost every type of weapon that we might come across, reading map coordinates, killing silently, or gathering intelligence. A team trained together so it could operate efficiently in the bush. When I was on point, for example, my eyes were continually sweeping the area in front of me, and wherever I was looking my weapon was pointing. Each member of the team operated off me. If I stopped and swung my weapon to my right, the individual behind me would immediately swing his weapon to cover our left, and so on down the line. We were better trained to work together than the Rockettes, and a lot more deadly, too.

When replacements joined the team, we had to take time training with them before we would take them out on a mission. We were only as safe as our weakest member. I remember when Mike Echanis joined my team. Mike was a martial arts expert, and eventually we would live and work and almost die together in Nicaragua. Mike was my friend. He was one of the toughest men I have ever known and a black sash in Hwa Rang Do. Mike also was his own man who wanted to prove himself. On the first recon mission we took him out on, we got into contact with a superior enemy force. The NVA strategy was to occupy your attention from the front and attempt to flank you so you would be surrounded. That meant when we were in a firefight with a superior force we had to keep moving. If we stayed in one position too long, eventually they were going to surround us. So during this firefight I decided it was time to break contact and high-tail it to our exfil point, but Mike decided to stay there and fight them. Mike was always wanting to try out his hand-to-hand Hong Kong Fooey, to see if his kicks and punches worked, so he starts going at it with this NVA. I looked at him and thought, *Are you shitting me?* So I just shot the fucker and told Mike, "Come on, Mike, let's get the fuck out of here. We got to go, amigo." He didn't want to leave. We had to go back and get him, which put the whole team in jeopardy. When we got back in the rear I fired his ass off my team; we couldn't allow one person to function independently. Instead he got put on convoy security, and as his convoy was going through the An Khe Pass sometime in 1970, they were ambushed. Mike got his leg shot up bad and lost the use of his foot, although he managed to overcome that. I liked Mike, liked him a lot, but when he showed that he couldn't be part of a team there was no place for him. He was in country for less than a month before he was wounded.

A LRRP wasn't much more than a walking arsenal. We carried everything we needed to survive and fight for four or five days on our back. When we saddled up, the least we would carry was an M-16 or other weapon, two claymore mines, thirty or more magazines, smoke grenades, frags, willy peters, maps, canteens, a compass, a first aid kit, two knives, and C rations. I carried my medicine bag hanging around my neck. In it I had my eagle feather and some other things that mattered. I also had a survival kit where I kept my extra compass, a second pistol, a signaling mirror, a fire starter, a strobe light, and a little beacon radio, the stuff I would need for E&E, escape and evasion. Everything was attached to web belts, taped down and tied down so six men could move through jungle, elephant grass, or rice paddies without making a sound or leaving a trace. As long as we were in the field, day or night, our equipment was never more than a foot or two away from us.

That was pretty much standard, but we all modified our personal equipment. In addition to the M-16, we carried all different types of weapons. A lot of point men carried a sawed-off M-79, which fired 40×46mm grenades—thumpers, we called them—as a secondary weapon. This was a real valuable weapon. If we walked out of the brush smack into an enemy patrol, for example, one blast would take a whole fucking head right off. That thumper made a loud and violent statement and it bought us the time we needed to switch to regular firepower. It also was a useful weapon when we had to blast open a door in one of their camps and we weren't sure what was behind it. When it fired it sounded just like a 60mm mortar, *whomp, whomp,* which made the enemy believe we had to be part of a bigger unit, a weapons platoon or even a company, because no six-man team could hump a mortar. That gave us time to maneuver while they were thinking about it. We found a lot of different uses for it.

When possible we preferred to carry Russian-made AK-47s that we captured from the NVA. An AK was more reliable than an M-16 in that climate; it was more durable and easier to keep clean, and even when it got dirty with sand and water it was still operative. The M-16 jammed too easily. Another problem with the M-16 was that it was such a high-velocity weapon that if a round hit a twig or something it could ricochet. I've seen people hit in their upper body with an M-16 round that traveled all the way through, bouncing off bones, yet there were times it wouldn't penetrate a target. An AK round was much more effective at busting through jungle growth, and we had plenty of captured ammunition.

Basically any weapon we could take off an NVA was valued. Not only were they good weapons, the sound they made was distinctive, so we could fire them without alarming the enemy. When we were going into an area where my sixth sense told me to be ready for some heavy contact, for example, I carried a cut-down M-60, a machine gun. "The pig," I called it, and my team referred to me as "the pig man." Normally that thing was too heavy to carry through brush for several days, but I cut away everything except what it needed to fire. I cut off the stock and replaced it with a homemade stock that held the buffer spring in, I took the guards off it and cut the barrel down. I took off the muzzle suppressors. I even designed a different trigger mechanism for it. Then I cut down an ammo bar I'd taken off one of our gunships and rigged it so my rucksack fit on it. I had a feed tray coming out of my rucksack underneath my arm right into the M-60. I loaded 1,500 rounds in the rucksack, so I could feed the pig straight out of that rucksack. Generally our whole pack weighed as much as 100 pounds, but even cut down, that pig weighed at least 25 pounds, not even counting the feed tray and ammo. It was a load.

As far as I knew there wasn't another weapon like that in the whole country. That motherfucker roared when I fired it, and flames shot at least 15 feet past the muzzle in a spectacular fireball. The NVA never knew what it was. They had never seen or heard a weapons system like that. It sounded something like a fast-firing .50 caliber. That thing created confusion on the battlefield, which was what we wanted to do. Normally one out of every six rounds is a tracer, but I loaded it special so that my first five hundred rounds were all tracers, so all of a sudden they'd see solid tracers coming at them and wouldn't have any idea who was firing what; they couldn't figure out how many people were out there. Let them think there was a whole weapons company firing at them.

That pig could make a big difference. One time we were not more than 300 yards from our landing zone when we got hit. We'd gotten off the bird and faded into the woods; we were waiting there for our senses to get up, to get the noise of the slick's engines out of our heads so we could hear the small sounds when we got in contact. Most of the firing was coming from in front, but then they began flanking us. We didn't know how many of them there were, but we always operated with the belief that there were more of them than of us. We formed our defensive semicircle; I was right in the center. When my team was delivering suppressing fire I stayed hunched down on my knees, but as soon as they started changing magazines I rose up and start spinning in a circle, continuously firing the M-60 right over their heads. You could see the rounds going through the barrel; hot brass was flying out of my rucksack. Flames were spitting out of that gun like it was a big flamethrower. I didn't see who I was shooting at. I was just spinning, spinning, firing continuously. Suddenly I heard my assistant team leader Steve Byer and Hardcore Kelly hollering at me, "Stop firing! Stop firing! You're catching us on fire!" We were bunched so tightly that my rounds were hitting them on the back of the neck and the flames from the weapon were heating up their rucksacks. After that they began calling me "the mad 60-man." We scared the shit out of those people—and my own team wasn't so comfortable either.

I depended on my knife, especially with the type of missions we were running in Vietnam and later when I was in Nicaragua. I always carried three knives with me. I had my little Randall knife, which was a really good handmade knife used by Special Forces. When I first got into the LRRPs I really wanted one, so I sent that company a letter asking how much it cost, and they sent one back to me. I also had a British Fairbairn knife, which was like an 8-to-10-inch long dagger sharpened on both sides, and a razor-sharp penknife I carried in my survival kit. I used the penknife like a scalpel if I had to cut something out. When I was in camp I was always sharpening my knives; they had a job to do.

I became an expert at the silent kill. Eventually I taught sentry stalking and silent killing at different schools for elite troops, but the first time I killed a man with a knife I almost sliced through my own arm. We was operating out of Pleiku, and an SF guy was teaching me how to kill a man with a knife. Practicing to kill a man hand-to-hand doesn't have too much relationship to the reality. When you're learning the technique, the one thing you know is nobody is supposed to get hurt. Somewhere in the back of your mind you wonder if you're capable of doing it for real. You never know until you know.

We'd discovered an NVA training base camp in an area known as the Fishhook, between Pleinong and Plebring where Vietnam borders Laos and Cambodia. It was real thick jungle. We was trying to get as close as possible to gather intelligence, like how many people were in there. Then we intended to pull back and call in air support. We were still outside their security perimeter when I walked up behind this sentry. When I saw him for the first time he was no more than 5 feet from me, facing away. I must have made a little sound, because he started to turn. I knew that if he kept turning he was going to see me and raise the alert. I didn't think, I responded to the situation. Like I'd been taught I threw my left arm around his neck, covering his mouth and his nose with my hand so he couldn't breathe or scream a warning, then with my right hand I stabbed him right through his neck with that Fairbairn knife. It surprised me a little how easily that blade cut right through his flesh and bone. What I did not realize, what nobody warned me about, was that the Fairburn blade was so long it would go completely through his neck and right into my arm. It ripped into my muscle and bone a couple of inches. I was stuck with this dead body hanging from the knife. He only struggled a little bit, but as I spun around and pulled out the knife I took him to the ground. I didn't have the slightest doubt or hesitation about cutting his throat, and I had no bad feelings about it either. Mostly I was just pissed at myself for putting that blade into my arm. It was an important lesson.

After I stabbed myself taking out that sentry, I knew I needed a special knife for the silent kill. The Fairbairn had three problems. Number one, it was too long; two, it was a dagger, made for stabbing; and three, for this work I needed a knife that would let me slit the throat, then come around and cut the spinal cord. I invented that knife in a dream. I saw it in my dream and I made it. I had learned blacksmithing and fabrication from my dad, so I could make pretty much anything I needed to. Basically, this knife looked like an Alaskan whaling knife. It wasn't much of a sticking knife, but it was an excellent sweeping and cutting knife. The handle was shaped something like a whale; the blade was sharp on one side, and as it came to a point it was sharpened on the other side. I made it out of a flat leaf spring that probably came off a deuce-and-a-half trailer. I cut a long piece of metal, curving it gently, sort of like the curve of a banana. When I used it I would yank back the sentry's head, reach across his neck and dig it in, then bring it back toward me, cutting his spine as I did. It was perfect for sentry removal. It was designed for one purpose only, to cut throats. It remains a beautiful weapon.

We basically created our own uniforms, dressing to fit the mission. We'd dyed our fatigues black or brown, so that when they were done the camouflage was visible but it was much darker than usual. We'd change our camouflage depending on the terrain we were going to be operating in. Sometimes we'd even change when we crossed from one area to another, from open areas to the jungle, to fit into the environment. If we were going into an area infested with VC, we'd definitely wear clothing that looked black at night or from a distance, which is what they wore, because if they saw us that split second spent trying to figure out who we were could give us an advantage. We'd cover all our exposed skin with camo. We never wore helmets. Helmets were too cumbersome and too noisy when we were moving through vines and heavy growth. Instead we wore floppy hats or just headbands to keep the sweat out of our eyes. Those headbands became important; some people had just one that they wore for a year or more, until it wasn't much more than a torn-up piece of material. We wore all different types of footwear, again depending on the mission and the terrain. Sometimes I wore boots, sometimes Ho Chi Minh sandals, which were cut out of rubber tires, and sometimes elk moccasins that my grandmother sent me. What we did with our boots was mold smaller footprint impressions on the soles, so anybody tracking us couldn't be sure whether we were Americans or Vietnamese.

I also had my bones, buffalo bones, which I wore in my ear, my war necklace, and my war shirt. I had the totems of war that a lot of us collected and didn't talk about, too, but that came later.

The LRRPs got assigned just about every type of mission you can imagine. We were the people who went into enemy territory and did whatever had to be done. Personally, I don't have any idea how many missions I went on, but I was in the field more than I was back in camp. While usually we were each assigned to one team, I would go out with all of them. I kept three rucksacks packed all the time. While I was out Steve Byer, my assistant team leader and a good country boy from Utah, would prepare my rucksack for the next mission. I didn't like sitting around in camp waiting several days to go. There were always these little Barbie details that had to be done, and

I didn't want any part of that. I earned a reputation as being a really good tracker, so teams wanted me to be with them in the field because they knew I was going to find the enemy. I had my recon map of all the terrains and the ridges, and I studied it, I analyzed it. I would go over it and over it. In my mind it was a topographical map; by looking at it I could see the hilltops, I could see the streams. I would know where a human could go in and how he would move.

At night, when I closed my eyes I would visualize where we would find him, where I would be if I was him. I would see in my mind where we would walk. In my dreams I projected myself as one of them, and there were times when we went out on a mission that I knew I had been there before. I had walked that trail, and I would know that down this trail the bad guys were waiting. It took me some time to trust these visions. They weren't like the visions I'd had as a child, staring into a fire, where the elders would come and teach me. These were different; I couldn't grab hold of them. Sometimes I didn't consciously remember them until I was walking the path.

I wasn't that little kid who'd peed his pants in that first firefight, I was a seasoned troop. A proven warrior. I thrived off the mission.

When I was in camp I wouldn't eat American food or use American soap, aftershave lotion, or anything that had a recognizable odor. I didn't want anybody smoking American cigarettes anywhere near me. It wasn't just the obvious odor on your skin, it was the scent of your sweat, your piss, and your shit. The NVA and Vietcong lived in the jungles; they literally could smell us coming. So I ate only Vietnamese food, mostly rice, and used local products. We would never cook in the field. Usually we would share one ration between two people. We'd bring dehydrated food packs with us or indig food, rice and fish, and just put it in our pockets to heat it up. Food was about the last thing we were concerned with in the field.

The mission began when we climbed on board a Huey, which was big enough to carry a six-man crew with all our equipment. There wasn't too much talking as we flew to our landing zone, or LZ. We were putting on our game face. We knew we could be staying in the field as long as a week, and a lot of that time would be spent just lying in a concealed position for hours or even days, waiting and watching anything that came by. Normally the slick would touch down and then lift right off in several different places, so that if anybody was watching or listening they wouldn't know precisely where we got off. It could have been any one of those places the slick hit the ground. The first thing we did when we got down was secure our perimeter and get into a listening mode. We had to adapt to our new environment instantly; we had to get in touch with Mother Earth. Once we felt in tune with our surroundings, we moved out of the area as fast as possible, just in case somebody had seen us coming in.

Many of our missions were beyond the range of our ground communications, sometimes even beyond our artillery. Usually there were several teams on the ground at the same time, but in different sectors. There were instances where different teams bumped into each other and there were casualties, but it didn't happen too often. Communications were the difference between living and dying. We always carried at least two radios, sometimes more. The terrain we were in made normal radio contact impossible, so we improvised. When it was possible we set up a camp in the area to relay communications, but mostly we were dependent on our observer.

My platoon leader was Lieutenant Gary Dolan, who was in position in a fixed-wing bird dog up above us. He had responsibility not just for my team but for all the teams on the ground. Gary Dolan saved a lot of lives. When we were down there it was comforting to know he was circling above us running the show. Besides relaying our communications, he was calling in gunships, fast movers, and artillery when we needed them and making sure the slicks got us in and then got us out quick when that became necessary. He was a vital part of our team; nobody stayed on station as long as he did, and I knew there were times he limped home on fumes. Those times he had to go refuel or the weather got too bad, we felt naked. We actually used to plan our activities around the times we knew Gary was going to be up there, and during the time frame he was off station we would curtail them and sometimes just lie low.

Gary and I were definitely living on the same wavelength. I used to carry the antenna of my radio beacon folded over in my rucksack where it wouldn't be seen, but when we needed assistance I'd pop it up. He knew to bring in guns when that radio beacon popped up.

When you live in the jungle like we did, you get accustomed to certain colors and shapes and movements. Anything different attracts your attention. My team was walking along an animal trail late one afternoon. I'd stop every few minutes just to let my senses explore the area. I always took a gulp of air, because your taste buds will respond to anything a little different. In this case I tasted smoke. Somebody not too far away was cooking. As we were the only LRRP team in the grid, whoever it was wasn't friendly.

We had come out of the triple-canopy jungle into an area of less dense bush. There were still some trees, but rays of sunlight were slanting through the branches, creating areas of light and dark shadow. In those conditions we had to be especially careful not to move from light to dark and back into the light, and never break a ray of sunlight, because movement across light attracts attention. We were moving very carefully—then we heard some muffled noises. We stopped. Someone in the area was practicing noise discipline. I scanned the area slow and careful, and finally off to one side I noticed an unusual shape. Next to the trail there was a dark rectangle in the upper section of a small hill. Nature doesn't create dark rectangular shapes, and the dinks did a rotten job camouflaging it. It looked like what it was: a slit cut into the side of a little hill. It was flat on top and they'd covered it with logs and brush. They didn't bother breaking up its straight lines. I knew right away it was a machine-gun bunker. Obviously they'd built it there for a reason. It was protecting some type of fixed camp.

Whatever it was, they didn't want it discovered. It had to be something large, or they wouldn't have made the effort to build a permanent bunker in the outer perimeter. Eventually we figured out that this was an NVA base camp and we'd been fortunate enough to come up on it between two bunkers. I pulled the antenna of my emergency radio out of my rucksack and turned on the beacon. Gary was up, and he recognized immediately that it was Double Deuce, it was me, and he knew from experience that if I had turned on my beacon I was requesting air support. He got a reading on the beacon's position and called in the gunships and fast movers, anything within range that could deliver firepower, as well as alerting a reaction team.

We withdrew to a safer place where I could actually talk to him on the radio. I gave him coordinates from the beacon, 200 meters north of it or whatever. Then we moved to a safe place. Those pilots weren't going to worry about us; they were going to shoot up anything moving in that area. Once they lit it up, the bees were going to be leaving the hive, and the assumption was that anything on the ground in that area was an unfriendly. It was up to us to evacuate.

After the air strikes we went in with the Korean reaction force. Our official mission was over, but this was too interesting to leave. It was a training area or a briefing area. There were command bunkers, weapons caches, piles of supplies, all of it set right there in the middle of the jungle. We had just stumbled upon it. Nobody had even suspected it was there, and it was only our ability to move silently that did not alert them.

As rewarding as a mission like that was, our primary job was to collect intelligence. We used to call it SALUTE: the size, activity, and location of the unit, the uniforms they were wearing, a description of the terrain, and the equipment they had. SALUTE. While we were in enemy territory we took samples of the soil, vegetation, and water. We took photographs with a little Olympus camera, and if we could sneak in and out of a camp we gathered up written intelligence.

Sometimes we also were assigned special missions—planning an ambush or capturing and bringing back a prisoner for interrogation. Two different times I was on teams searching for American POWs.

We had intel that American prisoners were being held in a certain area, and they wanted a team to check it out. Officially we weren't supposed to go up into Cambodia, but there weren't any lines on the ground like on a map, so we went where we had to go. This was the mission that we all had been waiting for. We knew the VC were holding Americans in the north, and it was frustrating not being able to help them. In my mind we were going to find them, kill everybody around that was holding them, and bring them home. I believed that.

We spent two days tracking them before we found their camp. It was empty. We found some cages, but no VC and no prisoners. We spent several hours under cover just watching silently, in case one of them came back for something left behind, but this camp had been abandoned. The prisoners had been moved. The stuff we picked up indicated they had been there within the last couple of days, but there was no way of telling where they had gone. That was as frustrating as hell, but there wasn't anything more we could do. Later I found out they were only about two miles away. We definitely could have gotten to them, but we didn't.

To me, the perfect mission meant getting in, obtaining all the information possible, and then getting out without being detected or a shot fired. If we came upon a sizable enemy force, before slipping away we could either call in a line unit or have the fast movers and artillery blast the shit out of them. I especially liked bringing in the Koreans because that country had not signed the Geneva Convention; when those people came out, they didn't leave anything living behind. Most of the firefights we got into, we either ran into the enemy point-to-point or we got detected and had to fight our way home.

One time, for example, my team was in the woods walking an animal trail above and parallel to a regular trail, just doing our usual snooping and pooping, and I sensed that the VC were there. We knew these trails were safe because if there had been booby traps the animals would have popped them. I was walking point. I stopped, and the instant I stopped my whole team froze. No movement at all. The way we operated, the team was a mirror image of the point man. Whatever the point man did, everybody mimicked. They were waiting on me. I was throwing my senses out there, trying to figure out what was going on.

Then we heard some muffled sounds coming up behind us. Using hand signals—we almost never spoke when we were in the field; we would literally go four or five days without speaking one single word—I told my team to get off the trail. We took one step, two steps off our trail into the grass and waited. We didn't move, barely breathed, waited. At that moment our only objective was to become part of the environment. We were in what was called hasty ambush position, meaning it wasn't the best possible location but it was all we had time to do. In that situation we could either let the enemy walk by and live or we could take him out, depending on the mission objective. After a few minutes the enemy came down the trail. It was a point element, a squad walking security in front of the main force. They were relaxed. There was no reason for them to believe Americans were this far north. We stood there for more than two hours watching as the whole main body of the company moved by us. They were no more than five or six feet away from us, and they never knew we were there.

When the main body passed we waited some more, until their rear security went by, then we waited a few minutes more and finally moved silently in the opposite direction. When we'd put some distance between us we called in artillery, fast movers, and gunships, then hightailed it to our exfil point for the pickup. Before we left on a mission we would designate several extraction points over several days. So if we couldn't get to the first LZ we knew the next pickup was in eighteen hours or twenty-four hours at another predesignated LZ. Sometimes we had to go a long way to get there, as many as 10 to 15 klicks (kilometers), which is a lot of ground to cover when you're moving carefully. Rarely did we go beyond a secondary pickup, but we did prepare for it.

Extractions weren't necessarily pretty, but they were always quick. In my years in country, never once did I see a pilot not make the greatest possible effort to get a team off the ground. It was dangerous enough being a small target with limited ground cover; those guys were big targets with no cover. They was risking their lives just as much as we were when they came in to get us.

They flew all types of aircraft under all types of conditions. Slicks were troop carriers, with two M-60s to protect against whatever was out there while people were getting on. They did not deliver the firepower of a gunship. A gunship was essentially a flying arsenal. Basically we had two types of gunships, the Charlie model and the Mike model. The Mike was a basic chopper with Cobra turbines and extralong blades and a strong transmission that hauled nothing but ammo. No passengers, just the two pilots and the crew chief/gunner. The fast movers were the F-104s that would come in and strafe, drop bombs, and shoot the shit out of the bad guys. Usually they were assigned to hit fixed targets, but we got their welcome assistance when we were in contact and they were already up on a mission. Too often the forecast was hot with a chance of bullets.

When a slick hit the ground we had seconds to get on board or we missed our ride. I own an old helicopter, got it out on a lot behind my metal shop in North Carolina. That bird comes right out of my old unit. It's in sad shape. I got it from range control at Fort Bragg, where it had been used for training and then basically abandoned. It'd been sitting out there for several years, falling apart. The people who ran that program knew it was surplus, so they asked me if I wanted it. I took it before I even looked at its records and realized it was the exact same bird that had once saved my life and the lives of my team!

I never did forget the number, 235. We were receiving intense fire, and the slicks couldn't get in to get us. They had already taken too many rounds. We were sort of stranded there until a gunship pilot decided he was going to get us. As he came in, he let loose with everything he had on the enemy. He lit up that jungle, and he bought us maybe thirty seconds. As we were running to jump on board he yelled at us, "You got one bounce to get on my aircraft," and he wasn't kidding. Everybody grabbed hold. There wasn't enough room for all of us on a gunship, so I just wrapped my arms around a rocket pod and held on tight. He was on and off the ground in maybe fifteen seconds. He got us to a safer LZ and set down, we got picked up by a bigger helicopter, and that gunship, 235, took off.

When the fire was too intense for a chopper to land, there were several other ways of getting teams out under fire including ladders, McGuire rigs, STABO harnesses, and extraction rings. Ladders were the easiest; the crew dropped ladders on both sides and half the team would snap into them on either side and just hang on as they lifted us out of the area. McGuire rigs were nothing more than a strap hanging from the slick that we snapped into and then held on tight. STABO was a harness, so it was a little better. We tried to avoid using any of them; it definitely was a last resort, but it also was definitely a lifesaver.

I probably had to get pulled out three or four times. The NVA hated the LRRPs, hated and feared us; so capturing a LRRP was considered a big prize. They even created their own "LRRP hunters," people they dressed up like us, with American equipment, then put them in the field to try to find us. So when they located a LRRP team they would bring as much force as possible. One time we were on our way to the designated LZ when we got compromised. We ran, but there were only six of us and the whole motherfucking North Vietnamese Army bearing down on us. We threw whatever we had at them, and we had gunships and fast movers coming in to keep them off us. Then a little slick came on down into a small clearing and dropped ladders. The crew chief and the door gunners were blasting the shit out of the tree line. Above them the gunships were putting rockets on the NVA to suppress fire. We grabbed on to those ladders. The pilot didn't waste any time trying to hoist us; he just took off to get us out of that area. It took a great deal of skill for that pilot not to drag us through the trees. Trust me, that did happen to people. During that extraction I took a bullet in the fleshy part of my right thigh. It wasn't much, considering all that metal flying around, and the medics pulled it out easy, sewed it up, gave me some antibiotics, and I was good to go. The fact was that any way you got out alive was considered a great extraction.

On the majority of missions we didn't make any contact with the enemy, but the ones I remember most are those missions where people died. Fortunately for us, it was their people.

CHAPTER THREE

Ten young men who had sworn to follow Crazy Horse "anywhere in battle" were standing nearby. He dusted himself and his companions with a fistful of dry earth gathered up from a hill left by a mole or gopher, a young Oglala named Spider would recall. Into his hair Crazy Horse wove some long stems of grass, according to Spider. Then he opened the medicine bag he carried about his neck, took from it a pinch of stuff "and burned it as a sacrifice upon a fire of buffalo chips which another warrior had prepared." The wisp of smoke, he believed, carried his prayer to the heavens. (Others reported that Crazy Horse painted his face with hail spots and dusted his horse with the dry earth.) Now, according to Spider and Standing Bear, he was ready to fight.

Thomas Powers, The Killing of Crazy Horse, *Knopf, 2010*

The more time I spent in the jungles as a LRRP, the closer I got to my native side. We basically were operating independently. The conventional rules of warfare didn't apply to us. Charlie Rangers would go places in Vietnam, Laos, and Cambodia that no other units would go. We conducted missions given to us by Special Forces and the II Corps commander. We were fighting a guerrilla war, and we were using the tactics indigenous peoples had always used. I had studied the tactics used by the Lakota Sioux, the Apache, and the Kiowa, all of them known for their fighting abilities. I had studied everything about how they lived off the land, tracked their enemies, and brought the spirits into battle with them. It turned out their tactics were similar in many ways to the tactics of the Montagnards, the Vietnamese indigs who lived up in the mountains of the Central Highlands and mostly hated the NVA and the VC. The South Vietnamese didn't like them too much either, but the VC were brutal to them. The Montagnards liked Americans, though, and we gave them respect. I would go up to their villages with an interpreter and ask endless questions; I wanted to know how they lived off the land, how they hunted, how they used their weapons. They taught me how to make spring traps from bamboo, which they used mostly to trap animals instead of men.

I really learned the jungle from these people. I used to take them out with my team on what I called training patrols into areas that we knew were decently safe, places it was unlikely we would stumble onto any enemy. They would teach us which plants were safe to eat and how to avoid poisonous snakes; they taught me how to tell if the vegetation had been disturbed and what I could learn from the animals, birds, and insects. Just like I did with the native people, I sat in their villages and watched their ceremonies.

We lived our life the LRRP way. The officers stayed back in the rear and either didn't know what we were doing or pretended they didn't know. That was better for everybody. We were warriors living in a constant state of war; people were dying around us every day. On a daily basis we made up our own rules. That's how I learned how to fly, for example. When I got my leg shot up, instead of sitting around pulling details, I started flying on little slicks as a door gunner. I had my machine gun and rockets, and I love to make a mess. I had a lot of fun blasting and shooting from the sky. In some ways it was the ultimate video game, except that the bad guys really were shooting back at us. There was one pilot that I flew with who got a little jealous of me having so much fun, and he wanted to learn more about the weapons. I agreed to let him play gunner if he would teach me how to fly that bird. So we would go up and he'd let me have the controls until I was comfortable. I didn't have any license or tests or scheduled training, and I'm pretty sure the people in charge would have frowned upon the fact that an officially untrained private was flying one of their expensive toys, so we didn't tell them about it.

This actually wasn't that unusual. The LRRPs were a small group of brave, thrill-seeking mothers who put our lives beyond the front lines every single day. Flying fast was fun, so some of us learned how to do it. I did take the controls on a few missions, and the pilot would sit in the back with the weapons. Only one time did that pilot get to direct fire at the enemy. We took some small-arms fire and we were both thrilled. We started hooting and hollering, and I circled around and went back over the area—and he let loose. Neither of us cared if he hit anything, and we never did find out if he did. I wanted to fly and he wanted to shoot.

Basically, we did what we wanted to do when we wanted to do it. We were living out there on the edge. With the risks we were taking every day, there was nobody that could control us. When we had a couple of birthdays to celebrate, for example, we'd all sit up on top of the bunker, get some beer and whatever, then get on the radio and tell them we had VC in the wire and we needed support. We knew the commander's call signs, and we'd use them to call in artillery and napalm. Then we'd sit back and enjoy the greatest display of birthday fireworks in history. "More firepower! More napalm!" We'd light up the sky. Headquarters didn't like it much because the whole perimeter would go on alert, but we definitely had some awesome nights to remember!

I was careful never to break any orders, instead I postponed them or manipulated them to fit the situation because those people giving those orders were in the rear and didn't know what was happening on the ground. As long as we gave them the results, they mostly left us alone.

Oh, we definitely gave them results—but we did it our way. War has no rules. The only way you win a war is to take war to war, to fight without rules. Nobody keeps score. The only thing that matters is who is standing at the end of the battle. We did what we had to do to live; the enemy was doing the same or similar things. Things happened in Vietnam that were tough to live with, things that changed you as a person forever. Maybe we started out one way, but that place changed everybody who was there. If we were among the good and the lucky ones who got to come home not all broken up, we came home different.

When I was still in the 173rd we'd go out on patrols around the base camp. There was a village a couple of klicks away that we would make a point of walking through on our way back to the base. This was a pretty safe area, and we got to know some of those people. It was a village with a few whole families, some families without the man, and a lot of kids; some of them were orphans. These were good kids, and we did what we could for them. Sometimes two or three of us would go down to the village to bring them food and clothing. It was the whole hearts-and-minds campaign. We got to know them and care about them, and when we walked in they were always standing there with the biggest damn innocent smiles you have ever seen.

Late one afternoon we were coming in off a patrol, and I was walking point. We didn't know the VC had moved into the village.

They knew we would be coming. They let me walk into the village, and then they opened up from two hooches on the rest of my patrol. The patrol was pinned down without any reliable cover. I worked my way through the village and around the back. I started blasting away at one of the hooches, which gave the patrol the chance to get closer and blast those dinks inside. There was a lot of fire still coming from the second hooch, and there was too much open ground for the patrol to cross to get close. They laid down a wall of suppressive fire while I low-crawled my way around it from behind. When I finally got close enough I took two grenades, pulled the pins, and shoved them in under the grass wall and dove down on the ground and got covered up. When the grenades exploded they killed the two VC in there.

As we discovered when we searched that hooch, my grenades also killed the five little kids and one woman that they were holding in there as hostages. I had no idea those kids were in there, nobody did. They were hunched in the back. There is no way you walk away from that without damage. I knew those kids, I played with those kids. There's nothing you ever did before that allows you to understand that moment. It's beyond anything I was ever warned was going to happen. That's the thing about being in a war. It's a one-way street for your mind, and once you go down it there's no turning back. You can't unsee what you've seen, and wherever you go after that you carry it with you. We brought our memories back with us from Vietnam just like the kids are bringing them back from Iraq and Afghanistan.

That's maybe the reason I never really wanted to come back. Instead I just kept finding new places to keep going down that street.

Whatever last hold on traditional American values I still had disappeared when I looked inside that hooch. After that I fought the enemy as viciously as I could every time I could.

Nobody was reading about stuff like that at home. We knew all about the politics that was dividing the country. The public never was told about a lot of the brutality that was a regular part of our life. A lot of people took war trophies: ears, hair, and scalps—and more. We took war to war. I separated myself from being an American. I went completely native. Some of our people wore what we called war necklaces around their necks when we went into battle; these were made up of ears taken off the bodies of enemy soldiers and strung together. There was a reason for this. A lot of times the REMFs, the rear echelon motherfuckers who had never been anywhere near a battle, didn't believe our body counts. They couldn't believe that six-man patrols were killing the number of enemy soldiers that we were reporting. They thought we were making it up. There was no way to bring back those bodies of our KIAs, but when they counted up the ears, they knew we were telling the truth.

One time a friend of mine got so pissed off at being doubted that he piled six bodies onto a chopper and made that pilot fly it all the way to the command post. While they were hovering over the headquarters he kicked those bodies out one by one and watched them bouncing off the tarmac. *Bam. Bam. Bam. Bam. Bam. Bam.* "It's raining dinks!" they told me he was shouting as he pushed out those bodies.

My ancestors believed that they could drain the strength from the enemies they killed. I never wondered if that was true, but when people put on their war necklaces, they felt fearless. We were the best men in the world at the job of war and we knew it. I knew that if any enemy looked me in my eyes he was going to see his own death. That's the way I felt every day I went into the field.

There was more. During one recon mission we found a VC camp right on the Ho Chi Minh Trail. We watched for a while, and suddenly there was a lot of traffic, a lot of movement around us. Our window of communication hadn't opened up, so I hadn't reported our position. We started tightening everything up, figuring we might have to move out fast. I wanted to get us into a safer zone before we called in air strikes.

We hadn't been detected. I wanted us to be higher up and far away, so we found an animal trail and started walking toward the ridge line. As we moved quickly along that trail we began seeing NVA boot prints. Then we began hearing voices. We started moving a little more quickly, but we couldn't get away from those voices. It seemed pretty obvious we were being tracked. As we moved up the mountain we stopped, and I set my team up in a hide site. Then I circled back with my Kit Carson scout. The two of us worked real good together when it came to moving in the jungle and stalking the enemy. We magnified each other.

We set up a hasty ambush off the trail and waited. There were two people coming up that trail. There were times they had as many as four people out in front, but it was only these two. We didn't know how big the patrol moving behind them was, and truthfully we didn't care. We didn't care too much about making noise, either, because I knew the trail ahead of us was clear and my team was waiting in ambush for anybody who followed us.

As these two people walked by us we took them out. I leaped out of the jungle and grabbed my guy. I was carrying a World War I bayonet with an 18" blade, like a short machete. I'd been practicing for this. I killed him almost without a sound. I was pumping so much adrenaline that when I hit him with that bayonet in the back of the neck it just took off his whole head. I didn't plan on that happening. I just intended to kill him, but once it was done, there wasn't any putting it back. My Kit Carson scout stabbed his guy in the neck and basically ripped out his throat, then threw him into the woods. I pushed my guy's body into the brush, but his head was lying there on the ground. My whole attitude was *Save my team,* which meant cutting off the pursuit. We definitely were in harm's way, and I wanted to send the enemy a message. Without giving it any real thought, I took the rifle that one of them was carrying and stuck the bayonet in the dirt. Then I picked up his head and shoved it down on the stock. Then we took off down the trail.

They quit following us.

When I caught up with my team we called in air strikes, then continued moving out of that area.

That wasn't the only time I did that. My Kit Carson scout and I would work out together in camp. I would visualize the whole attack, going through the entire motion but without a weapon in my hand. It's like shadow boxing. You practice a fluid motion, but the mental aspect of it is as important as the physical part. You have to visualize whatever type of knife or weapon you will be carrying in your mind; you have to make your movements with that weapon, knowing how long it is and how heavy it is, whether it's a pocketknife, a machete, or a submachine gun. You have to practice planting your feet and bringing all the emotion in your body into delivering the killing blow. It is the addition of that potent mix of emotion, that anger and excitement channeled into the physical act, that makes it so easy and so deadly. Bringing everything together into that one effort produces extraordinary results.

That was the same technique we used when we were taking out sentries. Silent stalking and the silent kill were what I became best known for and later taught to the Rangers and Special Forces. In Vietnam, Cambodia, and Laos we were operating mostly in enemy territory, so it was an essential survival skill. I only took out sentries when it was necessary. If it was going to jeopardize the mission or give away the fact we had been there I wouldn't do it, but my Kit

Carson scout and I became the experts at it. We had it all worked out. I would hit the target from the side and slice my knife across his throat while my scout would come from the other side and control the target's weapon so he couldn't fire it or even drop it as I took him out. Then we would leave his body somewhere in the woods.

One thing about being in the middle of a combat zone, nobody asked too many questions. Back in Saigon there were layers of officers protecting themselves by pushing papers, and we tried to have as little to do with them as possible. Sometimes it became necessary for us to resolve a situation without involving those people. For example, I kept seeing this Vietnamese worker outside a local village who looked familiar, but I couldn't figure out from where. I'd see him from time to time just like I saw everybody else, but I got this itch about him. There was something about him that was bothering me. I kind of thought he might be VC, but there was no way of proving that. We were in the middle of a civil war, and sometimes it got confusing figuring out who was fighting on which side. In that environment there were a lot of people whose loyalty I wondered about. There were very few locals I ever really got to trust. As far as I was concerned everybody else was a potential enemy. That was the best way to survive.

Early one morning we were out on a patrol and got into a firefight. Some people had been probing our perimeter. They weren't aggressive, just trying to determine our weakest points. Son of a bitch, I recognized that guy as he faded into the tall grass. He just moved in a certain way. There was absolutely no doubt in my mind that it was him. I had to assume he recognized me, too. I didn't know who he was or what he was doing, but he definitely was in places he shouldn't have been. My guess was he was just gathering intel and had the bad luck of being caught with the wrong friends.

What I should have done was report what I had seen up the chain of command. Eventually the MPs would have taken him into custody and asked him a lot of questions. When he finished explaining that he was just a farmer they probably would have let him go. *Where's your proof, O'Neal?*

I knew what I had seen. In those situations you did what you had to do. He just disappeared. Nobody seemed to miss him, and nobody ever saw him again.

When we were out on a mission, we tried hard to instill fear in the cold hearts of our enemy. The NVA referred to LRRPs as "green men with painted faces," the ghosts who shouted "Boo!" when they appeared out of nowhere and blew your brains out. The terrain we worked was mapped into square kilometers, 1,000 by 1,000 meters. When we went into an area, we were assigned so many grid squares to recon. We were real careful not to work in the same grids too often. The NVA never knew where we'd show up; they never knew what havoc we were capable of creating. We brought the war to places they considered safe havens, like rest camps in Cambodia, and we brought it there with the maximum firepower possible from a six-man team. We tried to sow fear and doubt among them. Every unit had its own calling card that they would leave on their kills. Ours was the Ace of Spades. I always carried a bunch of them with me. It was our message to them. *You don't see us, you don't hear us, you don't know we're here—but we are here, all around you, and we're coming for you.*

Fear can be a weapon; it can destroy you or it can empower you. If you can control your fear and channel it into action it is potent; if you can't it will cripple you. These people had been told that Americans were weak and that we would run if they fought us hard enough, so they didn't know how to deal with people who lived among them and appeared suddenly and killed viciously, then disappeared like ghosts back into the jungles. We were their nightmare. While our core mission was always recon and intel, when we had the opportunity we did like to leave an ace.

An ambush had three purposes. The first was to stop or slow down pursuit, the second was to spread fear that we were always there, and the third was to kill the enemy. I participated in all three kinds. For example, there was a time during the war when we wanted to let the enemy know that Cambodia was no longer going to be a safe haven for him, that we were going over that border and he could no longer feel comfortable. Command sent a heavy team of twelve men to set up an ambush on the Ho Chi Minh Trail, hoping to slow up the steady flow of reinforcements coming from the north toward Saigon. This was the largest mission I was on in the LRRPs.

We set up a beautiful ambush. At that point the trail was about as wide as a road but concealed from air reconnaissance by a thick jungle canopy. We had about 120 claymores, which were linked into different series with 1-inch det cords. Unlike regular fuses, which burn, det cords explode. They detonate. We wrapped 1½-inch metal spirals spaced about 6 inches apart on this det cord, so when it blew it would spread shrapnel like a grenade. We prepared the whole ambush site with rows of claymores facing in all different directions in anticipation of their response. We laid down det cords on all the potential escape routes. We set it up like leading rats into a maze. We figured how they would run to get away and then set up secondary kill zones in that area. Then we took positions on the right side of the trail. An advantage of a claymore is that it is a shaped charge, so you can sort of aim it. Anything in its kill zone is going to be ripped apart, but you could be pretty safe if you were 20 or more meters behind it. Then we waited. A lot of hours of my life were spent just lying and waiting in the jungles of Vietnam. Finally the company-sized force we were expecting started moving down the trail. Their security was not tight—they absolutely did not expect to be hit this far north. They were noisy and casual, definitely not prepared to fight. We let them through until the headquarters element walked into the kill zone. Then we simultaneously blew a series of claymores right into them and opened up slinging rounds at them.

They responded like we anticipated. There was a ditch running alongside the trail at that point, and they jumped off the trail trying to find cover in that ditch and the surrounding brush. We let them go that way; then we blew the det cord that we planted into those areas. The troops coming up behind them got off the trail and tried to flank us. We gave them enough time to get into position; then we blew the claymores we'd prepared for them.

There was air support standing off the station waiting to be called in, so after blowing most of our claymores we took off and let those assets blast the area. We'd protected our exit route with a wall of claymores facing out. As we hightailed it out of there, we turned those claymores around to face anybody coming after us.

We never did get a body count. Big, was about the best estimate they could make.

My team got assigned a lot of those special missions. One time the NVA was operating a mobile radar unit on the Cambodian border that enabled them to pick up on our aircraft when they crossed the border and start shooting at the slicks, which were vulnerable. We were having trouble locating it; they'd operate it from one position, then disappear and show up someplace else. They sent my team on a sniper mission to try to find it and, if possible, take it out.

I carried an M-14 with a scope. We spent several days humping around the boonies looking for those bastards, but we couldn't find them. We knew they were active in our grid, and it was frustrating as hell. Finally, after staying out for almost a week, we spotted them. They were set up, searching for air traffic. We were somewhere between 400 and 500 meters away. We called in air support, and when the radar system went active I started sniping. I didn't hit much, but I didn't care. I wanted to create havoc until the gunships got there to take out the radar. When they got on station they blasted the shit out of the gun and the crew.

By this time I was probably spending more time living in enemy territory than among the good people. When I was in the field I was living a spiritual existence. All of my senses were attuned to the environment. I would know things before they happened. I didn't question this information, I just followed it. When we were walking down a trail I would know what was waiting at the other end; I would know to go to the left instead of the right. When we were packing for a mission, I would know if we were going to get in the big mix. Just like a forest animal has an extraordinarily heightened sense of the environment, so did I. When we were fighting, my mind would see the whole situation as if I was looking at it from above.

I believed this knowledge came from my spirit guides. I paid my respect to them. I had my little ceremony both at the beginning and end of every mission. I carried my medicine bag with me whenever I was in the field. When I needed to remain perfectly still, even for hours at a time, I would give my mind over to my spirit guides, and they would bring me comfort.

Maybe that was my way of dealing with the death that surrounded me. Combat is very spiritual. Taking a person's life is very spiritual. When you kill someone you are taking God's creation. I honored life in all its forms. Even today, if a tree needs to be cut down, I will pray for it. *Thank you for your life and giving me firewood to warm my family.* This belief system is not any kind of religion, and I never treated it that way. It was the spirituality of the Native Americans.

Being in the field required as much mental discipline as physical conditioning. When you're moving around in enemy territory, knowing the only way you're going to get out is up in the air or buried in the ground, there isn't one second you can relax. If you let your mental guard down for that second, you could end up dead. It happened to good people. We weren't perfect. There were a couple of teams that just disappeared, and it wasn't unusual to take casualties. One little mistake was all it took to be found out. So the whole time we were out there we lived right on the edge, ready to spring.

One time we'd been out four days and were moving toward our designated LZ to meet our taxi. During that time we hadn't eaten a complete meal or slept for more than minutes at a time or cleaned ourselves except for a quick wash in the river, so we were hungry, tired, sweaty, and overall miserable. That was really the most dangerous time, when we were walking toward the LZ, on the way home. That's when you made mistakes. Sometimes after you'd been walking for several hours without contact there was a tendency to let your mind drift for a few seconds, but we didn't have that luxury. We couldn't put our weapons on our shoulders and carry them along; we had to keep them in front of us at all times, slowly swinging them back and forth. We were living one second from death. Remembering that keeps you alert. We were walking the main trail, and running parallel to that was an animal trail. Mostly they were separated by heavy vegetation, but at places the two trails converged. As we came close to one point where they touched, I started hearing strange sounds. I couldn't name them, but they made me uneasy. Just before we reached the bend I froze. Instantly my whole team froze behind me. Seconds later someone walked around that corner, dressed just like me.

I knew instinctively that it was a dink, a LRRP hunter. These people dressed like us, in stolen or captured American uniforms, they carried American equipment, and they went out trying to find LRRP patrols. It was a sound theory. If they ran into people dressed like them, they knew they were Americans; if we ran into people dressed like us, for an instant we might think they were Americans—and hesitate. We knew that was possible; LRRP patrols had occasionally been put down in the wrong grid and run into each other. We were aware that back in Vietnam the NVA had people patrolling in American uniforms trying to infiltrate line companies, but this was the first time we'd seen them in Cambodia. Didn't matter, I didn't hesitate, which saved my life. He hesitated, cost him his. I couldn't tell you how I made that deadly decision instantly, but I did. If that guy had waved to me, smiled or made any type of friendly gesture, I probably would have been dead on that trail, but he didn't. His weapon was shouldered; there was no possible way he was going to get it before I hit him. My weapon was leveled at my hip, but he was so close to me I didn't have room between us to swing it around. Instead I lifted it and slugged him in his face. Knocked him down. That freed up my weapon and I put *pop-pop-pop-pop* rounds in him. Meanwhile, my team was on the ground firing into the vegetation between the two trails. We were receiving beaucoup fire. Those trails couldn't have been more than 20 feet of thick vegetation apart. Nobody could see shit, but we were just blasting everything we had right through it.

The whole firefight lasted less than a minute. There were seven bodies on the other side, but we didn't know if anybody had gotten away. Even though we knew they were enemy troops, there was still something really uncomfortable about shooting people in our uniforms. We picked up all their equipment and started going through their pockets. None of them were carrying ID or any papers. We threw them in the brush and kept going to our exfil point.

It wasn't just the NVA that we had to watch out for; the jungle could be hostile, too. Getting too comfortable in the jungle could be just as deadly as walking into an ambush. When we settled down at night we tried to find the most inhospitable place as far from a trail as made sense. For us, that was the safest place to be. There were times we'd crawl through some bad stuff to get to a place where we felt comfortable. We'd crawl inside tight areas where there were animals, birds, reptiles, your chiggers and bloodsuckers and eight-leggers, biting ants, and insects like I'd never seen before. We had to contend with all of them and do so absolutely silently. I tried to project the energy that I was not a danger to those creatures, but we were invading their homes. There were some times we might have even welcomed a bullet, because we knew how to dodge bullets, but some of the biting things we ran into couldn't be avoided.

The jungle could lure you into a feeling of ease, making you believe that if you were respectful of the environment it would accept you. Like the Greek sirens who lured ship captains onto submerged rocks with their beautiful voices and music, the jungle could awe you with its beauty and its wonder. There was even beauty to be found in the darkness of the triple-canopy jungle. In the jungle, though, you just never knew what was waiting for you. There was a rumor that the NVA were bringing tanks down the trail, but no one had seen one. One night a LRRP patrol was lying down to get some rest when they heard something huge churning directly toward them. It got louder as it got closer, and it was louder than anything they'd heard in the jungle. At night that jungle was black; man, you couldn't see 15 feet in front of you. Not being able to see just added to the terror of the night. This thing kept coming toward them, until it came out of a tree stand and they lit it up. Killed that elephant in its tracks, but they also gave away their position and immediately had to evacuate that area.

I ran into a bad situation one time. We bumped into one of their patrols and started shooting. Instantly everybody went for cover. There was a rotten old log just off the trail, and it looked pretty good to me. Get down behind that thing and I had some good protection. I dived over it, rolled over, propped up my weapon, and kept shooting. Within seconds I discovered I had dived directly into a scorpion's den. I had people shooting at me and scorpions crawling all over me. The scorpions weren't very big, but there was a lot of them, and they were pissed off. I had to focus on the firefight, but between bursts I kept trying to pick off the scorpions. They were all over me; I could feel those fuckers biting me everywhere. That was the longest firefight of my time in Southeast Asia, and by the time it was over I was badly bit up. Soon as I was sure it was safe I got up and stripped and pulled them off. I can't remember what we were carrying in our medical kit. It may have been epinephrine, but whatever it was didn't help much. My whole body swelled up. It was like being stung by a thousand bees. There were many physical things that I had the ability to control with my mind, but this was not one of them. We had to make time back to the LZ, and I was in piss-poor shape when we got there. They got me back to camp and put me right into the hospital. My eyes were swollen just about shut. I hurt everywhere. It was almost two weeks before I was able to go out again.

Probably the most difficult kind of mission they gave us was to bring back a prisoner. Those requests usually came from Intel, and they never told us why they needed someone, just go out and bring back someone if possible. We'd go out to the dump and practice a lot for this type of mission because it required pretty exact timing. Thankfully they didn't happen very often. Generally a POW was a target of opportunity rather than a primary mission. If we had the chance to snatch somebody up, we would, then bring him back and turn him over to S2, the intelligence section. We did go out on a couple of snatch missions. I was just starting to get known for being good at this type of work. My ability to control my senses was especially useful when I was out front, out on the edge. When the military was starting up the elite organization that eventually would become Delta Force, which at that time was known as Blue Light, it would be a primary reason I got selected. I learned it in the jungles of Southeast Asia.

To start, we needed to find a perfect location on the trail, a place that provided good cover for us and maximum exposure of anybody walking down that trail. We would set up our ambush with an arc of claymores in front of us. When we fired them, anybody caught in that arc was dead. After we set up the claymores I stood up hidden in the jungle just off the trail. Then we waited. Unfortunately, most of the time that was the extent of it; odds of an NVA patrol walking down that trail into our trap at that moment were slim. On a few occasions, though, that's exactly what happened. When it did I'd wait until the patrol went by. When their slack man started cleaning up behind them I'd reach out and grab him by his collar and yank him into the bushes, generally behind some cover we'd prepared. I'd manhandle him, throwing him down and jumping on top of him. I'd hit him on the side of his face, his jaw if possible, with my wrist, which was hard bone, to force his mouth open. I exploded into him. It all had to be done quickly, before he could understand what was happening and even think about trying to fight back. I had to make him know that he was my prisoner and I had total physical control of him, that whether he lived or died was my choice.

As soon as we were off the trail, the team would blow those claymores and open up on the patrol. They'd all end up with an ace of spades on their body. Then we'd be out of there. Transporting a prisoner was not easy. We had to move rapidly and silently, bringing along a person who was dragging and screaming. The first thing we always did was strip the prisoner of any possible weapons, tie his hands with cord, and gag him. Everything was tied tight as we could make it, to reinforce the feeling that he was in our control. Then we had to move out of the area fast as possible to the predesignated LZ. If it was an emergency exfil we'd get to a nearby clearing, snap him into a ladder, and have them pull him up.

Once we handed him over, that was it. We never heard another word. We never knew who we got, what information they were able to get from him, or what happened to him after that.

I spent more than four years in country. I had the full experience. In that time there was one encounter that remains fixed in my memory. Although I wouldn't know it for more than a year and a half, it was the day I won my Silver Star.

We were out on a recon mission. It wasn't my usual team; I had two new guys with me, which was unusual, one Korean and my scout. Our forward air controller was Gary Dolan, so I felt comfortable pushing hard. Knowing he was there gave me leeway; if we got into it and anybody could get us out of it, that was Gary Dolan. It was a weird thing—we were out for four or five days in this area, and every morning I would hear a gunshot, just one, and again in the evening, just one. Two shots, every day, then quiet. It made no sense to me. I knew the NVA was out there, but we couldn't find them. We couldn't find any evidence that people were anywhere around there, but we knew they were. Sound bounces all over the place in the jungle, making it impossible to determine where those shots were coming from. The not knowing was frustrating as hell.

I extended our mission because I knew they were there and I was determined to find them. We beat around, we beat around, we stopped and set up an ambush, we tried every tactic we knew, but still, one shot in the morning, one shot in the evening. After almost a week I accepted that it was time to pack up. My team was hungry and tired, we were running out of supplies, and I could see our alertness was starting to dwindle. No matter how badly I wanted to stay out there, my responsibility was to my team. It was time to get back to camp.

I intended to go in, get resupplied, get some rest, and then get right back out in this area. I wasn't about to give up.

We had missed our primary pickup, so we started humping to an alternate LZ. It wasn't too far, but to make the rendezvous we had to hustle. As it often did in the afternoon, it started raining. While usually I didn't like walking in a stream because it left you exposed, that was the quickest and the easiest way to make time. I figured that if there were any NVA in the area we would have made contact with them by that point, and the rain would provide some cover. Of course, the problem was that it inhibited air support because the aircraft had to stay above the clouds. They couldn't see a damn thing on the ground.

The water in that stream was clear and cold and about up to my calves. I was walking point, and as we moved along I started to get the feeling that there were people around us. It was a chilly feeling that had nothing to do with the temperature of the water. I alerted my team, and we slowed down. I got them out of the river and began moving forward with my Kit Carson scout.

When we heard voices we froze. We stood still as those little rubber World War II soldiers I'd played with as a kid. A few seconds later an NVA female—later we found out she was a nurse—came out of the grass carrying a bucket. She filled it and stood up. If she'd turned the other way she never would have seen me and we could have gotten out of there. If she had turned the other way there's a lot of people who would have lived. But she didn't. She turned and looked right at us. It took her a few beats to understand what she was looking at, and then she started screaming. She turned to get away and I lit her up. There was no thought involved, no hesitation. I was running on instinct. I wanted my bullets to alert them that we were there, not her screams.

My scout and I opened up. For several seconds there was zero response from them. They had no idea Americans were in the area.

If they had security out we never saw it. When you have the element of surprise, the best thing to do is grab hold of it and thoroughly exploit it. Sow confusion. Don't let them get organized. I thought my team was following close behind my scout and me, but it turned out they weren't. We'd broken visual contact with them. It was just the two of us, but the NVA didn't know that. For a brief period of time, neither did I. We charged right into their camp.

We were creating such havoc that the NVA had no idea how many of us there were. They figured they were being overrun by a much larger force. Who would have believed two men would attack an entire camp! Turned out that this was a hospital and rest camp, and they had been using the stream as their trail. That's why we never saw them in the jungle. They weren't on any type of alert; we were the last people they expected to see. My scout and I just kept moving forward, firing continuously, changing magazines on the run.

That camp was in chaos. People had been doing their regular jobs, or just lying around in their hooches to be out of the rain, and suddenly we were on them, shooting AK rounds. I always cracked my AK first to create additional confusion, because that was "their" weapon. We were dressed in dark fatigues that looked enough like what they were wearing to cause them to pause. We knew that everyone who wasn't the two of us was the enemy, so we didn't hesitate; if it was moving we shot at it. They were being attacked; they were scared. This being a rest area, there were not many trained or experienced soldiers, so they started shooting recklessly. They created their own targets, and some of them started shooting at their own people. There was shooting coming from areas we hadn't even been near.

That camp was in complete disarray. Grenades were going off everywhere, bullets slinging all around, guns blasting, explosions coming from every side. This camp was not set up in one large clearing carved out of the jungle; it was spread out, separated into smaller areas by thick vegetation. That worked to our advantage. At some places the vegetation created a protective barrier for us. If it was thick enough, bullets, and even grenades, couldn't get all the way through it. In fact, if it was bamboo, grenades would just bounce off of it. My scout and I were battling side by side, protecting 360° around us. We'd race from one area into another, our movements shielded by the tall grasses.

We just kept smoking our way through the camp, screaming like banshees, trying to make as much noise as possible. We were firing our weapons, throwing our grenades, continuing to press our attack. In a situation like that, where you're battling, you want to project the most evil, animalistic creature that ever walked the face of the earth. Be the aggressor. In any type of combat, be the aggressor, keep moving forward, keep attacking. The instant you back off is when you begin losing control. By moving through the camp, we came up behind some of the bunkers on the perimeter. We blasted them. I knew the rest of the team had to be coming up quick, but we weren't about to wait for anybody.

I was existing in a different realm. I was without fear, relying entirely on my warrior training. When we ran out of ammo I started swinging my weapon like a club, slamming people with it. I used anything I could grab as a weapon, my entrenching tool, my knives. I was slashing, stabbing, kicking, punching, ripping, tearing; I was a whirlwind of destruction. I hit and kept hitting, I didn't stop, I couldn't stop. We were in face-to-face combat and I just kept moving, fighting. I was unleashed. It was uncontrolled lunacy. I was operating in pure survival mode.

Finally we made it to an empty bunker and got settled down. Turned out this was an ammunition bunker, and weapons and ammo were stacked up in there. It was reasonably secure, made out of logs. I knew that as long as we didn't get attacked by grenades or rockets we could survive there for a while. We were being sniped at, but there wasn't a lot of convincing fire coming at us, and I could still hear firing from other parts of the camp. That meant that except for those people who had watched us go into the bunker, they weren't really sure where we were. That gave us an opportunity to get a breath. My scout and I were alone. Because I didn't hear rapid firing, I figured the rest of my team was down and we were the only ones left. Then I heard the sweet sound of M-16s firing from the other side of the camp. That meant somebody was still alive and we'd best get to them as rapidly as possible. We loaded up every bit of firepower we could carry and got ready to go again. I was always partial to grenades, and there was a sufficient supply in that bunker. The last thing we did before getting out of there was toss a couple of those grenades in the weapons bunker—then we took the hell off, raging back through the camp.

The rain had slowed, but it still was coming down pretty good. We were throwing grenades everywhere around us because we were booking through that camp. The chaos had worked for us. One thing the NVA knew was that we controlled the sky; they knew that when they got discovered we were going to drop a shitstorm on them. So by the time we took off again they were already moving out of the area as rapidly as possible.

My scout and I kept low, kept moving, and kept firing. Having fought our way through the camp once, at least this time we had some concept of which direction we needed to go. Their return fire was more organized, but there was a little less of it. I don't think they anticipated us coming back; it was not the obvious route to safety. We were fortunate their attention was focused on the river side of the camp, where they were engaged in a firefight with the rest of my team. There were beaucoup bodies on the ground, and even above the roar of our weapons I could hear yelling and screaming. People were hit and in pain.

Both of us got hit with shrapnel as we fought our way back

through the camp, but we wouldn't realize it till much later. During the fighting we were in that mindless place where you just don't feel anything. If you intend to stay alive, you've got to keep going. When we got back to the river, then across it, we took cover behind an anthill. The anthills over there were as tall as a man and as hard as bricks; they made great protection. There was still a lot of fighting going on. As soon as we made contact with the team I raised up the beacon of my PRC-10 emergency radio to let Gary get a read on us. Within minutes that large enemy camp was going to cease to be. The reaction force was already on the way. Soon as we regrouped we faded back into the brush and hightailed it to a safe LZ. As usual, I never heard a body count, but without any question, it was hundreds.

Eventually we found out what that single shot in the morning and evening had been all about. They were killing a monkey for fresh meat.

Almost two years later I learned I had been awarded the Silver Star for what happened that day. Truthfully, I don't remember the details of that day too much, but other people's memories have helped me describe it. The way my citation reads is basically:

> O'Neal, Gary, Specialist 4, Company C (Ranger), 75th Infantry (Airborne), awarded Silver Star, 10 August 1970.
>
> For gallantry in action in connection with military operations involving conflict with an armed hostile force . . . while serving as Assistant Team Leader of an Airborne Ranger team . . .
>
> Extremely adverse weather prevailed as his team observed several enemy soldiers . . . The enemy detected the team . . . Specialist 4 O'Neal, recognizing the vulnerability of the six-man team's position, and disregarding his personal safety,

> charged the enemy bunkers attempting to silence the enemy weapons employed against his men. Hesitating only to throw grenades, which were forcing the enemy to abandon their positions, he carried the assault into the bunker positions. Throughout this action he was aware that the team had no communications and he was completely on his own resources.

I left the jungles of Vietnam physically in December 1971, but like so many of the people I served with I never completely left them behind. For the rest of my life, in so many different ways, I have been carrying that place with me.

One thing the army had failed to teach me was how not to be a warrior. That was what I had become, and without any preparation I was expected to come home and be something else entirely. They put me on a plane and flew me back to civilization. My young wife and my son were waiting for me, but I wasn't the person she was expecting. I was a completely different person when I came back, and I was returning to a completely different world. So it was not surprising that I had a difficult time adjusting. I had the tools to live in the jungle; I wasn't so good in the city.

When I came back I didn't cleanse myself. The first thing I should have done when I got home was put myself through a native cleansing ceremony, but I didn't. I reeked with death. I would walk into a room and my son would start crying. Children could smell it on me, but the adults couldn't figure it out. My wife couldn't figure it out either, but I knew it. It was confusing, it hurt, but I didn't know what I could do to change it.

I couldn't let Vietnam go. I slept only in short bursts at night. I'd snap awake not knowing where I was. During the day almost anything would set me off. I was always anxious, constantly looking around at my surroundings, although I didn't know what I was looking for. People didn't know anything about PTSD, post-traumatic stress disorder, at that time. They didn't understand why I couldn't just be normal. The reason was I didn't know what their normal was. Normal for me was never being out of reach of my weapon, living on the edge of combat. That didn't change for a long time. One time, years later, when my son was a teenager we were in the kitchen eating dinner. A pitcher filled with tea was sitting on the glass table. My son got up from the table and casually tossed a spoon or a fork into the stainless steel sink. In my mind that sounded like the the safety lever of a grenade being pulled, and I responded instantly. I flipped over that table, dived down behind it, and grabbed for my pistol. I was ready for combat. The table shattered, and the pitcher hit my son in the back, knocking him down.

So it wasn't surprising that my wife got scared of me when I got home. I would never do anything to hurt her, to hurt anybody I loved, but the possibility I'd lose it was definitely there. We were living with her parents, and it was tough for all of us trying to figure out who I was.

In Vietnam, the war was still being fought, and I was desperate to get back into it. I knew I belonged there. Although I'd been designated a Ranger while I was in country, I was not officially Ranger qualified. I couldn't wear the black and gold tab, although I was permitted to wear the Charlie Company 75th Rangers patch. If I was going to stay in the army, which I wanted to do, I needed that school, so I applied and was sent to Fort Benning.

The Rangers can trace their history back to 1675, when a unit of the Massachusetts militia known as Church's Rangers fought the Indians. Rangers were always small commando-type units, known for using creative guerrilla tactics to fight and harass the enemy, a lot of times behind their own lines. Robert Rogers, who fought in the

French and Indian War, is known as the "Father of the Rangers" and he wrote the 28 Rules of Ranging which still were relevant in Vietnam. These standing orders, as we referred to them, included:

1. Don't forget nothing.
2. Have your musket clean as a whistle, hatchet scoured, sixty rounds powder and ball, and be ready to march at a minute's warning.
3. When you're on the march, act the way you would if you was sneaking up on a deer. See the enemy first.
4. Tell the truth about what you see and what you do. There is an army depending on us for correct information. You can lie all you please when you tell other folks about the Rangers, but don't never lie to a Ranger or officer.*

Rangers fought on both sides in the Civil War. They fought in World War II and in Korea, where according to General Lawton J. Collins their mission was "to infiltrate through enemy lines and attack command posts, artillery, tank parks and key communications centers or facilities." As soon as General Westmoreland arrived in Vietnam in 1964 he realized that there was a need there for a Ranger-type unit who could operate in enemy territory.

Ranger School is the army's toughest school. You're under relentless pressure from the moment you get there for eight weeks; you never get a second to relax, you never get enough to eat, and you never get enough sleep. Students average less than four hours sleep a night through the whole course. RIs, Ranger instructors, are constantly pushing you, trying to test you every way possible. I did what I needed to do to get through the course. One of the phases you have

*This is how the orders are explained by a character in Kenneth Roberts's novel *Northwest Passage* (1937). It is the version that has become Ranger tradition.

to pass is land navigation, which requires you to use a map and compass to complete a route within a specific length of time. It starts in the middle of the night and ends in the morning. At each station we had to take an azimuth reading and stamp a card proving we'd been there. They put me with two officer trainees from Singapore, two men who spoke no English and had no idea how to use a compass. I tried to communicate with them, but they weren't too interested in listening to me. They thought they knew a lot more than they actually did, and I wasn't about to let them cause me to fail the course. So I tied the two of them to a tree; the Singapore Sling, I called it. My goodness, they did yell about it. I did them a favor though. I took their cards and went through the course by myself. Then I went back and untied them and handed them their checked cards.

The hardest part of the school for me was dealing with military procedure. I had to remember that I wasn't in my own army anymore. If I pissed off one swinging dick, he could end my career. There were a lot of RIs there who believed that the United States Army knew more than I did. After four years of combat it took me a little while to accept that concept. Of course, I knew some of the instructors. My problem was they knew me, too. They knew what I could do, so mostly when we went on training missions I carried the M-60 or the radio. The instructors also paired me with the weaker officers so I could assist them when they needed it. I wouldn't tell them what to do, I would simply make suggestions.

One of the instructors I served with was Sergeant Lincoln—I never knew his first name—who had been with me in Charlie Company in Vietnam. There were four phases in the training: city phase, mountain phase, desert phase, and Florida phase, where we ran around patrolling in jungle-type conditions. Sergeant Lincoln was the NCO in charge of the mountaineering phase, which we did in Georgia, and the first thing he said when he saw me was, "What the hell are you doing here?"

I told him, "I'm going through Ranger School because I'm sick and tired of these shake-and-bakes telling me I'm not Ranger qualified, even though I got more than two years of Rangers in Vietnam. That bullshit ends right here."

Sergeant Lincoln was not about to let me go through his training unscathed. We never did get enough to eat during the training, but at one point we were allowed to go through this 10-square-foot cabin that was full of what we called pogie bait, which was lickies and chewies, candy and gum, every type of sweet you could imagine. The purpose was to get us some quick energy. You were permitted to eat as much as you wanted to, but only inside that cabin. You were not allowed to take anything out with you.

Not allowed. To me, that was practically a challenge. They checked our pockets and rucksacks when we came out, so I definitely could not hide anything there. Instead I took two giant-sized Hershey bars and taped them to my belly. Fooled them suckers.

I thought. This was definitely not their first rodeo. Sergeant Lincoln never said a word, but as we were humping through those hills he was right there alongside me every step of the way. It was hot in Georgia, and I started sweating, and that chocolate started melting directly down into my crotch and then down my legs. Naturally it attracted the flies and the bugs. When we took a break I couldn't sit down because the ants were waiting for someone like me to come along. I looked like the cartoon character Beetle Bailey, an army of bugs circling my body. The first stream we crossed, I pretended to slip and went into that beautiful water. I ripped that candy off me. When we got back on patrol nobody said anything for a while, until Sergeant Lincoln walked up and said, "Hey, O! How was your chocolate?"

One of the proudest moments of my life was receiving my Rangers tab. There hadn't been a lot of victories in my childhood. I hadn't even finished regular high school and had to get my GED during my first tour. So becoming an Airborne Ranger was a real big deal for me. As soon as I graduated I knew exactly where I wanted to go. Charlie Rangers was being pulled out of Vietnam, but the toughest unit over there was known as MACV-SOG. Military Assistance Command, Vietnam—Special Operations Group (later Studies and Observations Group), which conducted the most unconventional warfare missions of the war. We knew it as CCN, Command and Control North. These guys were the elite of the best warriors we had, including Army Special Forces, Navy SEALs, air force and marine personnel, and CIA operatives. It was the type of unit that eventually evolved into Delta Force and SEAL Team Six. Among the people serving in that unit was Bob Howard, who was awarded a Congressional Medal of Honor and was nominated for it two more times. That was the quality of people up there. The missions of this unit were classified, but throughout the war they were regularly making combat parachute jumps into Laos and Cambodia. At the beginning it was run by General John Singlaub.

Everything I'd done in Vietnam was aimed at getting into this unit. Finally, after becoming Ranger qualified, I was accepted into it. It was being run out of Da Nang, and I went up there, but by the time I got there it was being closed down. The United States was closing up shop in Vietnam, bringing troops home, cutting back on missions. We had settled into a defensive strategy, while I wanted to attack. I spent about two months there basically just packing up papers, listening to the stories of what they'd done. I never got near the jungle again. So there wasn't much there for me to do, but I did meet some people I would work with on other assignments later in my life.

The defense of the United States of America is a big business, and a lot of different branches and agencies play a role in it. Some of the people who were running those operations began to know about me. I was earning a reputation of going out and completing the mission without making a fuss. Like in any organization, there is a small group of people who meet when they're young, and as they earn more responsibility and move into higher positions, they bring the people they know and respect up with them. While I was real disappointed that I didn't get to go out on any missions at CCN, my acceptance into that unit was an acknowledgment that I was capable. It meant that I had proven that I could work on that elite level.

I went back down south to II Corps and eventually got reassigned to 75th Infantry Rangers at Fort Carson, Colorado. This time I knew when I left Vietnam I wasn't going back. That war was over for me, although I would spend the rest of my life looking for it.

The flight back to the States was supposed to land in Oakland, but we were diverted to San Francisco. It was a strange flight back; rather than anybody celebrating the fact that we had survived, it was very quiet. I wondered if it was because we knew what we were bringing back with us or because we didn't really know what was waiting for us when we got home. I had been back several times, so I knew the whole political situation, but when we landed in San Francisco it was in my face. The airport was crowded. In addition to the soldiers coming back there were Hare Krishnas chanting and long-haired hippies and antiwar demonstrators who blamed us for protecting their right to blame us. With the draft there were a lot of people who had no real choice; it was either serve your country, leave your country, or go to jail. It was total bullshit, and this airport was the wrong place for these antiwar people to try to make their point. Basically, we got off that plane with fuses just waiting to be lit, and these people wanted to be the sparks.

After we landed I picked up my kit, and I was walking toward the bus when someone threw old vegetables at me and someone else spit at me. There was a line of cops there, and that was the only thing that kept me out of prison. I was ready to go after these people. Obviously my government did not want me to do that, so instead they handed me a high-powered rifle and sent me to Miami Beach to work security at the Republican National Convention.

Are you kidding me? There were thousands of people at both parties' conventions marching up and down protesting the war. I was a sniper in Miami Beach. In retrospect maybe I wasn't the best choice for that job. I'd stay up on top of a building working with the Secret Service. My job, I decided, was to sit there during the day looking through the scope of my rifle trying to pick out the best-looking women. If things got out of control I guess I was supposed to help restore order. Fortunately it never came to that.

At night, when we were off duty, I'd put on these red, white, and blue pants with peace symbols all over them and a fringed shirt and pull down my hair. I was camouflaged! Then I'd go out trying to pick up women. Legally I was still married, but that was just a formality. I wasn't emotionally capable of being married to anyone at that time. Like always, I didn't have a home. I lived wherever I was staying that night or wherever the army told me to be. Reality had become elusive for me. I was moving from one extreme directly to another without even pausing in the middle. I'd gone from taking ears in the jungle to wearing beads in the middle of Miami Beach in a matter of months. I no longer even had a concept of normal. Everything swirling around me was crazy. The one thing I did learn was that many of these antiwar protestors were committed people, and what they were committed to mostly was having a good time. I know it was supposed to be a protest, but mostly it was just a big party. I had no problems with that—I liked to party.

One afternoon I was walking along in my fatigues and saw a guy also in uniform who looked familiar. It turned out he had been in

Vietnam, too. "I was with Charlie Rangers," I told him, "Everybody there called me Big O."

He knew the name. I'd heard his name, too. It was Bones, and he was known to be about as crazy as I was when we were over there—crazy being a good thing if you liked being alive. Bones had become well known in Nam for bringing his surfboard with him and going out surfing on the South China Sea. Nobody actually knew how he got it over there. It definitely didn't fit in a rucksack, and they didn't encourage us bringing recreational equipment, but somehow he got it over there. People said that he had been the model for the famous surfing scene in *Apocalypse Now.* Bones and I hung out that whole week, partying and drinking and meeting some interesting women. Things were different in those days; sex was safe and skydiving was dangerous. So we played it safe as often as we could.

At that point I figured we had won the war and we were leaving that country with pride, but the truth was that the American people were just tired of seeing people being shot up on TV every night and demanded that it end—it made for bad TV. Truthfully, I missed it. If I could have gone back there I would have, but the army was bringing people home. My enlistment was just about up, and I had to decide what I wanted to do. I began looking around to see where I might have the best chance of finding combat. Some people I knew were accepting jobs around the world as soldiers of fortune. The pay was good, although the joke of that was assuming you lived to collect it. For whatever reasons it just didn't appeal to me. The easiest thing for me to do was stay in the army. I talked to a lot of people, and the consensus was that the people with the best chance of seeing combat somewhere in this world were the Special Forces. The Green Berets had become soldier superstars early in the war, mostly because of a popular song, "Fighting soldiers from the sky, fearless men who jump and die."

That die part seemed pretty dramatic, but the Green Berets were real good. If this country needed to send troops, especially to fight an insurgency, which seemed a lot more likely than another big war, the Special Forces would be the first to go. They were based at Fort Bragg, North Carolina, so I knew that somehow I had to get back there. I found out that the Golden Knights, the army's demonstration and competition parachute team, was also stationed there. That was perfect for me. I loved jumping out of airplanes, and I was very good at landing exactly where I intended to land, so I volunteered. I'd get to work with the Golden Knights and be close enough to Special Forces to get to go if they were needed.

I just needed to find me a war.

CHAPTER FOUR

I proposed to him that in the spring of 1919, when I would have a great force of bombardment airplanes, he should assign one of the infantry divisions permanently to the Air Service, preferably the 1 Division; that we should arm the men with a great number of machine guns and train them to go over the front in our large airplanes, which would carry ten or fifteen of these soldiers. We could equip each man with a parachute, so that when we desired to make a rear attack on the enemy, we could carry these men over the lines and drop them off in parachutes behind the German position. They could assemble at a prearranged strong point, fortify it and we could supply them by aircraft with food and ammunition. Our low flying attack aviation would then cover every road in their vicinity, both day and night, so as to prevent the Germans falling on them before they could thoroughly organize the position. Then we could attack the Germans from the rear, aided by an attack from our army on the front, and support the maneuver with our great air force.

Colonel Billy Mitchell writing of a meeting with General John J. Pershing, as quoted from Mitchell's memoir in The Sword of St. Michael *by Guy LoFaro*

I jumped out of an airplane for the first time when I was thirteen years old. It was in western Kansas. I'd seen people skydiving on the TV show *Ripcord,* and it looked like fun. I bought a parachute rig at an army surplus store for twenty-six dollars and just got in line. The rules back then were pretty much if you had the five bucks to pay for your jump nobody was going to stop you.

Physically, jumping out of an airplane is easy. You just take one step out the door. Mentally, it is one of the most difficult things an individual will ever do. Every jump you make, you're dead until you choose to save your life. You are dead until you pull your rip cord, get a good canopy above you, and land unhurt; then you saved your life. There are very few things most people do in regular life that actually put it on the line like that. There are times when a chute doesn't open right, the cords get tangled, and you don't get air in your canopy, so you die. It doesn't happen very often, but it does happen, and everybody knows that. That possibility of death is the aspect that gets your adrenaline flowing. I've seen people in the plane freeze and refuse to jump. I didn't have that problem. I couldn't wait. I didn't have any real instruction—just go ahead and jump out of the plane and remember to pull the rip cord before you hit the ground. I figured, how hard could that be? Then I made that first jump.

Maybe I was fearless, but it definitely got my full attention.

I'd never experienced anything like it. It was absolute and total freedom. I was flying. Flying! Of course, I was also falling. The ground doesn't exactly sneak up on you. You look down and it's there. You see it coming, and it's coming fast. My heart was pumping. I tumbled and tumbled until I yanked the cord; then my canopy popped open, filled with air, and pulled me up, and I floated down like a feather. I hit the ground hard and pitched over, stumbling to get control. That took me a little while, but as soon as I got myself organized I wanted to get back up and do it again. I was an adrenaline junkie, and jumping was an absolute adrenaline rush.

Eventually I started playing chicken with the ground, seeing how close I could get before I pulled the cord. I needed the rush; once I proved I could do something, I pressed a little harder. I waited a little longer. I got a little lower. There was no combat jumping in Vietnam beyond a few Special Forces insertions, but unlike the paratroopers in Europe during World War II we didn't have to go too far to find the enemy. I didn't need skydiving to get my thrills in Vietnam; there was always another firefight. I saw somewhere that during World War II infantrymen were in combat 10 days a year; in Vietnam infantrymen spent 240 days a year in combat.

I did do some recreational skydiving in Vietnam. When I had some time I'd go up to Long Thanh, one of the most beautiful places in Southeast Asia, where the Special Forces was doing HALO/HAHO training. American paratroopers had jumped into combat for the first time in 1942, when a team from the OSS, which became the CIA, jumped into Sardinia in Italy. We had been training Airborne troops since then.

Sergeant Major Frank Norbury was operating the HALO school in Long Thanh, and he gave me the opportunity to do HALO jumps without officially being enrolled in the school. The highest jump I did in Vietnam was 10,000, maybe 15,000 feet. I didn't do any real high-altitude jumps until I got back to the States.

In combat, the military makes static line jumps. The opposite of that is free falling, where you dive through the air until you decide to pull your cord. The mission always dictated the altitude of the jump, but most combat static line jumps are made from an altitude of about 800 feet. HALO (high altitude, low opening) or HAHO (high altitude, high opening) is totally different. They are techniques used by Special

Forces or undercover operatives to infiltrate a denied area without being detected. You leave the airplane at 25,000 feet or higher and can float as far as 30 miles or more before landing, which allows you to get into an area without your airplane showing up on the enemy radar.

HALO/HAHO is the best ride in the world, but doing it right is a learned skill. You are up there by yourself, often at night, sailing through the cold, cold air trying to hit a landing zone about a yard wide 25 miles away that even if you could see that far it might be obscured by cloud cover. When you leave the aircraft the upper winds are blowing in a certain direction, but sometimes as you get lower the crosswinds are coming from a completely different direction. In free fall you're dropping about 176 feet a second, or about 120 miles an hour, with your normal body weight in a flat and stable position. With all your equipment, as much as an additional 100 pounds, you're going to fall a lot faster, so there are a lot of calculations that have to go right for you to be able to stick that landing on a 5-centimeter disk.

When I got back from Vietnam, free falling became real important to me. I needed the charge that I got from it. If I couldn't be in combat I would train to be in combat, and skydiving was the closest feeling to being in combat I could find. It gave me the sensation of being back on the battlefield; the fear unleashed my adrenaline, and the chemical changes in my body reminded me of that feeling I got when I was in combat. When I jumped my mind was moving so fast that everything around me slowed down. When I was jumping we pulled our rip cords on a thirty-second delay or a two-minute delay, and it felt like it lasted for hours. I was riding on the edge again.

It was this desperate need for excitement that probably cost me my first marriage. I'm not contending that it would have lasted much longer anyway, but this brought it to a rapid ending. I was trying hard to bond with my little boy. During the week I'd sometimes bring him to work with me. I'd stand in formation with him on my shoulders. We got close. In addition to what I was doing during the workweek, I'd go jumping on the weekends, and I would bring him with me then, too. He got used to watching me jump; he could even pick me out at 4,000 feet. "That's my daddy! That's my daddy!"

Eventually I made him a little jumpsuit and a little parachute harness, and he'd run around practicing like he was jumping. Back then we could get away with a lot of things that would be impossible now. For example, I went to the 34' jump tower and strapped him on me and we practiced jumping and swinging. He loved it, and he did it right. Naturally it occurred to me, if he can do this, why don't I just take him on up with me? I did. We did a tandem jump. It was beautiful, sailing through the air together, completely free. After we landed safely I told him we had a solemn bond—he was not to tell his mother. Under no circumstances was he to admit to anything. "This is a man's secret," I told him. "Do not tell your mother or anybody else." *She'll kill me if she finds out about this,* I figured.

We were able to keep it our secret, at least until we had that malfunction. On our thirteenth jump the main chute didn't open, and we had to pop our reserve chute. It happens. He was so excited that as soon as we got home he told his mother, "Guess what? Daddy and I had a malfunction."

I laughed and explained, "He means Daddy had a malfunction." She believed me, at least until she heard the real story from the other people who had been there. It's real hard to keep that kind of secret at Fort Bragg. She pretty much packed up and left that week.

I always tried to make every jump as difficult as possible for myself. More accurately, I tried to make every part of my life as difficult as possible for myself. Jumping was just what I was doing at that time. I would set up new challenges. I had to land on this exact spot, I had to wait a few seconds longer before pulling the cord, I had to carry 8 pounds more than I did my previous jump. I had to inject more risk into it. Some jumps I waited and I waited and finally pulled the cord, canopy opened, lines stretched, hit the ground, boom, boom, boom, boom. Several years later, when I was with the Rangers as a trainer, I was the first person to jump with a square canopy instead of the traditional round canopy. Square canopies were new and were not being used by the military or approved for military use, so I went out and bought my own rig. The toughest competition I had was myself. I drove myself harder than anyone else could have possibly pushed me. Every practice jump I made had a purpose. I made myself get better every jump.

I got real good at accuracy. Landing exactly where you intend to land requires pinpoint concentration and a complete awareness of everything that is happening around you, just like in combat. To control my landing I had to react instantly to every change in the wind and the weather. When that got too easy I'd always do something to make the jump more difficult, knowing that the penalty for failing potentially was splat. It was a way of keeping my mental skills sharp: I had to stay ahead of every problem because I knew that if I got behind it there was no catching up. Every mistake I made got magnified, and the closer I got to the ground the more magnification there was. It was a life-and-death test of all my skills.

I learned to jump in every possible environment. In December 1972, when I was in B Company, 75th Rangers at Fort Carson, we suddenly got orders to go to Alaska to show the flag to the Russians. We had been spending most of our time training for antiterrorist missions, especially taking control of airports. Alaska was basically a training exercise. There were a lot of scientific missions going on at the North Pole, but the Russians apparently had moved some troops into that area. We wanted to demonstrate to them that if necessary we could mobilize rapidly, so the brass decided to send the Rangers.

I'd only been back from Vietnam, where it seemed like the temperature always was over 100°, for a few months. We were issued cold-weather gear, which most of us had never seen, much less worn. In addition to the thermal jackets we were given what we called Mickey Mouse boots, which had an air pocket built into the heels. It created a thermal barrier between the zero cold and your boot, like an air curtain. The amount of air in there could be adjusted with a little valve on the side of the boot, but nobody told us anything about that. We took off from Fort Carson, Colorado, which was at an altitude of about 6,000 feet. They just put us onto C-141s and flew us up to Alaska for a mass tactical jump.

It was about –30°F when we jumped. That was cold, so cold that our mustaches and eyebrows froze up and if you rubbed them, little pieces broke off. We didn't know that we were supposed to unscrew the valves to let all the air out of our boots. When we jumped we were below the altitute from which we had taken off, so the air in our boots began to expand—and when we hit the ground they started exploding like balloons. It sounded just like we were in a firefight in Vietnam. *Pow. Pow. Pow.* Those boots were exploding all over the place. I don't think it scared the Russians. The army had to send an emergency resupply of those boots up to us.

Skydiving filled in some of the emotional pieces I was missing after Vietnam. I tried out for the Golden Knights and was accepted. When I first came in directly from the Rangers I had a nice big Fu Manchu mustache. The Golden Knights were clean cut. The sergeant major of the team, Bob McDermott, looked at me when I reported and asked, "How badly do you want to be on the Golden Knights?"

"I want to be here, Sergeant Major. I really do."

He opened his drawer and took out one of those old double-edged Gilette razors and tossed it to me. "Go outside and cut off that mustache and we'll talk about it."

I took several steps outside his office and started dry shaving. I cut that thing right off, and when I went back into his office I was dripping blood on his shirt and on my uniform.

He smiled. "Now we can talk. You know, I can take a soldier and I can make him into a skydiver, but I can't make a skydiver into a soldier. You're a soldier. Welcome to the Golden Knights."

The Golden Knights consist of several teams, including the Black and Gold demonstration teams, which perform at public events, and the competition team. I spent my first few months with them on the Gold team, just traveling around the country to fairs and air shows, jumping out of airplanes and performing tandem jumps. Years later during my second tour with the Golden Knights, we jumped into major football stadiums like the Gator Bowl and Orange Bowl. When we weren't doing shows we were practicing, jumping ten or fifteen times every day.

I got to know the people on the competition team, including Skydiving Hall of Fame member Gene Paul Thacker, Charlie Hall, and Chuck Collinwood. One Saturday afternoon they asked me to come out to do some style jumping with them. I had never turned style before, so they taught me the basic techniques—turning left and right, back loops, fallaways. On Monday they put me on the style and accuracy team.

I wanted to do everything right away. One afternoon I was so focused on getting my maneuvers right that I lost track of my altitude. That is without doubt the worst thing you can possibly do on your way down. I pulled the cord at the last possible second; if my canopy had surged or hesitated before opening I was dead. Thacker was duly sympathetic, telling me to get right back up there and go through all the moves again, "but maybe this time you'll want to start a little higher or open up a little sooner."

I agreed that was a fine idea, which I intended to put into practice.

Within fifty jumps I was working alongside world champions and holding my own. My first skydiving competition took place in Jackson, Mississippi—and I took first place in style and accuracy and first place overall. I was doing real well on the Golden Knights and I was enjoying it, but there is something about me that just can't be satisfied. Many people get their pleasure by doing what they know and enjoy over and over, but that has never been me. My pleasure has always come from reaching farther, and maybe tweaking the system a little bit along the way. In the military that is officially frowned upon but privately appreciated by many individuals, so long as you don't get hurt or screw up anybody else.

My attitude did cause some problems. I was always experimenting with new or different equipment. I was always looking for better methods, equipment, and technology to make our combat troops more efficient or to make infiltration and extrication easier and safer. I was always modifying my rucksacks, testing new rigs. I just wanted to see what would happen if. That "if" basically was wide open for suggestions.

I was intrigued by the square canopy. In the early 1970s square or rectangular parachutes were becoming popular with skydivers, but the military wasn't interested. I thought it possibly had some real advantages; they thought it was a bad canopy. With the round canopy you had to do a downwind landing, stretching out full bore to hit your mark. The precision definitely was hit and miss. With a square canopy you could sink right into the wind and land standing straight up. A square canopy had a much better landing ratio, and it was easier to maneuver in the wind, which meant you could jump in various weather conditions. It made sense to me. I'd done numerous jumps with a square canopy and wanted to continue to test it for accuracy. The army wasn't interested in my opinion.

So one Saturday I took my ParaPlane Cloud square chute over to Louisburg, North Carolina, where a friend of mine operated a drop zone. I made several jumps that day, and I was getting good results. I was playing with my equipment to see what effect each small change would have. Late in the afternoon as I was coming in for a landing, a crosswind came in on me when I was about 44 feet high and collapsed my canopy. I slammed straight down into the ground and broke my foot and my wrist.

I screwed up and I got hurt. I didn't tell them it happened that way, of course. Instead I told them that I had a flat tire and while I was fixing it the jack slipped and the car fell off the jack, causing my injuries. "Damn thing just slipped. I'm lucky I wasn't killed," I said convincingly. At least convincingly to me. There was a little bit of truth there. I did have a flat, and the car did slip off the jack—but only because I couldn't do what I needed to do. It turned out that none of those old ladies in the drop zone could keep a secret, so I got my ass chewed for lying and got knocked out of competition for more than a year. What hurt most was knowing I had let the team down. They were depending on me, and I screwed up.

That event marked the end of my first tour with the Golden Knights. More than a decade later I got back to the team in a very different position. I loved jumping. In fact, I estimate I've made more than 18,000 jumps in my career. For a time I was assigned to work with Colonel Nick Rowe, one of the men I most admire, on what was known as the HALO Committee. We were tasked with developing new combat delivery systems and infiltration tactics using HALO capabilities. As we were winding down in 1983, I decided to compete in the All-Military Parachuting Competition, which was being held at Fort Bragg. This was a jumping competition between all the military services, army, navy, air force, and marines. I hadn't jumped in competition since I'd left the Golden Knights. I didn't do any training, any preparation—but I smoked them all. I finished first in style and accuracy.

By that time I was in a position to have some choice about my next assignment. I was looking around for something interesting, and I found out the Golden Knights did not have a team leader. The thought of going back there seriously interested me. So I got myself attached to the Golden Knights as an instructor assigned to the competition team.

There wasn't too much I could teach these people about the physical aspects of skydiving. These were already some of the most talented people in the world. What set me apart from everybody else when I jumped was my mental attitude. What I was able to teach them was creative visualization. How to see what they were going to do in their mind before they did it with their body. I was able to teach them that their mental preparation was equally as important as their physical training. There were techniques they could use to be mentally prepared. So while they were still in the airplane they visualized everything they were going to do on the jump. It was exactly the same technique I had used in Vietnam in an ambush or taking down an individual; I had seen it in my head step by step, and then I just let it unfold. When my people left an airplane they were completely relaxed and already moving. In their mind they had already made the jump, and their body knew what to do. That put them far ahead of every other team in the world. We went out and became world champions.

In 1986, I believe, we went to the U.K. for the British National Parachute Competition. We were able to get in a few jumps before the heavy weather rolled in and kept us on the ground. After a couple of days everybody was bored. I created some indoor competitions on the training equipment. We were spinning around the floor on carts on wheels, we were jumping for accuracy on the swing landing trainers, anything to keep busy.

Anything. With time to kill, the whole team was walking in downtown London, and we happened to run into a group of punk rockers. Nice-looking gentlemen, spiked pink hair sticking straight up, lots of piercings, chains stuck through their ears. We were wearing our Golden Knights jackets and couldn't have been more clean-cut. These punk rockers started talking crap to us, and one of them made the serious mistake of spitting at my captain. I just reached over and grabbed hold of his face chain and tore it out. I ripped that pin out of his ear and shoved him up against a wall. "You son of a bitch," I told him. "You do not spit on an American." I didn't know if he was one of those bleeding hearts, but I did know for certain he was a badly bleeding ear. We ran the rest of them off.

The fact is that me with too much time on my hands could be problematic. I became friendly with some members of the Red Devils, the English team, and one day they took us to see Stonehenge. Nobody knows much about Stonehenge, which consists of forty-three large standing stones that had been arranged in a circle as long as five thousand years ago. It touched that mystical part of me that is appreciative of all the gifts left to us without any explanation by our distant ancestors. So naturally I began wondering, has anybody ever done a parachute jump into Stonehenge, landing inside the circle?

I found out it never had been done. The Red Devils liked the idea and ran it through the chain of command. Eventually we got permission to do a joint Red Devils–Golden Knights jump. I led the formation because it was my idea and I was the senior American. In addition to individual jumpers, our national accuracy champion, Jim Nipper, was going to do a two-stack—two canopies hooked together—with a Brit. In the days leading up to the jump I started prancing around. A lot of people were wondering what I was doing. When they asked me, I told them very seriously, "I'm practicing my rock surfing."

"Rock surfing?" Nobody had ever heard of that. "What's that?"

"That's when I land on one of the rocks and hop from one to another knocking them down. Oh yeah, that's gonna feel good." I knew I was teasing them—I was not going to be the man responsible for knocking down Stonehenge—but I think some of them weren't quite sure. I remember looking a British officer in the eyes and explaining to him in great detail how I intended to do it, by approaching one stone from the side with enough height and leverage and hitting it at the very top, and then it would be like dominoes. As I was telling him this I was showing him with the palm of my hand how they would all fall over. I was completely making it up, and he was just as completely engrossed in what I was telling him. There was no question that he definitely did not think I was funny.

There was a lot of American and some very anxious British brass at Stonehenge when we made the jump. I was coming in, coming in, getting closer, maneuvering carefully, and I hear this clipped British accent screaming at me, "You touch my stones, you're going to jail, O'Neal! Do not touch my stones!"

I lifted my legs as I sailed over the top of the stones and became the first parachutist to land inside Stonehenge. I landed almost directly in front of the generals and drew up to attention and saluted. Even I could see the look of relief on those British generals.

When I'd left the Golden Knights for the first time I was looking to go to Special Forces, but the army reassigned me to the 82nd Airborne. At that time the army was looking to disband Special Forces, so they were cutting back assignments. Fortunately Pappy Wells was 1st Brigade sergeant major, and he brought me in as his NCO in operations.

I was only there a few months, which turned out to be just long enough. While I was there I wrote the manual and SOP for the Dragon, a hand-fired tube-launched antitank missile that was developed to replace the 90mm recoilless rifle. It was a miniature TOW missile. Also while I was there we had the annual Division Competition, in which everyone competed for best company, best shot, best weapons platoon, best mortar. It was a great competition; we all got to blow up a lot of shit. To train B Company I put in a request for ammunition: Dragons, TOWs, 60mm and 81mm mortars, 106mm recoilless rifles, .50 cals, M-79s, M-60s, M-16s, whatever weapons system we were using in the competition.

As an E-6, a staff sergeant, I had no real authority, but I did have a long tradition known as "midnight requisitions" behind me. I filled out all my forms and went up to Major James Lindsay, who eventually became a four-star general, to get my request approved. I didn't have much hope that he would approve all of it. He wasn't there, but the sergeant major was, and when the sergeant major had to leave the office I noticed that Major Lindsay had left his rubber stamps on his desk. Approved! Approved! Approved! Major Lindsay's rubber stamp approved them all. When he came back he did sign and stamp the first allotment, except he didn't know it was only the first allotment.

I got some trucks and went over to the motor pool to pick up my ammunition. All of my ammunition. We burned up the division's annual ammunition allotment in a couple of months. It was no surprise when we won the division that year—the rest of the companies didn't have any ammo to practice with.

It was at the 82nd I also met Charles Wesley Evans, who had come into the army from the Seabees because he wanted to go to Special Forces. He ended up working for me, so I sent him to Special Forces school. He didn't have any orders, but I had a lot of friends in SF, so me and the XO, we just sent him up there. That was the way SF used to be run, people helping people. While he was training we covered for him, marking him present for duty, and if anyone was looking for him we invented some excuse. "He's running down some papers for me." "He's on a detachment." He was good except for the last three weeks of the course. We got a new first sergeant and XO, and everything changed. When they found out where he was, at first they couldn't believe it; there was a lot of "He's where?" "Finishing SF school, First Sergeant." Then they were angry. They wanted to bring charges against him for being AWOL. That was ridiculous, the man was doing exactly what we told him to do. He was already up at Robin Sage, the last part of the program, so I called in some favors, and as soon as he graduated from the program they cut the orders for him to go into the program. CW may well be the only Green Beret to be accepted for training after he'd already graduated.

Primarily because of what I did with the ammunition, I was assigned to the Recondo School as the chief instructor for tactics and combatives. Recondo School is basically LRRP school. My job was to teach people to survive in enemy territory by remaining undetected or, if necessary, fighting their way out. I taught movement, stalking, ambushes, POW snatches, sniper tactics, hand-to-hand, and escape and evasion. They gave me seventy-two students, and at the end of the course one person graduated. People told me that might have been the single worst ratio in any school the army ever had conducted. My problem was I thought that was a compliment.

By 1975 the military was getting to the lower part of the barrel. The draft had been ended in 1973, and we'd moved to an all-volunteer army; the problem was nobody wanted to volunteer. Vietnam had left a big scar on the military. Good people were getting out, and less good people were coming in. I had people in my class who were there by choice, the army or jail. I had drug abusers. I had school dropouts. Most of these people didn't care about flunking my course. In fact, they wanted to get out. There definitely were a lot of whiners in that class. At times I thought the only person who wanted to be there was me.

The army wanted to hold on to every body it could rope. I definitely was a hard-ass. I knew that the enemy didn't grade on a curve; if you didn't know what you were doing you got yourself killed, and maybe you got your buddies killed, too. I was not going to put anybody in the field who would be a risk to other people. Our commanding officer was a Vietnam vet who knew his stuff and gave us great latitude. I set my own rules for the course and did things my own way. I did it the old-school way. They wanted me to teach people what I had learned in Vietnam, so I made the training as realistic as I possibly could, from the POW camps and the hand-to-hand combat to the patrolling and ambush tactics. I didn't do it the conventional way, and I found out that if you tie up and interrogate just one single trainee people are going to be upset.

I was teaching Introduction to Escape and Evasion for POWs. It was held in a long, narrow room in a square tin building sitting off the ground on cinder blocks. I had seventy-two students in there, plus some cadre, all of them sitting comfortably in school-type desks and chairs. What not one of those people knew was that I had planted smoke cans and artillery simulators all around the building, and I had everything wired to a toggle switch. I was never perfect at calculating how much explosive is enough, so I used the reliable P for Plenty. There definitely was plenty.

I had the toggle switch to blow it up on the podium with me. I was introducing the material to them, emphasizing the fact that you always have to be prepared for the unexpected, when I blew it. First smoke, then *BOOM!* My mistake was that I didn't realize how powerful those simulators were; that whole entire building got lifted off its foundation. I blew it right off those cinder blocks with myself, my students, and other instructors in there, and it landed cockeyed. Then the doors flew open and I had people rushing in shooting—blanks, this time—up into the air and screaming. They put burlap bags over the heads of the students, and we marched them out of the classroom into trucks and drove them to our POW camp. That was their introduction to hostage resistance.

The hand-to-hand combat might have also been a little rougher than the cadre preferred. They didn't want to get these people hurt, while I wanted to teach them that this whole thing wasn't some big joke. I did professional, realistic training. I took it to the point of death; I had my hands around every student's throat, and I took them as near to passing out as possible. I knew exactly what I was doing, and nobody suffered any damage beyond fear. Those people would look at me and never be certain how far I would go. *Just how crazy is this guy?* I destroyed all their perceptions of safety. I wanted them to experience fear, and if I kept them within the boundaries of "regular" that never was going to be possible.

It was at that time that I first began teaching the most deadly individual combat system ever devised, the American Warrior Free Fighting System, which I helped invent. I would always begin my demonstrations of this technique by taking an ice pick, sticking it through the front skin of my neck, and using it to lift a 50-pound bucket of water. I promise you, that got everybody's attention. I did it every Friday for three years while I was teaching a new class, to demonstrate that I could manage my pain and control my bleeding. I started learning how to do it in Vietnam. I stuck an ice pick through the flesh on my arm and used it to pick up my M-60. It isn't a trick; it is exactly what it appears to be, the use of your mind to control pain.

As I have always taught people, the only limit to your capabilities is your mind, and the ability to control your mind is the strongest weapon you ever will have.

I would do a lot of crazy stuff to prove that. In addition to picking up buckets of water and weights, one time I stuck that ice pick through my neck, hooked the ends onto a car, and pulled that car across a parking lot. I would also park an army jeep on my belly and demonstrate how to fieldstrip an M-16 while it was parked on my gut. The purpose of doing this was to demonstrate that you can control your breath flow, your emotions, and your fear, and if you do that you can even use your mind to control your bleeding. I associated the penetration of the pick with a bullet wound. In Vietnam I had seen people die of a flesh wound because they went into shock, while other guys who had their guts hanging out, their brains hanging out, lived because they did not let their fear overcome their will to survive. I told my students, if you can survive having a 3,000-pound vehicle parked on your gut, the next time somebody slams you in the stomach you are going to just look at him and ask, "Are you kidding me?" I wanted my students to understand that they hadn't started to explore their physical capabilities.

The American Warrior Free Fighting System was born in Vietnam and developed as I moved along. It is an accumulation of pieces of various fighting techniques, from the Native Americans to combat weapons. I called it free fighting because there is only one rule:

Win. It doesn't matter what you do, win. In Vietnam I began learning the traditional martial arts, but I focused mostly on Muay Thai, which unlike most other martial arts uses all eight of the striking points on your body—your fists, feet, elbows, and knees. Most of the hand-to-hand combat I did in Vietnam, I had something in my hands to hit people with, but after that battle at the hospital camp when I literally was fighting with my hands, I wanted to learn a technique to take out an individual by bringing the maximum force against the points of least resistance with the least energy expended—basically, using the least amount of energy to create the maximum amount of damage. When most people fight, they just flail out. They have no technique, so they aren't committing the maximum possible force. They're just striking out at people. If you teach your body a technique and continue to practice it, when it is needed it clicks in automatically. It allows you to conserve energy in combat, which is like filling your car up with gas.

Martial arts is both a mental and physical discipline. I made the mental aspect of the Free Fighting System every bit as important as the physical requirements. The mental aspect has nothing to do with conscious thought. If you think, it's too late, you're dead. You have to react, and the actions that you take are learned and practiced skills. If someone throws a kick at you, for example, you need to be able to block it without thinking about blocking it. The mental aspect means being able to put yourself in a state of relaxation by controlling your breathing, and eliminating fear and pain to allow yourself to totally focus all of your energy and all of your senses on one point. Our fighting capabilities exist inside us. We were born with them because we need them for survival. Every living thing has a survival gene. Bugs don't understand concepts like life and death, but they run when they sense a threat, and when necessary, they fight back. We're the same way. We've got all that inside us; we just need to bring it to the surface and learn how to control it.

There is a reason all of the ancient warriors—the Mayas and the Incas, the Aztecs, the Native Americans, the Montagnards in Vietnam—prepared for battle by listening to drumbeats or chants or repetitive music for hours and hours. It put them in an almost hypnotic state of pure relaxation. It's possible to do the same thing by controlling your breathing. By practicing, I learned how to put myself in a state of relaxation in three breaths. I actually learned how to control my heartbeat through my breathing; I could speed it up or I could slow it way down, which a few years later would save my life.

We taught our students to "think black," think nothingness. The example I used was that if a man is firing his weapon without consciously thinking about it, his energy is focused entirely on that action, but he if he is wondering, "What happens if I miss?" he's lost focus. He's allowed his fear to influence his actions and possibly cause him to miss his target.

When you are able to go into battle without being handcuffed by fear or pain, you have the ability to bring out the greatest power inside yourself. I was wounded a lot of times, but it never prevented me from continuing to fight. When your mind gets cluttered with pain you've lost the battle, so you have to isolate it and release it through your breathing. If you allow your mind to dwell on your pain, it magnifies it. Like a toothache, for example. If you have a toothache at night when you're lying in bed, it's all you can think about; it kicks your ass. That same toothache during the day becomes manageable, and you may even forget it because you're not bringing attention to it. Pain is manageable if you train yourself.

I took every opportunity to learn as much as possible about anything that might benefit a warrior in combat. When I was with the LRRPs/Rangers in Vietnam, I went to the field medic courses so I could serve as a team medic if necessary. While taking those courses I also learned about the most vulnerable points on the human body. In hand-to-hand combat those places are your targets.

When I hooked up again with Mike Echanis a few years later we began adding the techniques of Hwa Rang Do, a Korean martial art that had been founded in 1960 and involved both hand-to-hand techniques and fighting with weapons. At one point Mike brought in Joo Bang Lee, who with his brother created and named Hwa Rang Do and was naturally the Supreme Grandmaster. He was an arrogant son of a bitch. I wanted to be trained by him, but he told me that first I would have to carry his bags for six months, I had to bow to him, I had to do all these things to learn humility. There was exactly zero chance of that ever happening, so we did not get along. Eventually, though, I did get my black belt from him.

I didn't press the American Warrior system on those people I was training. While I was tough on them, nobody got seriously hurt, but I didn't let them pussyfoot hand-to-hand combat either.

The thing I really did get in trouble for was my live-firing exercise. I believed in real-world training. What happened wasn't completely my fault. Nobody told me I had to use blanks. So I set up an ambush with live claymore mines, suppressive fire with an M-60 and M-16s, TNT, grenades—I had it all. The brass didn't like it, because I didn't do it on a so-called official range. I told them, "You telling me that in combat you fight on a range? Get real." They were still very upset and wanted to know how I'd gotten hold of all those explosives. Where did all those claymores come from? I told them I'd made some phone calls, or I went over to people and scrounged, and then I did the training.

The 82nd finally had enough of O'Neal. They told me to go find a job. When they told me I wasn't fitting in, I responded, "You think?" I had been in the jungle, I knew what was waiting out there for these people if they ever had to go, and I wanted to prepare them for it.

I don't think my superiors cared where I went, as long as I went there quickly. I upset people, and some of them were concerned that my presence in their outfit might be detrimental to their careers. They didn't know what I was capable of doing. These were not the fighting people for the most part, but the paper people. Leaving was acceptable to me; I hadn't wanted to be there in the first place. I asked them to send me over to Smoke Bomb Hill, where John "Skipper" Coughlin was helping to organize what eventually would become Delta Force.

I'd first heard about Skip in Vietnam, where he was building himself into a legend. He was a LRRP, and in battalion recon we called him "the wild man." He had been born in Northern Ireland and emigrated to the United States when he was a kid. He was one of the Son Tay Raiders, a Special Forces team who flew deep into North Vietnam, to a prisoner-of-war camp 30 miles outside Hanoi, in an attempt to rescue U.S. POWs. They successfully got inside the prison, shot up some NVA, and got back without suffering a single serious casualty—but the intel had been bad, and the prisoners had been moved out of Son Tay months earlier. Skip won his Silver Star that night. The raid proved that Special Forces could operate anywhere in the world, and because it took place, the North Vietnamese started treating our POWs much better. The fact that more than forty years later the SEAL Team Six raid that resulted in the killing of Osama bin Laden was carried out in a remarkably similar way did not surprise me, because Skip was one of the people who helped create our special ops teams.

I'd met him once in Vietnam, when I went up to the brigade area for a briefing. I transferred out of the 82nd into 5th Group, where Skip was training a team in antiterrorist tactics. The experience in

Vietnam had finally proved to the military that in the type of wars we were going to be fighting, small, highly trained assault teams capable of operating deep in enemy territory would be essential. In a large bureaucracy like the military where everything has to fit into an organizational structure, these types of units cause a lot of headaches, because no one knows where they actually belong, and they suck the best combatants and materials from other units that can use them. So Skip was fighting a lot of paper battles to create an elite HALO/Combat Diver–trained unit that could infiltrate anywhere in the world to carry out any type of mission. It consisted of two assault teams and a support unit. As far as warriors, this was the most capable company in the military. We had Green Berets, Rangers, Recon veterans; we had the top demo-trained guys in Special Forces; our senior medic was a physician assistant who'd quit his practice to join Special Forces. This was an elite team.

We were training for any type of mission. We were capable of dropping down on the enemy from 25,000 feet and popping up on them from a nuclear submarine. We practiced landing on beaches and in populated areas, moving silently through drainage systems, or fighting in the mountains. We locked in and out of submarines and jumped from 30,000 feet. We worked with every type of weapon and generally trained with live explosives. While I wasn't SCUBA qualified, I learned on the job, being taught by the best people in the world. We trained with the navy's SEAL Team Two on the East Coast. We taught them techniques on land, they taught us techniques in the water.

We did more PT than any other unit in the military, we shot more, we swam more, we jumped more, we were continually training hard. We took every type of class—medical classes, tactics, intel, anything we might need to know.

Even with all that training, what was missing was realistic

instruction in hand-to-hand combat. They were still using old techniques. At that time I was living at Fort Bragg with CW Evans, Chuck Sanders, and Mike Echanis developing our American Warrior system, and we wanted to set up a course to train Special Forces. We needed permission from both the operations side and the school side to start up the school. We went to a colonel from ops, and he agreed that if his counterpart at the school approved it he would give permission. Then the colonel running the school agreed that if ops approved he would get it set up. So in that situation I did the only thing that made sense. I went in and typed up the necessary paperwork, got a rubber stamp, and got a two-week school approved.

The problem we had was that we needed Mike Echanis, and he was a civilian who was not Ranger qualified or Special Forces qualified—although he had served in combat with 75th Rangers. He also was disabled from being shot up in Vietnam. While his foot was still attached to his leg, it was pretty much useless unless he was wearing a special boot, but he'd overcome that to earn his black belt in several martial arts disciplines. So while he didn't have the qualifications the military demanded to teach, he did have the knowledge we needed. What I did was take my 201 file and white out my name and Social Security number, then write in his name and number. Just like that Mike became a Ranger and SF qualified.

We were an impressive, destructive group. Chuck and Mike had grown up together, and I had become friends with Mike in Vietnam. CW was a street fighter, and Mike was expert at all that Hong Kong Fooey stuff. Chuck Sanders was a hell of a combatant—a wrestler/judo champion and maybe the strongest of any of us. I fought a completely different way because I had fought in the trenches where there were no rules. We created a system of hand-to-hand fighting the only way possible, by fighting. This was completely against regulations, but that hadn't stopped any of us before. What we would do was go out in back of the building or out to a training area and fight. I mean fight. We wore combat boots, web gear, rucksacks, everything we would be carrying on a mission, and we began with the premise that, OK, we're out of ammunition, now what. "What" was the American Warrior Free Fighting System that I had created. We would fight full blows with half-gloves on, which are open-fingered gloves that reduce some of the shock when you get hit in the face. There were no rules. If you weren't good enough to block a blow you'd get kicked with combat boots anywhere in the body. We all got hurt. We jammed fingers, broke bones; I even had my left eye popped out. Surprisingly, popping out an eye is easy. You can do it with just a little flick, and it isn't that painful. You still can see out of it, and it goes right back in.

The four of us wrote three books together to promote this type of fighting, *Knife Self-Defense for Combat, Basic Stick Fighting for Combat,* and *Knife Fighting, Knife Throwing for Combat.* Because CW, Chuck, and I were still on active duty, we all agreed that Mike would put his name on the covers and get the credit. It was a four-man show with a one-man billing. Because Mike had been the martial arts editor of *Soldier of Fortune,* we were able to get several stories about the course published, in addition to our books. Mike then went ahead and sold the same rights to several different people, but that was Mike.

After we'd convinced each of those two colonels that the other one had given approval to start the course we went ahead and got it set up. It was fifteen days long, and it was brutal. It was an all-volunteer course, and we would lose as many as ten of our twenty-five students the first day. They thought we were crazy. They probably weren't completely wrong. Mike was a complicated person who had a tendency to exaggerate and obfuscate, and he created a legend for himself, and like in Vietnam there were times when he went a step too far. Crazy or not, we successfully created the toughest course any of these people had been through. Mike outlined it once for *Black Belt* magazine, and he was accurate about it. "This will be the most sophisticated approach to hand-to-hand combat, knife fighting, sentry-stalking, hypnosis for combat, defense against armed attack, riot control, mind control, breath control, acupressure massage, standard punching and kicking techniques, throwing, joint-locks, choking and neck breaking techniques." In addition we taught them knife throwing, short stick fighting, and the use of garrotes and crossbows. We showed them the concealment techniques that I'd learned in Vietnam, using shadow and light to make yourself almost invisible and conforming to the terrain. It was fifteen days of hell.

Even with all the fighting the four of us did, there was only one time when an injury caused me problems. One time some soldier from Fort Bragg just went crazy and killed his Korean wife, put her body in the trunk of his car, and drove it into a lake. A helicopter spotted the car about 10 feet underwater. The MPs got called in and they asked 5th Group to go into that lake and search the car. While I wasn't officially combat SCUBA qualified, I had been well trained by other members of the team. Skip never made a big fuss over paperwork; you either could do the job or you weren't there. I put on the tanks and went down there with the team. We searched the bottom, and when I came out of the water to get another tank Col. Montell, the commander of 5th Group, was standing right there. Colonel Montell looked at me and asked, "Hey, O'Neal, are you SCUBA qualified?"

I gave him the only answer possible at that moment, "What

does it look like, sir?" and kept walking. I put on another tank and went back to work. He was still standing there when I came out again. "Get those tanks off, O'Neal," he said. "You are not SCUBA qualified. I already spoke with Skip, and you're going to the next SCUBA class."

I shook my head. "No, sir," I said. "You can't do that."

"Why not? Why don't you want to go?"

It was ridiculous. My attitude was the same as it had always been. *Put the rucksack on, grab a weapon, and fucking go. Whatever happens, I'll figure it out.* I explained, "The team is going on a sub op, and I need to go with them."

He shook his head. "No. You're going to SCUBA school first, and then you can go." Even I couldn't figure out a way to beat this one. Unfortunately, the night before I was supposed to report to the school to begin SCUBA training, I was out practicing sword fighting with Mike Echanis. We were using wooden swords, and he hit me in the groin with a cheap shot. It opened up something inside my body, and I was leaking semen. Semen is a foreign object in parts of your body, and its presence will cause an infection. My entire groin swelled up. I was doing all that running and swimming, and I was hurting. I had serious trouble just walking, but I was determined to get through it.

I can tell you, Skip did not help me at all. While the team was off training to evac from a nuclear sub, I was bobbing up and down in a swimming pool. I was angry, thinking that I should be with my team instead of wasting my time in a tank learning how to bob. We were in the water bobbing one afternoon when the door opens and Skip walks in. Everybody in the Special Forces world knew Skip. He was my personal hero and my friend. There have been few people I admired more in the world than him. He had a cigar in his mouth and was wearing a black T-shirt. He waited until he had our attention, then he said, "O'Neal says that this school sucks and all the instructors are pussies." Then he smiled at me, turned around, and walked out.

That was all our instructors needed to hear. They had a shark frenzy. They had us bobbing and bobbing and bobbing for hours until my SCUBA partner collapsed. He wasn't going to quit; he actually drowned. They dragged him out of the water and revived him; then they had to medevac him out. The rule was that when you were in the tank, at no time were you permitted to be more than an arm's length away from your partner, so when we dragged him out I was ready to get out with him. The instructor told me, "You get back in there and bob, you son of a bitch. You think we're pussies? You fucking bob until you die."

I bobbed. I bobbed for what seemed like hours. I was going to die before I gave anyone the satisfaction of making me quit. I bobbed until I was exhausted. I had fins on my hand and I could barely move them. I could hardly keep my mouth above the water, so finally I sucked in as much air as I could through my nostrils and went down to the bottom of the pool.

We carried tanks with full air in them, but we did not have a breathing apparatus. We wore the oxygen tanks for the weight and bulk, but we didn't need them to breathe, as this was a survival exercise. So I sat down on the bottom of the pool, pulled out my dive tool and opened up the tank, then cupped my hands in front of me and sucked in air bubbles. I was furious but determined. Some people came down and signaled for me to go up, and I flipped them off. Anybody who came near me, I was ready for a fight. I signaled them that I was okay, I was just resting, but I warned them to stay away from me. I meant it, too. I stayed down at the bottom of the pool until they went and got Skip and he signaled for me to come up. When I popped up, he still had this big smile on his face about the joke he had played on me.

By the end of that class I was hurting bad. My nut sack had swelled up like a tennis ball and was extremely painful. To pass the course we had to complete a 3,500-meter swim and a 9-mile run. There was no time limit. My instructor wanted to put me on profile, which meant I'd go on medical and could complete the training when I recovered. I tried to talk my commander into allowing me to lance it and let it bleed out but he turned me down. We argued about it. I told them there was no way I was going back to Coughlin's team without my fucking bubble. I was leaving with a badge or I wasn't leaving. Finally I lanced it myself. Man, nasty-smelling black pus just poured out of my groin sack, but it relieved the pressure and I was able to complete the swim and the run. I got my bubble and returned to the team.

The regulations had permitted me to wear a green beret because I had been attached to Special Forces in Vietnam, but I wouldn't wear it because I had never been through the school. It didn't make any difference to Skip, I was already doing everything an SF guy could do, but everything I ever got in the military I earned, nobody gave me nothing. If I was going to wear that green beret, I was going to go through the whole program. I went over to Camp Mackall to go through the training.

People in the military are as competitive as in any corporate situation. There's a lot of scrambling for promotions and assignments, and when people don't get what they think they deserve or what they want, there is anger and jealousy. If you're in the military long enough, you're going to make some good strong friendships and allegiances, but you're also going to make some enemies. Phase I was qualification, where people who don't have either the physical or the mental ability to complete the course get weeded out. Phase II was MOS training in light and heavy weapons, communications, demolition, medical, and intelligence, and more people got cut during that phase. Finally we went over to Robin Sage for Phase III, unconventional warfare, which is a field-training exercise designed to test everything the candidates have learned. Students live out in the field and organize guerrilla actions against role-players. Several of the instructors knew who I was and knew what team I was on, so they expected more from me and gave me more responsibility. There were also a couple of people there who didn't like Skip one bit. They thought he was trying to run his own little army, and they wanted to show him up by seeing me fail.

The cadre made me a class leader. The "enemy" was the school cadre, so I felt in some ways like I was competing against the people I knew. The exercise takes place over a wide area of North Carolina that includes all different types of environments. I wanted to make this as real as possible, so I got our own communications frequency from friends from the Signal Company, which meant the "enemy" couldn't listen to us. In addition to our own communications network, we set up our own escape and evasion network, with safe houses and meeting points, and our own command and control network. We even arranged our own transportation. We were operating totally independently of the normal chain of command. We were set up to wage unconventional warfare against the school.

The 5th Group commander, Bob Montell, and the school commander, Charlie Beckwith, as well as a few of the instructors, knew what I was doing, but I didn't even give them all the details. I had my own plans. In some ways this was a test of the cadre, too, to see how good they were. I got myself a set of fatigues that might have belonged to a Major Sanders, if there actually had been a Major Sanders. I took a cold bath in a stream, shaved, put on my stay-pressed uniform and highly shined jump boots, pulled a green beret down over my forehead, and got into an official army vehicle supplied by friends in the auxiliary. I drove that car up to the cadre field safe house, where they did all the command and control of the students. I got out carrying a clipboard with official forms attached. I walked in there like I belonged. The school staff people didn't know who I was, and if any of the NCOs recognized me they didn't say anything. I said I was evaluating the training; my job was to find out where the students were, what their status was, and what their operational plans were. I went into the ops center, and the entire cadre plan was posted there. It specified what their team was going to do, when they were going to do it, and where they intended to take any "prisoners" they captured. I had the "enemy's" whole strategy. I had a pin double-e camera that took sixty-four pictures, so I took pictures of everything, then put on my cammies and went back to my team with the intel. We developed the pictures in the field.

By the time the cadre attacked our base camp, we had already moved to another location. They were not happy about that, because in these exercises the cadre is supposed to win. For students, being taken prisoner is part of the Robin Sage experience. They couldn't find us. They were wondering where the hell we'd gone.

Part of the exercise requires working with "local guerrillas," and the one person who wanted to see me fail gave me a "guerrilla chief" who didn't want to be there. This role-player was a cook who was getting busted out of the army because he was a heroin addict. The last thing he wanted to be doing was running around playing some kind of war game. I couldn't get that SOB to do a damn thing, and he was going to end up costing my whole team its grade.

There were a lot of things I could tolerate in the military, but I could not forgive laziness or sabotage. This fucking junkie was angry at the world, and he was intentionally trying to screw us up. I never did know how to play at war. In my mind this guy was putting my team in jeopardy. Maybe I did get carried away, but I brought an unauthorized pistol into the field with me. I was going to make him move. I was going to give him a choice. He was either going to do what I told him or I was going to shoot him. I pulled it out and cocked the trigger. Would I really have shot him? Truthfully, I'm not sure. It was possible, I was that angry.

Turned out that threatening a soldier with a loaded weapon was a serious offense, potentially a career ender. It wasn't like putting an officer's stamp on some papers. My TAC, tactical assistance cadre, who was supervising the entire exercise, saved my career. Without any question, he saved my ass. When I cocked that hammer he grabbed the weapon. He took the ammo out of it and put it in his pocket. I got sent back to the rear. I was completely aware how much I'd been getting away with, how I had been rounding the edges in a lot of situations and taking advantage of the fact that the army was transitioning to peacetime, but this was different. This could have gotten me court-martialed.

They held a hearing right away. Charlie Beckwith was there, Oley Meyers was there, plus the senior NCO, my TAC, and one uptight, officious NCO who wanted my ass. My TAC stood up and vouched for me. He said I was using an empty weapon as a training aid. He explained that everybody wanted to learn my technique for sentry stalking, so I was teaching hand-to-hand fighting techniques, in this case disarming someone with a pistol. My TAC said it was his weapon, and he was just letting me use it. He was amazing. Thanks to him, when they passed the weapon around it wasn't loaded. I really did believe there was a real chance that my military career was done. I felt awful about it. Whether they believed my TAC or not, at least he gave them something plausible to use in my defense. That's if they wanted to use it.

Meanwhile, when my assistant team leader found out that I had been "captured" and sent back to headquarters, he sent the prearranged signal out on our network that we had been compromised, and everybody on the mission, three twelve-man teams, went into the E&E mode and headed directly to the safe houses. They just disappeared. They did not show up on any school frequency. The school reached out but couldn't make contact with them. As far as the school was concerned, they had three teams lost somewhere in the woods. Everything stopped. They didn't know what was going on. As far as they knew those students might be injured or in danger. They started putting people in the field searching for them.

That hearing lasted a long time. That sorry-ass NCO really felt like he finally had me where he wanted me; my career was in his hands. He was what we called a "garrison troop," meaning he looked great in a uniform but didn't like to get it dirty. They were trying to figure out what they wanted to do with me when they got a phone call reporting that three student teams were missing. It was a pretty simple equation: They had me, but my teams had disappeared. Obviously there was a connection. The NCO questioning me went near-ballistic. Suddenly the hand he was playing wasn't so strong. He demanded that I tell him where my people were, threatening to boot me out if I didn't tell him. "I don't know," I said.

He persisted. Finally Colonel Beckwith came in and asked. "C'mon, Gary, you know where they are. We need to know."

"Well, sir," I said, playing the only cards I held, "if I tell you where the teams are, I want my diploma."

He shook his head. "We'll talk about that later. Right now I need to know where these people are."

I asked him, "Sir, what were the instructions? If any member of the team got compromised they go into E&E mode, go underground until they get further word. That's the way we were briefed. They ain't doing nothing they weren't told to do. We just modified it a little bit."

"But we can't find them."

"They're in their hide sites, and they're safe."

That NCO was still adamant that I must have done something wrong, but I laid out the entire scenario for them. I told them exactly what I had done. I dumped out my rucksack, and out came the keys for the vehicle, my shined jump boots, the starched "Major Sanders" fatigues, and my green beret. I explained how we'd moved from our base camp so the 82nd couldn't find us, and our plan was to set up an ambush when they came looking for us. We'd set up our own E&E network and got our own communications frequency. We had played by the rules, but we played better than they had expected.

The fact that my TAC stood up and claimed it was his weapon took a lot of pressure off me. Finally the colonel told me, "Okay, this is what we're going to do. You are not going to make honor graduate. In fact, you don't even get to go to graduation, but you will get your identifier diploma, and you graduated. Now bring the teams up."

I sent out the proper call sign and told everybody to return to their last known position. After that they went on a mission I had planned, a hostage-type scenario to get cadre out of an old schoolhouse building. It was a pretty successful mission, although I was not permitted to participate. I took my diploma and went back to Skip's team to continue my training.

It was becoming pretty obvious that I fit much better in a combat situation than in the peacetime army. This was not an easy time to be in the military. The anger from the Vietnam War was still smoldering. People were blaming the soldiers for the decisions made by the politicians. This was probably the first time in American history that our soldiers weren't even appreciated, much less honored. Naturally that did not set well with me. I'd seen too many people die or suffer terrible injuries in combat. They weren't doing it for the glory or because there was some big payoff waiting for them. They risked and sometimes lost their lives because they were Americans and they were doing their duty. Now suddenly there were places where we were being told it wasn't a smart idea to go wearing a uniform? Are you kidding me? Admittedly, there were some nights when somebody said the wrong thing to me after I'd had a few drinks and I responded. Trust me, I responded. I was a coiled snake, ready to strike. For me, like for so many other people who had shared those experiences, it would have been very helpful to have an outlet of any kind, to be able to talk about it and try to understand what we had seen and done. That didn't exist. It was just the opposite; nobody wanted to know anything about it. The country wanted to forget it or pretend it hadn't happened. So we kept it bottled up and tried to pretend it wasn't there.

The army had been battered by the war, too. For the previous decade there had been a massive explosion of personnel, equipment, and missions. Then it ended, and the fallout from that was still settling. Almost everyone who had stayed in the army had entered during Vietnam, so we didn't know what was expected of us during peacetime. The politicians were still trying to figure out how to use the army, what our mission was going to be. There wasn't a lot of support anywhere in the country for any type of large use of the military. We definitely were slimming down. There were still a lot of people competing for a reduced number of slots, so the competition for rank and assignment was extreme.

Rank didn't mean anything at all to me. Rank is just a pecking order, a pay scale. The money didn't make much of a difference either. There were a lot of higher ranks than me who had none of my experience or training, but they pushed papers neatly, took no risks, went along with the system, and didn't get in trouble. That wasn't me. That definitely was not me. I just liked working the edges of that system. In the special ops community, which is where I wanted to be, rank is a lot less important than ability and accomplishment. The people who needed to know my qualifications knew them. I was respected as a hellacious fighter who would do whatever was necessary to carry out the mission. I was already getting known for my knowledge of sentry stalking and the silent kill.

The Department of Defense was finally comprehending that the nature of warfare had changed. The new enemy was terrorist groups in small cells and operating in urban areas. The DoD was concerned that we were going to be facing the same type of hostage situations that the Israelis had been dealing with. As the Israelis had proved in their successful raid on Entebbe Airport in Uganda, a lot of the missions in the future were going to have to be done by small, well-equipped, well-trained, and heavily supported units that could move quickly and operate anywhere, clandestinely when necessary—LRRP-type units but with more capabilities than we had. In the past when a unit like that had been needed, it had been created by drawing in people. The DoD wanted to set up a permanent antiterrorist organization. Colonel Montell told them that 5th Group already had a team like that in training. Charlie Beckwith also was putting together a team to respond to airport seizures and hostage situations. Fifth Group was given the name Blue Light; Colonel Beckwith's team was Delta.

Blue Light consisted of Skip's team plus several people requisitioned from other units in 5th Group. No one really knows for sure where the name came from. I always thought Montell used it because it was the name of an undercover OSS mission in France during World War II. We were a top secret organization, and for more than a year the DoD even denied Blue Light existed. They moved us into a large, long-abandoned training area in Fort Bragg where we were far away from regular training. It's pretty much impossible to keep secrets in the army. Too many people have a piece of every unit from supply to S2, so eventually the word got out. We were the nation's first official antiterrorist team.

Our mission was to be ready to meet threats from terrorists, to offer individual protection measures, and to learn resistance to interrogation, how to manage hostage situations, surveillance, improvised explosives, kidnapping, vehicle and personal ambush, escape from captivity, and sentry stalking and silent killing.

We had a sniper team, an intel team, a security team, us, and two assault teams. We were the people who kicked down the doors and went into the compound. We trained to work in cities and buildings. We practiced daytime and nighttime helicopter landings on buildings. We had HALO and SCUBA insertions. We learned how to get over or under electrified fences, bust through walls, move through confined areas like embassy buildings, and take out hostages from trains, buses, airplanes, and any other places where hostages might be kept. We learned target recognition, shooting underneath cars, shooting off the pavement, and the use of a variety of stunning and killing weapons. All those things that have become part of our regular life were new then, and we were learning and training and testing.

We were hardcore. There was a lot of politics going on at that time between Blue Light and Delta to see which one would get picked to be the permanent team. Through the years we heard all types of stories about the connections Colonel Beckwith had in the government that caused them to pick Delta. That decision was unbelievably tough on us. We knew we were as good as any fighting unit in the world when the DoD disbanded Blue Light. Blue Light was turned into the Special Operations School, which taught all SF troops door busting, sniper support, demolitions, all the things that we had learned.

As good as Delta Force is, I always thought that decision was a mistake, that this small, mobile antiterrorist force should have been kept under the beret. After the decision was made, some of the people from Blue Light went over to Delta, but I didn't. I had some other offers that I decided to pursue.

CHAPTER FIVE

> The Christmas party raid provoked Somoza to launch a major counterinsurgency campaign during the 34-month period from January 1975 to October 1977. The FSLN found itself placed in a defensive posture as clandestine networks, urban cells, and rural guerrilla forces were discovered and dealt heavy blows by Somoza's agents and the National Guard. Much of the credit for the Guard's success may be attributed to the existence of a highly trained group, known as BECAT (Brigada Especial Contra La Acción Terrorista or the Special Brigade Against Terrorist Action), and the elite, 400-man "General Somoza Garcia" combat battalion.
>
> *Bynum E. Weathers Jr., "Guerrilla Warfare in Nicaragua, 1975–1979," Center for Aerospace Doctrine, Research, and Education*

I was a warrior looking for a war, and finally I found one.

When Blue Light was disbanded I didn't have anything to do. I didn't want to go over to Delta; that wouldn't have been a good fit for me at all. I also knew it would be at least three or four years before they were really up and running. At that time a lot of really good soldiers I knew were leaving the service to train combatants around the world. The romantic way of describing them was soldiers of fortune, but it probably was more accurate to describe them as mercenaries. Soldiers for hire. In fact, the concept was so popular that a whole magazine about it had been founded, called *Soldier of Fortune, the Journal of Professional Adventurers.* At that time there was a strong demand for the services of well-trained people, especially if you didn't get overly concerned about the local politics. I also knew that even if I left the military I had enough contacts that if there came a time I wanted to go back in, they would find a place for me. So I decided to test the skills I'd been teaching in a real-life situation.

I was hearing from different people I knew around the world, describing their own "professional adventures." Among those people who contacted me was my company commander in 5th Group, Colonel Juan Montes, who had gone down to Nicaragua as the military attaché to the Mil Group commander. He invited me to come down to be a "consultant."

At that time Nicaragua was being run by President Anastasio Somoza, who had been educated in the United States and graduated from West Point. He was a friend to America; he had allowed the air strikes supporting the Cuban exile invasion at the Bay of Pigs to leave from the coastal city of Puerto Cabezas. After that invasion failed, Cuban premier Fidel Castro began supporting the Sandinistas, a rebel army attempting to overthrow Somoza.

I had my own connection with the Somoza family. I had trained the president's son, also named Anastasio Somoza, when he was going through Special Forces school at Fort Bragg. I liked him, but he was a spoiled rich kid, so we had to establish priorities with him. Took a little time, but eventually he got the message. When he went back to Managua he somehow managed to earn a promotion to major and led their SF units in the fight against the Sandinistas.

Somoza wanted me to come down to Nicaragua and train his special troops as well as his personal bodyguards to fight the guerrillas. Chuck Sanders got out of the army several months before I did, and I arranged for him, Mike Echanis, and a third close friend of ours we'd brought back with us from Vietnam, Bobby Van, to go down there and start getting things set up. They were all traveling as American businessmen. Chuck's cover was that he was working in the medical field, Mike was a contractor, and Bobby was a chef.

Bobby's green card was in the name of Nguyen Van Nguyen, which was the Vietnamese equivalent of Smith, John Smith, but he was always Bobby. He was a Vietnamese who had been fighting the VC and NVA since he was about eleven years old, when they had killed his parents. He killed his first VC when he was twelve and grew up to become one of the best soldiers I ever met. He was running recon at CCN, which is where we met, and when it disbanded we got him back to the States. Bobby believed in America more than many people who had been born here. He was a great cook, and he was working as the chef at the Sheraton in Fayetteville when he heard about our mission. He told me he was bored out of his mind cutting meats and vegetables and wanted to go with us. We were pleased to have him.

When I got my discharge, instead of immediately going to South America, I went down to Fort Myers, Florida, and started working for Worldwide Steel. This was a company run by a good friend who'd been shot up when we were in the 173rd. I never told anyone at the company, including my friend, that I was there to build a background for a government assignment. Later people would claim this was a CIA front, but it wasn't. It was a legitimate company that built bridges, laid rebar, and provided reinforced concrete for high-rises. I worked there for several months letting my hair grow out, getting a good tan, learning Spanish, and establishing a believable cover as a consultant for this company. I had intended to stay there until I was close to fluent in Spanish, but I got a call one day from Chuck telling me to get down there ASAP because Mike was getting a little crazy and "I can't control him anymore."

Mike was a unique individual. He was dreaming that he would be the next Chuck Norris or Bruce Lee and was doing everything possible to get publicity, writing stories for *Black Belt* and *Soldier of Fortune* magazines, letting his photograph appear in the local newspapers. He was so busy creating an image for himself that sometimes he forgot we weren't in a Chuck Norris movie, we were in the middle of a dangerous military situation. He kept hinting to people that he was some kind of superspook, making all these claims about his military background that weren't precisely true. Mike actually hadn't been in the army that long before he'd been wounded and discharged, and while he was excellent in hand-to-hand combat, he certainly didn't have all the experiences that he liked to talk about. The problem was that he was talking too much and too loud; he was becoming too high profile, which is exactly what we didn't want to happen. I told him that all that attention eventually was going to bite him in the ass, but Mike heard only those things that he wanted to hear. The situation was dangerous enough without drawing attention to our presence there. As we learned later, Mike's talking would have its consequences.

Before I left I also had a conversation with a government agency that had a real concern about knowing what was actually going on down there and asked me if I would provide some of that information for them. I'm a patriot; when my country asked me to do something, I was in the habit of doing it. To me the sides were pretty clear down there. One side was led by a West Point graduate who had been close friends with all our presidents since Franklin Roosevelt and had allowed us to use his territory to launch the invasion of Cuba; he was one of the few leaders to support Israel when it was established in 1948 and provided weapons for them to fight the Arab armies. On the other side was a rebel army trying to overthrow him that was being supported by the Communist governments of Cuba and the Soviet Union. There were a lot of Americans complaining about human rights abuses in Nicaragua, but I remembered that when Castro had taken over he'd lined his enemies up against a wall and killed them, which definitely could be considered an abuse of their human rights. I'd spent five years in Vietnam fighting the Communists, so it didn't seem like a difficult decision to me at all. So while I never officially worked for this government agency, I considered myself a consultant.

By the time I got to Nicaragua I had long hair, a mustache, and a beard. Every time I looked in the mirror it took me a split second to get comfortable. Chuck picked me up at the airport. The three of them were living together in a tin-ass double-wide trailer outside the city. There was one lazy guard in front of the place. I took one look at it and told them that they couldn't stay there. I checked into the American Embassy hotel. Actually, the embassy had several hotels down there, and they weren't doing a lot of business. Two of them were run by a German family. I rented one of them, which was more like a giant hacienda than a tourist hotel. It was what we needed; it was surrounded by 12-foot walls, and it had big rooms, a large kitchen, even a swimming pool. It was so nice that Bobby's and Chuck's girlfriends eventually came down to live with us. I encouraged that; I thought it helped provide cover.

One of the first things I did when I got down there was meet directly with President Somoza. He brought me into his office and closed the door. Just the two of us were in there, and he told me that he wanted me to train his elite unit, a company capable of carrying out Special Forces–type missions, from hostage rescues to sabotage. I did notice he didn't seem to be especially worried about the rebels, but he wanted to make certain he was ready for whatever happened. Revolutions were part of life in South and Central America, and with Castro stirring up revolution in the region it was smart to be ready. He told me that I would be working directly with General Reynaldo Pérez Vega, the chief of staff of the National Guard, as well as his own son, Major Somoza. Chuck, Mike, and Bobby had already begun getting the facilities organized. All I had to do was tell Somoza's people what I needed, he said. Training equipment, uniforms, weapons, ammunition, whatever we needed they would get it for us. Nicaragua was getting their weapons mostly from Israel, he explained, and there was no shortage. Pérez would select the troops, but I could set my own standards for their training.

This definitely was an exciting opportunity for me. It was a chance to train troops to fight Communism using the methods I believed were most effective. It was a chance to see my teaching come alive on the battlefield, a chance to fight tyranny and make a difference in the world.

Nicaragua is a beautiful country, a combination of the modern cities of South America and the jungles of Vietnam. Being back in the jungle, knowing there was an enemy somewhere out there, was a comfortable feeling for me. When I was there, when beams of sunlight were shooting through the trees, it felt like I'd never left Southeast Asia. The situation when I got there in early 1977 was manageable. The Sandinistas weren't more than a deadly irritant, confined to making hit-and-run attacks. The Somoza government was still in absolute control of the country.

I went to work right away establishing my cover as an engineer for the Worldwide Steel company. I began touring the country inspecting bridges and bunkers, which gave me a perfect excuse to move around and make myself familiar with the situation. When I was in Managua I'd leave the hotel each morning dressed in work clothes and eventually make my way to the military compound. If anybody was watching me, that wouldn't be surprising. The military probably had more construction projects in progress than private industry, so it was natural for an engineer from a steel company to be working there. Once I got behind the gates I'd go up the hill to an area we called "the cave" and change into a private's camo uniform. Then I'd ride with the soldiers to a training area and instruct classes in a variety of antiterrorist skills, from kicking in doors to taking out sentries.

I had my first little taste of what was to come about a month after I arrived when the Sandinistas attacked a National Guard post not far from the northern border with Honduras. There were about fifty members of the National Guard in a big building under attack and I asked Somoza to let my troops respond. I thought it would be excellent training for them.

By the time we got there several hours later, the rebels had the building surrounded and were pouring fire into it. I maneuvered my people through the streets and through some buildings, setting up ambushes. We were in contact with the Guard in the building, so we were able to set up a crossfire. As we got closer the Guard shifted their fire away from us. My people weren't well trained yet, but we had superiority of firepower and position. We basically trapped the rebels between us and the building. The battle didn't last long once we got there, and we had quite a few enemy KIAs.

For me, it was awesome to be back in combat. It was everything I'd been training to do, and it definitely established our credibility with Somoza. Within months we had our training areas in full operation. We had a compound, but we also trained in pastures and on ranches and farms out in the country. We had a mix-and-match of weapons ranging from M-1s to 57 mm recoilless rifles, Israeli Galil assault rifles, Uzis, and as much ammunition as we needed.

The people we were training were known as the Black Berets, and by the time we graduated them they were hellacious fighters. We taught them how to function as an army—patrolling, tactics, setting up an ambush, communications, E&E, infiltration and exfiltration, all the SOPs that an army needs to operate. This was hardcore training in unconventional warfare, so there was no slack. These people were going to be in combat; they were going to be putting their lives on the line for their country, and I was going to make damned sure they had the proper training to succeed. One time, I remember, I had a student fall asleep during my class on water survival techniques. So I put him in a wall locker, closed the door, and tossed him in the pool. The metal locker sank right to the bottom. That thing started rocking as that student struggled to get out. Finally I let another student dive in and open the door. I guarantee you that I didn't have another student fall asleep in class again.

Mike took charge of teaching close-quarter combatives, primarily hand-to-hand and small-weapons techniques. We used to drill in a dugout training area covered with a bed of sawdust that we called "the Bear Pit." It was about 8 feet deep and 20 yards by 30 yards wide. Mike would be down there waiting somewhere in the pit, but he would be camoed up so he could blend in with the shadows and the sides and was almost invisible. When the student went down into the pit, Mike would come out of the shadows.

In addition to the physical techniques, we also taught the application of mental power. Both Mike and I would do the ice-pick-through-our-neck demonstration, or we would lie down and let a jeep roll over us. We showed them what was possible with intense focus. Another thing we would do was lock up, grab hold of each other, and then challenge the entire class to try to move us off dead center. It didn't matter how many people were working together, they could not move us one inch. As we used to lecture to our students, it's easier to be the mountain than to move the mountain.

The training course lasted six months. We had them out by 5:00 A.M. starting the day with an 8-mile run. These people were called the BECATs, and I was El Tigre Negro, the Black Tiger. By the time they earned their black berets they were equal to any commando unit in the world. There were times we would take them into the field for real-life missions. At one time we learned from our intel that the rebels had a small base camp down in the south, toward Panama. We didn't have good air support, so we moved mostly by vehicle. Our mission was to snatch a Sandinista officer, to bring him back alive. I took a small force of my black berets with me, maybe a dozen men, and we went into the jungle.

This is when I was at my best. While I understood the city, I belonged in the jungle. It was where my skills had the most value, where all of my senses were engaged. The concept of sneaking into an enemy camp in the jungle and grabbing a Sandinista officer sounded like an extremely difficult mission. In fact, it was a lot less complicated than it appeared to be. It had to be carefully planned and carried out professionally, but we had the huge advantage of surprise.

We moved through the jungle for most of the first day in two vehicles. When we reached a predetermined point several miles from the camp, we stopped for the night. At first light I left two men with the jeeps, and we began fast-moving through the jungle. It wasn't exactly like Vietnam because there weren't anywhere near as many guerrillas as there had been NVA and VC, and there was no reason for them to be patrolling in the jungle, so chances of us running into any of them were very small. We also didn't have to worry about booby traps. They weren't expecting us. I kept a good pace because I wanted to push my people. I wanted to see what they were capable of doing. Most of them had already seen fighting in this war, but until I saw them under fire I didn't have complete trust in them. It took pretty much the whole day to get to the camp. That was fine; I wanted them to get acclimated to the environment. We located the camp not too far from where our intel told us it would be. We'd seen smoke from their fires first and circled in on that. The camp was under some trees, which provided more protection from the sun and weather than concealment. We lay in the grass just observing. I had no intention of going in there until it was dark anyway. I kept my eye both on the camp and on my people, but they were pretty good following my lead. Late in the afternoon the clouds rolled in, and it started raining hard. That was a gift. It was obvious the people in this camp felt safe—they were far away from any city, and it was well known that the National Guard didn't like to go into the jungle. If they had even bothered to set up perimeter security we never saw it. Inside the camp they were going about their business. The rain just provided additional cover. Most of the people in the camp were forced inside a hooch, trying to stay as dry and warm as possible, and the sound of raindrops banging on the environment can actually be pretty loud, literally drowning out any accidental or unusual sounds.

The rain started and stopped for several hours. We watched, we waited, we learned. We had ponchos pulled over us, but we still got soaked. After a while it became pretty obvious which hooch belonged to the commander. It was a little smaller than the communal places, it was set off by itself a little, and it was the only one with a sentry on it. Physically, it was typical of these jungle huts anywhere in the world. It was raised off the ground about 2 feet, and it had a thatched roof and openings in the front and back that were covered by what looked like parachute nylon. I studied the sentry. He definitely didn't want to be there, and his actions made it pretty obvious he wasn't taking his job too seriously. He probably thought it was a waste of time, the way recruits in basic feel about guarding a Dumpster. There was no reason for government troops to attack a small camp hidden deep in the jungle.

He had pulled the hood of his poncho over his head to shield him from the rain, but every once in a while he'd stop and cup his hands around his mouth. I could see a quick glow as he snuck a puff on a cigarette. This was one unhappy sentry.

We waited until way after dark, till after people had eaten and had gone back to their shelters. There were only a few lights shining anywhere in the compound. A few people with flashlights were moving around in the distance. They were dressed in camos very similar to what we were wearing. I set up my extraction corridor, placing men on either side of a narrow corridor leading into the jungle. If we had to get out quickly, they would provide cover fire.

I pulled my own hood over my head and checked to make sure I had a pack of cigarettes. Then my sergeant major and I strolled casually into the camp. There is an art to the snatch. One of the most important parts of it is projecting that you belong there. I've always described it as camouflaging yourself in open sight. Wherever you are, you have to take on the mannerisms of the people around you. Generally you don't have to speak, but you do have to move as they move, mirror their behaviors, and do absolutely nothing that will draw attention to you. If you're going into a fancy restaurant, you wear a nice suit and tie and in your mind you become a successful businessman. If you're an engineer for a steel company, you put on a hard hat and work clothes and you examine steel structures. At one time or another everybody has been at a party or in a place where you don't feel comfortable, and eventually you begin to believe that everybody else there knows you don't belong. They probably do. Your actions have made it obvious. You've backed yourself into a corner, you're not moving around, it's obvious you feel you don't belong there. You are projecting a negative aura. It bounces right off other people. People notice and wonder, who is that guy? Who's he with? What's he doing here?

I was trying to teach my people to project a feeling of complete comfort. I taught them they had to stand up straight rather than skulk around. They had to walk casually rather than appearing to be in a hurry or glancing nervously around. I taught them that if they encountered someone, they were supposed to look them right in the eyes. Make them back down with a hard stare.

I didn't really expect we would have any trouble. My sergeant major was a fine soldier, and I took him in with me in case we needed to converse in Spanish. There were a few people moving around the camp, but it was quieting down. Rather than walking at the edge of the camp we walked right across it, like we belonged there, like we knew exactly where we were going. The sentry we had been watching was still on duty, walking distractedly around the hooch. As he walked around the back, my sergeant major walked out in front and lit his own cigarette. As I approached the sentry, he looked up at me—and then started moving toward me. He was leaving his post, but he didn't seem to be challenging me. It took me an instant to figure it out—he was leaving to take a piss. We were mostly out of the light, so I waited until he passed me, then I turned around and took him down. I put one hand over his nose and mouth and locked my other arm hard around his throat. I did not take him out violently like I'd done in Vietnam; I didn't have to manhandle him, I just used centrifugal force to rip him off his feet. He was out before I laid him down on the ground. I don't think he was dead, but I didn't really care. I laid him down in the brush, completely out of sight. Then I took his place in front of the commander's hut.

I did a couple of circuits just to get a feel of the situation. My sergeant major faded into the shadows. There was one lamp burning in the hut. I couldn't really see much inside; both entrances were blocked by parachute sheets. It looked like the usual open space, probably with a desk and a bed and little else. I'd seen a thousand huts just like it.

The camp was really quiet. There were only a few people moving around. I could hear voices, even occasional laughter, but every sound seemed muffled. After a few minutes I heard some movement inside the hut. One lamp went out, but a second one stayed lit. I could see the glow moving toward the back of the hut. I kept walking, stopping on occasion to take a puff of a cigarette, just like the sentry had done. Finally the second lamp went out. We were now working in the dark. My time. I walked slowly around to the back. The sergeant major was right next to me. With one motion I swept the sheet back and stepped inside. I heard more than saw someone on my left make some startled noise and start to rise up. I was on top of him instantly. I chopped him hard as I could in his solar plexus, knocking the wind out of him with one big grunt. I grabbed him and pulled him toward me, wrapping my hand over his jaw and mouth. I didn't give him any chance to feel like he could gain control. I wanted him to feel total panic. I wanted to scare him speechless. It's hard to describe exactly what I did, because it all happened automatically. He moved, I responded to his movement. There was no thought involved, just conditioned response. I'd done this numerous times, only this time it was for real. I know I yanked him toward me, slamming him hard in the throat with the side of my hand as I did. There's a nerve running underneath your jaw that if you hit it right it'll temporarily paralyze you. I kept one hand squeezing his throat so he could barely breathe, and we locked up his arms. He was completely stunned, absolutely disoriented. Good. All this happened in a few seconds. He didn't even struggle; his mind was running way behind whatever was happening to his body. The sergeant major grabbed his hands and tied them behind his back.

I snatched his ass up and pulled him out the door. I tossed him over my shoulder, and we faded into the jungle through the escape corridor. My team folded up neatly behind me. When we got clear we radioed the jeeps, and they drove toward us as we raced toward them. We were long gone before anybody even knew we had been there. There was no pursuit. When we reached a clearing in the morning, a helicopter came in and picked up our prisoner. That was the last I saw of him.

Within several months I had settled into a pretty good routine. Nicaragua was a comfortable place for me to be. I was doing what I loved to do, and I was doing it in a good environment. I had never really thought of myself as having one place that I called home; I knew where I came from, but I had nothing pulling me back there. Nicaragua didn't feel like home, either. I had no deep roots planted, no place where I was supposed to be during the holidays; my home was wherever I was living at that time. I didn't mind it. I didn't feel like I was missing anything at all—except my son, and I was doing the best that I could to be in touch with him. The best I could, but that didn't mean it was enough. I didn't allow myself to feel any regrets. His mother and I had gotten officially divorced somewhere along the line. I was living the right life for me, in the middle of an adventure, with the people I wanted to be with, doing the thing that I most loved to do. My friends, the people I was working with and fighting with, the soldiers, they were my family. The one thing I did not expect at that point was to fall in love.

Women had passed through my life, but with the exception of my wife years earlier none of them had stayed very long. It seemed like there was always a woman there when I needed someone, but there was no one that stuck. That was fine with me. I didn't want to be attached. I needed to be free to go when I needed to go. The world that I was living in was a man's world; fight and train during the day, drink and tell lies at night, go home happy. My only responsibility was keeping my people alive, and anything else detracted from that effort. I never had to worry about paying the mortgage. I never had to be concerned about somebody else's feelings. Maybe it was selfish, but for me that was enough. A relationship wasn't something that I had the time or the need for. I was never lonely for a romance, never. That just wasn't an emotion that was familiar to me.

This relationship started out as an arrangement suggested by General Pérez. He felt that our presence was becoming way too visible. Mike in particular was seeking publicity. He wrote an article for *Black Belt* magazine in which he and Chuck were "chief instructors for the personal bodyguards of President Somoza, his special elite guard and the Black Berets, a newly developed commando unit for antiterrorist activities." It was completely unnecessary. I loved Mike like a brother, and he was a good soldier, but as Chuck had warned me, no one could control him. It would be pretty obvious to anyone paying attention that if I was living with them I damn sure had to be working with them. General Pérez suggested an alternative for me. He thought I should get married.

Not a real marriage, just a show marriage. He thought it would provide me an extra level of cover. He had a few women in mind, women who were working for the government in different capacities. I met Maria at a little cocktail party at the home of an officer after work one day, nothing fancy, just beer and pretzels. She was a lovely woman, small and dark but very confident. You could see that confidence in her brown eyes. A lot of Spanish women have a habit of looking down in deference when they speak; they don't meet your eyes. That wasn't Maria at all—that woman grabbed hold of your eyes and would not let you go. It was almost as if she was issuing a challenge.

As I later found out, she was a widow with three little children. Her husband had been an officer and had been killed. I never did learn exactly how he died, and it wasn't something she talked about easily. This first time we met we had a nice conversation, like people do at cocktail parties, and we discovered we felt the same way about a lot of things. Maria was very smart; her English was pretty good, and she could speak in several Spanish dialects from South and Central America. One thing I learned right away. She was a patriot who loved her country, and her husband had died for it. She hated the Communists, and I think she felt a need to play a role in defeating them. She didn't tell me what she did for a living. For a little while she let me believe she was a secretary or an assistant to some bureaucrat in the government. I guess she had her cover, too.

During the next few weeks we spoke several times, getting to know each other, but never talking about the real issue. That was going on quietly behind the scenes, where we both were being questioned about whether we could work together. We started going out in public, doing typical dating things. We didn't try to draw any attention, but if anyone was curious there was nothing unusual about two people who seemed to enjoy each other's company spending time together. As far as sex, there wasn't any. Nicaragua is a predominantly Catholic country with strong traditions, so it wasn't at all unusual that after a date I went home by myself. I also got to know her kids a little, two boys and a girl who were three, five, and eight when we met. They were great little kids, ready to take on the world. Maria and I got to know and like each other, and eventually we agreed to get publicly married. Then we moved into a nice house out in the country.

I picked the house carefully because it was away from other places and we could see all the approaches. There was always at least one guard around the house.

We lived a comfortable life. It many ways she acted like my wife, although we slept in separate bedrooms. In the morning there would be clean clothes laid out for me, and when I came home at night there was a hot dinner waiting for me. Like regular couples, we grew closer together, although in our situation the way we did it was a little unusual. She wanted to understand more about what I was doing, so I started teaching her some basic hand-to-hand fighting techniques, and sometimes we'd go out in the back and practice shooting.

In response, she let me get involved with her business, which was running hookers. One thing that has always been predictable anywhere in the world is that when men travel, some of them are going to want to meet women. They are in a country where nobody knows them, and they're often traveling on an expense account, so they want to get a nice meal, a good drink, and some great sex. This was especially true of lower-level businessmen from the Communist countries, where their opportunities at home were much more limited. Maria, later with a little of my help, provided those women. Basically, the government wanted to keep track of who was coming in and out of the country. Where were they from? Were they Cubans? Russians? What language did they speak? What was the purpose of their visit? How did they feel about the "problems in the countryside"? Maria had these girls working for us and paid them for the information they provided.

Most of Maria's girls worked out of a popular dance club in Managua. This was a clean, well-known place. The men would dance with the girls, buy them a few drinks, and then rent a room. The girls were instructed about what questions to ask and how to ask them. It was nothing too technical. These girls weren't any Mata Haris; they were working girls looking to make a few extra dollars. Once Maria got the information we would pass it along to General Pérez.

The relationship between us grew pretty quickly from like into love. It was more weeks than months. She created a home for us. I never had to do much talking, but if I wanted something it just was there. Our life became comfortable and predictable. The kids adapted easily to it, as kids do. They were regular kids; they loved watching cartoons and kiddie shows and playing kids' games. Sometimes we'd go out in the yard and kick a ball around. For their protection they didn't get on a bus and go to school; instead we had tutors come to the house to teach them.

We never discussed the fact that we had fallen in love, we just accepted it. We had fixed up a little area in the house as a bar, and at night we would sit there and talk. One night we had a couple of glasses of wine and a couple of shooters, and we finally relaxed with each other. We spent that night together, and after that it became normal. Our marriage became real, and the more time we spent together the stronger it got. I was in love with Maria and our kids.

I bonded with the kids. I'd be working at my desk and the boys would sneak up on me and sit in my lap, jabbering away in a mixture of Spanish and English. We figured out how to converse with each other. I got used to being with them all. It was a strange situation. This whole family structure that had been set up as cover for me turned out to be the only loving family relationship I'd ever had. While Maria and I never talked about the future, I think we both believed we would be together. At that time I didn't see any reason I wouldn't stay in Nicaragua.

During that first year I was down there, the government maintained its control over the Sandinistas. The guerrillas were a lot like bees in the summer. We had to be aware they were there, and sometimes they would sting, but we didn't believe they would ever be strong enough to make a significant difference. Each time they showed up we would slap them down, but they were well equipped by Castro and the Soviets. Probably the first time we were forced into an uncomfortable defensive position was in the summer of 1977, when President Jimmy Carter's wife, Rosalynn, was making a goodwill tour of South America. She was going to visit Costa Rica, Ecuador, Peru, Brazil, Colombia, and Venezuela, and the State Department asked the Somoza regime if it was safe for her to visit Managua. President Carter was not a friend of the Somoza government. He was focusing on what he called human rights abuses without understanding the fact that this government that had been supportive of America was fighting a Communist rebellion. Carter's first week in office, he had imposed a ban on all U.S. arms shipments to Nicaragua, and when Congress overruled him he did it through executive order. Fortunately the Israelis had picked up a lot of that business.

The Sandinistas were calling themselves freedom fighters, and there were a few different political factions involved, but mainly it was a Communist movement. The Somoza government did what they had to do to survive, but at least some of the things they got blamed for were done by the guerrillas to turn people against the government. One time they dressed their people in stolen National Guard uniforms and attacked civilians, killing several people, and just like they intended, the government got blamed. There was a lot of propaganda being released that I absolutely knew wasn't true.

I could never forget what the Communists had done to those five kids in a little hooch in Vietnam. Those kids were living in my mind. By this time the whole world knew what the Communists did when they won control of a country. We'd seen the mass executions in Cuba, Vietnam, and Cambodia. Carter still decided to come down hard on the Somoza regime.

While I had nothing to do with the final decision about whether or not to allow Mrs. Carter to visit, they did ask my opinion. I went to a staff meeting and told them that I could not guarantee her safety. This is crazy, I said. This is a war zone. You can't have the first lady of the United States visiting a war zone. We hadn't had enough time to train people to be a dependable security staff. The American Secret Service sure couldn't protect her. There was no way we could ensure that the Sandinistas wouldn't fire a rocket from a mile away, or try to shoot down her plane or plant bombs along the motorcade route. This is an unnecessary risk, I told them. You just imagine what would happen if the first lady of the United States was attacked or hurt. The government finally advised the U.S. State Department that it could not allow her to visit.

It turned out to be a real problem for us. The Carter people decided that the real reason we didn't want her to visit was that we were trying to hide what was really going on in Nicaragua. Therefore all those claims the Sandinistas were making about the government committing atrocities must be true. In response Carter began squeezing Somoza, basically demanding that he fight the rebels with kindness.

I don't know everything that went on in that country, but I do know at least some of the claims made by the rebels weren't true. As the Sandinistas grew in strength, they began attacking some of the smaller cities. They were looking more for propaganda victories than military successes. These rebel troops weren't particularly well trained or well armed, but they were brave and they were dedicated. We used these attacks as training exercises. They attacked in the city of León, Somoza's hometown, figuring they would embarrass him. President Somoza did not intend to be embarrassed. We responded to the attack with a well-trained force armed with .50 caliber machine guns mounted on jeeps. It was a classic response. We had them outnumbered, and we basically circled the city and then closed the ring building by building. I wasn't in the fighting; I was advising the officers leading the battle. That was my job, train them to fight this war, although if somebody took a shot at me I shot back. It was a brief but intense fight. We closed in on them, and eventually the rebels were forced to take refuge in the local church, the cathedral.

We caught more than a hundred of them in there. The priest was working with them. We caught him smuggling weapons inside under his robes. He was smart enough to make sure the newspaper reporters and the television cameramen were around to record what happened. Then he claimed that he had granted the men in the church sanctuary and we couldn't go in and get them. It was a standoff.

When General Pérez asked my advice I told him straight out, kill them. Just drag them right out and kill them all. To win a war you have to take war to war. These people are your enemy, I said; they wouldn't hesitate to kill you if the situation was reversed.

When the generals and government officials came in, I backed out of it. This was a political decision. The government did not want to mess with the Catholic Church. So the politicians finally decided they had to let them go. The TV cameras were running and I guess they wanted to prove that they were merciful; this was their way of proving they were not guilty of the atrocities they were being accused of committing. So they made all of the rebel fighters hand over their weapons and equipment, then let most of them go home. They did keep a few of the leaders. I didn't like them letting the rest of them go; to me that was just putting guerrillas back in the field, but there was nothing I could do about it.

We were winning the fighting but losing the politics. In January 1978 Pedro Chamorro, the editor of the opposition newspaper,

La Prensa, was shot in his car. Everybody assumed that the government had murdered him. Maybe, though I knew nothing about that. I was always real careful not to get involved in politics. It wasn't my job and I didn't know enough about it. Whoever killed him, the result was that people rioted in Managua. They attacked government cars and buildings. The government imposed more control, and the unions responded by calling a general strike. It was becoming obvious that the government was losing control of parts of the country.

The situation was definitely heating up. In late February the National Guard killed one of the guerrilla leaders, Camilo Ortega Saavedra, brother of Daniel Ortega. Ten days later General Pérez went to his mistress's apartment in Managua and three guerrillas were waiting there for him. Supposedly they were going to kidnap him and trade him for political prisoners, but when he fought back his mistress slit his throat. How they intended to get him out of an apartment in the middle of the city I had no idea, but that's what they claimed. That success shook up a lot of people. For the first time government officials felt vulnerable and started moving away from Somoza. We all started to take additional precautions. All of us except Mike, who believed he was invulnerable. He continued to put himself out there. He wouldn't listen to anybody else. That was Mike.

The most serious attack of the war took place in July 1978, when the Sandinistas tried to assassinate Somoza. They fired three 3.5-inch rockets from the seventh floor of the Intercontinental Hotel in Managua about 150 feet across the road into the National Guard compound where Somoza's headquarters were located. One rocket hit the mess hall that Somoza had just left, a second rocket landed in an open field, and the third rocket was a dud. A few people got cut up a little, but there were no serious injuries. In response, the troops just opened up on that hotel; they took out probably half the windows as well as huge chunks from the front of the building. After the firing stopped, somebody had to go into the hotel and clean it out. I was in the compound with Mike and Bobby when it was attacked and General José Iván Alegrett, who was the National Guard's operations chief, ordered the Black Berets to do that job.

The first thing we did was cordon off the hotel so nobody could get in or out. The ground floor was the restaurants, banks, and shops, so we got all the people out of there through the back. They were mostly tourists. We knew exactly where the rockets had been fired from, but what we didn't know was how many guerrillas there were in the hotel and exactly where they were. We had been training in the old Sheraton for a similar scenario, in which we had to rescue hostages from a hotel. In this situation there were no hostages, so it was just find them and shoot them.

The only problem was getting up there without being killed. Ideally you want to move down from the roof—that's an advantage of HALO, you just drop in unannounced—but in this situation that wasn't possible. The Intercontinental Hotel looks like a pyramid; it was built to be quakeproof after the great devastating earthquake in 1972 that wiped out the whole downtown. That meant the floors got smaller as we went up. They knew we would be coming; they had the opportunity to prepare for that. The hotel was calling their guests, telling people just to stay where they were and not open their door until somebody came for them. We could hear people crying in some rooms. As we went through the halls there were some people who couldn't wait and opened their doors. Every time a door opened we backed off and got ready to blast them. I was carrying an MP-5 submachine gun, a Browning Hi Power, which is a 9 mm pistol, and my .45 pistol.

We went methodically floor by floor, room by room, getting people escorted safely outside, then locking the floor down tight.

Obviously we weren't getting on any elevators. We were moving slowly but steadily. Chuck and I went first, sniffing out a floor before the rest of the squad came up. I had just passed a stairwell door on the fifth or sixth floor when it suddenly got flung open and smacked into the back of my arm and my heel. It threw me off balance for a second, and as I turned the first thing I saw was the barrel of an AK. Whoever threw open that door was also surprised when it hit something and bounced back on him, and he briefly lost his footing. I couldn't turn around quick enough with my weapon, so I just reached down and grabbed the barrel of his weapon in my hand and twisted it up and away. I'm guessing his index finger was on the trigger, so when I twisted it I probably snapped his finger. All I know is he let go of his weapon. That is the last thing you want to do if you plan to survive. I hit him right in the head with its butt, opening up a gash and staggering him. His eyes rolled back in his head, and as he was going down I grabbed him by his hair and slammed my knee into the back of his head. Then I whipped the point of my elbow into his back, trying to sever his spinal column. He hit the carpet and just lay there motionless.

Adrenaline was ripping through my body; I was one tensed nerve, ready to explode. What felt like an instant later I saw two people dressed in civilian clothes casually jogging down the hall to find out what was going on. Of course, they also were carrying AKs. Fuck them. The open door was between us, so I had a big advantage. If they saw me they didn't react. I sprayed them both with the MP-5 and they went down.

The entire corridor seemed like it was vibrating from the sound bouncing off the walls. I couldn't hear a thing, but it didn't matter. Chuck had my back. Trust me, no one else was coming to help them. We kept moving until we reached the seventh floor. We didn't have to look hard to find the room they had fired from—the door had been blown right out of its frame. That 3.5-inch rocket has got a serious backblast. It had just blistered the paint right off the walls. In a closed room the echo from that blast had to have been enormous. Three men were sprawled on the floor. All three of them were bleeding out of their eyes and ears. Two of them were dead. The third person was only half-dead. He was sitting on the floor leaning up against a wall, his eyes open and staring straight ahead; he had no idea where he was, and he didn't try to resist. My people took him out, and that was the last I saw of him. The attempt on Somoza's life was unsuccessful because they had missed him, but they had made a much bigger, much more important point—they had proved that they now had the capability to attack the government at its heart. The last thing you want to have happen in an insurgency is to allow ordinary people to start believing the guerrillas might win; that's when they begin hedging their bets, and they slow down their cooperation with the government. Psychologically this was an important victory for the Sandinistas.

A month later I was training, up by the Honduran border, when I got an emergency message to get back down to Managua as quickly as possible. A twenty-five-man Sandinista force led by Commander Zero (Edén Pastora) had taken control of the National Palace. They had dressed in National Guard uniforms and were taken there in what looked like army trucks, so they had no trouble getting inside. One soldier had challenged them and had been killed. They had taken almost two thousand people hostage, including congressmen, cabinet members, government workers, journalists, and visitors, as well as several members of Somoza's family.

This was like marching into Washington and capturing the House of Representatives. We had been advising the government that the security needed to be improved, especially after the attack on Somoza's compound, but nothing had been done. When you've had total power for so long, it's hard to accept the fact that you're vulnerable. The National Guard had responded to the raid by ringing the National Palace with tanks. The guerrillas had issued a list of demands. They wanted a $10 million ransom in small bills, the release of a hundred Sandinista prisoners, the publication of a Sandinista communiqué in the national media, and guaranteed safe passage out of the country for all the Sandinistas inside the palace.

The guerrillas threatened to begin killing hostages if their demands weren't met in eight hours, but then they extended that deadline another day. Somoza's officers wanted to fight, but there really was nothing that we could do. We didn't have any reliable intelligence about what was going on inside. They held too many hostages spread out over too wide an area. We also believed they had parts of the building wired with explosives, and we didn't doubt that the guerrillas were willing to die. If the Guard made a frontal assault with their tanks, they could break into the building, but hundreds of people would die. If the Black Berets tried a rescue operation, a hundred people would be dead by the time we got ladders on the walls, and even then there was almost no chance we could free the hostages. I told Somoza's people matter-of-factly, "There's no chance we can get in there without a lot of people dying. You need to negotiate this one." I told Somoza the same thing—if we attacked, his nephews and his friends inside the building were going to die.

Mike Echanis disagreed with me. At that point he was running security for Brigadier General José Iván Alegrett. General Alegrett wanted to launch a frontal assault; he wanted tanks to blast holes in the wall and then send people running inside. Alegrett estimated three hundred people would be killed in the attack, but he warned Somoza that if we didn't fight back "It will cost three thousand lives before it's over."

It was frustrating as hell. If I'd thought there was any chance of freeing those hostages without hundreds of people dying, I would have urged them to take it, but there wasn't. Eventually the government met most of the demands, although the payment was reduced to $500,000. Echanis was furious about that decision, and he couldn't keep his mouth shut. He started talking to reporters, boasting to the Associated Press that he was in charge of counterintelligence for the National Guard and he would never have allowed the Sandinistas to get out of the palace alive. "What did they do?" he asked. "They freed fifty-nine political prisoners. They gave the Sandinistas back all of their generals and political chiefs. Politically, it was the only thing Somoza could do. Militarily, it was a disaster. It demoralized my troops. I'm sending my commandos back into the jungle. We'll shoot every day, and we'll work them back up."

Mike was becoming much too visible. He made himself instantly recognizable—he had these wide sideburns and a Fu Manchu mustache—and he took few precautions. He would drive all over the city in an open jeep, telling anyone who would listen to him about all the battles he had led against the guerrillas. Everybody knew who he was, and people started calling him "Mike the Merc." He thought this publicity was great and he'd end up in Hollywood making movies. I told him he didn't understand what he was doing and he was putting everybody at risk, but as usual there was nothing anybody could do to quiet him down.

At least some of the Sandinistas released from prison accepted an invitation from Castro to come to Cuba. As far as I was concerned, that was a clear message to President Carter who these people were, and I couldn't understand why he was siding with the Communists. The United States continued to put pressure on Somoza. They stopped sending any economic or military assistance and tried to prevent other countries from offering aid. As a result, for the first time we were beginning to run low on ammunition. We had to go to other countries to buy it, which was expensive, and sometimes it was hard to ship.

The attack on the National Palace got a lot of attention around the world. It really shook people's confidence in the Somoza regime. It also made the Sandinistas seem to be much stronger than they really were; this bandwagon was starting to roll downhill, and people were jumping aboard. With more support the fighting picked up. The situation there was definitely becoming more dangerous for us.

The government had a very small air force. We had some helicopters, some combat-armed Cessnas, and the old reliable DC-3s, which were used mostly for resupplying troops. Sometimes the choppers would be used as makeshift bombers, and troops would drop everything from 500-pound bombs to grenades on the guerrillas. When I had the opportunity, and the time, I liked to get up into the air. A few weeks after the attack on the palace I was flying the right seat on a DC-3 that was delivering supplies and ferrying some troops to a small city in the north. The DC-3 is still the single most reliable aircraft ever built. You can practically hold it together with baling wire and bubble gum and it'll get you where you need to go. I have a deep and lasting affection for that airplane.

We were taking off after delivering our cargo and picking up a few people. As we circled over the jungle to gain altitude, we started receiving fire from the ground. They shot out a couple of cylinder heads on our right engine, so we had to shut it down and feather it. Several bullets came up through the fuselage and got me in my right leg and arm. Ripping through that metal had slowed them up pretty good, so they didn't have quite as much punch as they otherwise would have. I was a lot more concerned about the airplane than myself, but it barely even flinched. It shuddered once or twice and then just kept climbing.

Once again I got lucky. My wounds weren't too serious, although

I was bleeding pretty good. I wrapped my bandanna and a piece of cloth tight around my leg and my arm to slow down the loss of blood. We made it back to Managua without any real drama. That airplane knows how to fly.

One thing I had never been very good at was letting somebody else take care of me. I hadn't had too much practice in that. Besides my grandparents, there just hadn't been anybody in my life to rely on. When I'd been wounded before, the medics did their jobs and passed me along. I'd become friends with that surgeon in San Francisco who sewed my jaw back together and taught me how to play chess, but that ended when I went back to the war. This time, though, when I got home Maria was waiting there for me, and she insisted on being my nurse. Truthfully, I didn't know how to deal with it at first. These weren't life-threatening wounds, and I just wanted to get sewed up and get back to work. It was not easy for me to all of a sudden start trusting another person with my emotions. I made the effort. I lay back and pretended I needed her more than I really did, and we both benefited from that.

Except for the military there had been few things of permanence in my life. I wasn't a person who made long-term plans. The only future I thought about was being trained for the next battle. Without saying one word about it, Maria was changing that. She was making it so comfortable to be with her, without asking very much of me.

Maybe Chuck and Bobby were a little envious of what I'd found. Both of them had American girlfriends. One day in the office I heard Chuck talking to his girlfriend on the phone, and I said to him, "Why don't you guys just get married, man?" He didn't take much time to think about it. Both he and Bobby sent one-way plane tickets to their ladies, who flew down to join them. Bobby married the all-American girl, a beautiful blue-eyed blonde who loved him dearly.

Neither couple had a big ceremony. They got their marriage

certificate, stood in front of a judge, and became man and wife. I don't think any of us had expected to find what we discovered in Nicaragua. We had gone down there to do a job, which we hadn't expected to last long. A year, we'd guessed. It would not take Somoza's well-equipped troops any longer than that to put down a raggedy-assed rebellion. Then we would pack up our rucksacks and go home and start searching for our next assignment. Instead we were welcomed by nice people to their beautiful country. Nice people except for when they were shooting at us, of course. We were being decently paid, and most of our expenses were taken care of. It was possible to live very nicely on our income. I think all of us began to realize that when this war was over it would be easy to stay there.

We had gotten comfortable, which in my life has always been an error.

CHAPTER SIX

When it comes your time to die, be not like those whose hearts are filled with the fear of death, so that when their time comes they weep and pray for a little more time to live their lives again in a different way.

Sing your death song, and die like a hero going home.

Chief Tecumseh, Shawnee Nation (1768–1813)

In early September Mike, Chuck, Bobby, and General Alegrett were killed instantly when General Alegrett's Aero Commander 114-A exploded over Lake Managua. I was stunned. As wild as Mike could be, there was something about him that made you believe he was a survivor. Chuck was the stoic. He never said too much, he just got things done, but he was able to control the situation. Bobby—man, Bobby had worked so damn hard to get to this place in his life. He had survived so much tragedy and violence in Vietnam to finally find a wonderful woman; he was going to become an American citizen, which was his dream come true. The three of them, gone, on a sunny morning.

That news was unbelievably painful for me, and my first reaction was to be furious with Mike. I'd tried so hard to warn him. Over and over I'd told him, keep your fucking head down, there are too many people looking to shoot it off. As usual, he hadn't paid attention. All of us had been told to be very careful about getting on airplanes because bombs had been found on the tarmac and in the hangar. It turned out later the general's people hadn't even done a minimal preflight check. Nobody ever found out exactly what caused the explosion. Mike was going on some type of mission with the general and asked Chuck and Bobby to come along for the ride. When the plane got out over the lake, it exploded.

Then they were dead, three of my close friends. There were a lot of stories, a lot of claims; the one thing that was absolutely certain was that it was not an accident. They were killed. Some people believed the Sandinistas had shot the plane down. A few years later a story in *Black Belt* claimed that Somoza had found out that General Alegrett was plotting with the CIA to overthrow his government and replace it with a coalition including the Sandinistas, and a bomb with an altitude trigger had been planted in the wing. Another story was that Mike was out having a good time dropping bombs and grenades out of the airplane on suspected Sandinista positions and one of them went off prematurely. Whatever evidence existed was lying on the bottom of the lake.

It didn't matter to me, the result was still going to be the same. I was up near El Salvador taking peeks across the border when they were killed. The Sandinistas were firing mortars on the border, and I went up there with my people to check it out. A helicopter picked me up and flew me directly to the lake to supervise the recovery of the bodies. There was a lot of media on the site because General Alegrett was a very powerful government leader. The newspapers were speculating that this was another successful Sandinista attack. I had to be very careful to stay in the background during this recovery operation; I knew how dangerous it would be for me to be closely associated with the victims. I stayed away from any cameramen.

When they brought up the bodies I identified them. I was sure they all died instantly. Mike had been sitting in the left seat up front, Chuck had been behind Mike, and Bobby was behind the general. Mike was still wearing the religious medal that he always had with him. His body was intact except his eyes were gone. Bobby's body was shredded. Chuck's left arm was severed, and it looked like something had blown upward from below, because his legs were all torn up. There was considerable shrapnel in all of their bodies, which was what would have been expected if a grenade had gone off close by. That's what I told people later, but there was no way of determining the actual cause of the explosion. It definitely was some kind of explosion. The Nicaraguans weren't that interested in figuring out the details. People dying in explosions down there was not that unusual. We picked them out of the water and put their remains in lead-sealed metal coffins.

The one thing I insisted on was that their bodies be treated with respect. Both the Somoza government and the American Embassy wanted to bury them right there on foreign soil until the situation had calmed down and then dig them up, but there was no way I was going to allow that. These three warriors had earned the right to be buried in American soil, and I was going to make damn sure that's what happened. I went to the American consulate, but nobody there was willing to give me any help. Mike used to brag that he'd gotten a letter from Secretary of State Cyrus Vance telling him that he was a disgrace to the United States and urging him "not to violate any human rights and don't kill any noncombatants." Mike used to joke that this letter gave him permission to kill combatants, and "U.S. officials freak out when they see me in my National Guard uniform, but there's not a damn thing they can do about it." Well, this was their opportunity to do something about it. The consulate had no intention of making the situation any easier for me. I knew better than to approach that other government agency that was paying some of our bills. As far as that agency was concerned they never heard of Mike the Merc, Chuck, and Bobby. Or even me.

The Ranger creed is pretty specific, you never leave a comrade behind. My people have always lived by that rule. Just about a hundred and fifty years ago, in November 1864, my great-great-granduncle Emanuel O'Neal left his duty with the Pennsylvania Infantry during General Sheridan's Appomattox campaign and traveled back to Bedford County, Maryland, to bring home the body of his first sergeant and cousin, Jonathan Snider, who had been killed at Cedar Creek. I could do no less for my brothers.

I went directly to Somoza and told him what I intended to have happen. By that time he knew me well enough to understand that this was important to me. I never knew if he liked me or not, and I didn't really care, but he knew I was honest and loyal and had done a good job for him. If he had a beef with Echanis, he didn't indicate it to me. He seemed genuinely sorry about the situation. He told his people to make the arrangements to ship the bodies home to the States.

The Nicaraguan military flight landed in Tampa, Florida. The bodies were transferred onto a civilian aircraft and flown to Boise, Idaho, and from there up to Oregon. I was with them the whole trip, which as it turned out was a mistake. The fact that three American Vietnam vets had been killed fighting Communism was an important story. Mike was well known in the martial arts community, and all the different magazines, especially *Soldier of Fortune* and *Black Belt,* covered his death. It did not occur to me that photographers were going to be taking pictures and I could be seen standing in the background. It was exactly what I had tried so hard to prevent.

With the permission of Mike's family, we buried Mike and Bobby together in St. John's Cemetery in Ontario, Oregon. Some of their family members did not want to recognize Chuck's or Bobby's wives as being legal, claiming they were gold diggers. The government didn't want to give them their widow's benefits because the marriages had taken place out of the country. All of that was a damn shame, because those people loved each other. I was there. I saw the way they held hands, I saw the way they kissed. I could recognize real love when it was in front of me.

A lot of the people we'd worked with managed to get out to Oregon for the funerals, including Coughlin. We wanted to have them buried with full military honors, but some people objected to Bobby being buried with an American flag because he wasn't officially an American citizen. That made me furious. Bobby had spent his life fighting for American causes; he had gone on some hellacious missions with SF troops and saved more American lives than just about anybody I knew. I would not let them start the funeral until we got that situation settled. I got in my car and I drove the sixty miles to Boise, where I bought an American flag for my friend's coffin. When I got back we folded it in the correct triangular fashion, opened up his coffin, and laid it on top. Only then would we allow them to put him in the ground.

Unfortunately, there were more photographs taken at the funeral.

Chuck was buried in his family's place.

For me, being back in the country was a strange feeling, and I had a difficult time relating to it. I was living in the middle of a war, my three best friends had died in that war, and except for the people we'd served with, almost nobody even knew the war was being fought. Most Americans could barely locate Nicaragua on a map, much less explain the political situation there. Not only didn't they know, they weren't interested in learning about it. Vietnam had made America tired of war. We'd left, Vietnam eventually had fallen to the Communists, and it didn't seem to have a noticeable impact on America. I didn't talk politics to anybody while I was in the country, but it had become clear that Somoza could not depend on getting any help from America. The American people did not care at all who controlled Nicaragua. If it didn't affect the cost of putting gas in their cars, they just weren't interested.

I didn't want to leave Maria alone in Nicaragua too long. I knew she could take care of herself, and we did have some good security, but the situation down there was changing quickly. People were taking sides who surprised me. I believed Somoza could maintain control as long as he continued to get supplied. Carter was making that tougher and tougher, although Israel had proved to be a loyal ally. We were buying 98 percent of our arms and ammunition from them, and the pipeline was flowing. Even so, there was no question that the Sandinistas were continuing to get stronger. For the first time I began to think about the possibility of getting my family out of there.

I was out of the country only a few weeks, but even in that brief time the situation continued deteriorating. Soldiers were more visible in the streets, stationed in places I hadn't seen them before. It was like the whole country was feeling the tension, waiting for whatever was going to happen to happen. For my personal security, I hadn't told anybody when I was getting back. When I did, I drove right out to my house to see my family. As I got closer I just sensed that something was very wrong. When I saw that the guards weren't there, I knew it.

I don't know how I got compromised. I've always believed it was the photographs that appeared in *The Miami Herald* and *The New York Times*, but it could just as easily have been a few words from someone who had decided to get in the middle. However, the Sandinistas found out; they learned I was training Somoza's elite troops. They may have even known I was a contract employee of the agency. Once they found out, they took action against me.

The house had been ripped apart. There could not have been any reason for it; there were not enough people in that house to have resisted any type of force. It was a simple message: *Look what we can do.* The people who worked for us were either dead or missing, and Maria and the three kids were gone. Maria's bodyguard had been beaten and tortured before he had been killed, then left there on the floor for me to find. I found a second body out in the back.

The people who had done this also left a note for me in Spanish-English telling me where to go to find my family. I read it and reread it. Then I got careless. I'd spent my military career teaching people to wring the emotion out of combat, emphasizing that when you allow anger or fear or compassion to get between yourself and what you need to do, you hesitate or you make mistakes. There needs to be a direct line between you and your enemy; anything that intersects that line will prevent you from acting at the peak of your ability. I knew that; I'd practiced that and preached that. I took great pride in my ability to be completely dispassionate, to be the warrior.

This time I couldn't prevent my emotions from interfering with my good judgment. The deaths of Chuck, Mike, and Bobby had thrown me off balance, and then I'd gotten hit with this. Instead of being sensible about the situation, all I wanted to do was get my family back and strike out at these people. I didn't know if my family was dead or alive, but I knew I had to get to them as quickly as possible if there was any chance of saving them. I wasn't thinking straight; I was as close to panic as I had ever been. I know what I should have done. I should have put a team together and gone about this in the correct way. That would have taken time, though, a day or two days to get organized, and I couldn't wait. I notified my company what had happened, then loaded up my kit and went looking for my family. I was carrying as much firepower with me as one man can hump. I didn't know what I was going to find waiting for me, but I didn't pause to think about it. I had done everything wrong, and I was paying for it.

I drove my Land Cruiser way out into the country. I knew the area they were directing me to because we'd trained around there. It was a little less than two hours away. I tried not to think about what I was going to find when I got wherever I was going, but that was impossible. The rage was building inside me. I pulled my vehicle into the brush a few miles from my destination. I didn't want to get too far into the area without knowing what was waiting for me. I figured they'd set up some type of trap. I couldn't know how much Maria had told them about my work; for the safety of us both, I hadn't told her everything, but my guess was that she hadn't told them anything. She was as tough as she was smart.

I hiked into the area. It was mostly farmland, so there wasn't a lot of cover. Maybe I should have waited till after it got dark, but in that situation the night would have benefited them more than me. I didn't have a night scope. It was late afternoon before I got close enough to the place to see what was going on. It was an old ranch; it had a barn, some sheds, and a small stockyard with a few skinny cattle grazing. I lay there for a while observing. There were some people moving around, but they were ranch workers doing chores. There was nothing I saw that made me believe my family might be there. I was wondering if maybe I was in the wrong place when a soldier wearing mismatched fatigues walked out of the barn.

I had started moving into a better position when they spotted me. I opened up on them. They returned my fire. I got grazed in the left side, but I didn't even realize it. The only possible advantage I had was that they didn't know how many people were with me, and until they could determine that, they weren't going to be overly aggressive. They knew I wasn't going anywhere as long as they had their hostages.

I didn't know how many of them there were either, but I knew it was more than I had. I kept firing until I ran out of ammo; then when they came at me I used my weapons as clubs. It didn't take them long to overpower me. Then they started beating on me.

I lost comprehension of time. After that things happened when they happened; I had no way of putting anything in context. It might have been a minute or an hour. I felt my hands yanked behind my back and tied up. Then they drugged me and put me in the back of a vehicle. I have some vague memory of being bounced around.

I came to inside a barn.

They started beating on me right away, and never did stop. They enjoyed it. The truth is I was grateful when I was unconscious. I don't have any idea how many days I was hanging there or how many times I lost consciousness, but I will never forget what happened in that barn.

They interrogated me, asking me all kinds of questions about different people. I don't know what they thought they could learn from me, but there was nothing I was going to tell them. I focused on the techniques I'd been teaching people about how to resist interrogation. The most important thing was not to resist the pain but to accept it, absorb it, and control it. This required absolute mental discipline. The most important thing I could do was to keep the pain from cluttering my mind. That was my only means of fighting back. If the pain became so intense that I couldn't focus on anything except that pain, I was done.

You have to be able to take the pain and move it to a different part of your body, rather than allowing it to be centered in a specific place. I could move it from my shoulders to my legs, for example. Or you have to be able to project yourself outside of your body so that you can leave the pain in a body without any feeling. In my mind I had to be somewhere else. I looked into the fire, just as I had done growing up on my grandfather's farm.

I tried every technique I knew to deal with it. Eventually I reached the point where I could absorb the physical pain. My body became used to it, and it didn't seem like it could get worse. The intensity was so strong that I barely felt it when they hit me; on the pain scale it didn't measure up. Maybe they knew that; maybe they understood there wasn't any valuable information I would give them. This wasn't an interrogation, I eventually understood that; this was punishment. Nothing more. This was their vengeance for what Somoza's army had done to them. Their desire was to make me suffer, and they did. They took me to the extremes.

In my mind there is no order to the events, no logic. Things happened and then they unhappened. Everything was hazy, not even like a dream but more like a different reality. There are times after a firefight when you can look back and you can remember things and they're real and you know they're real and they happened, but these memories are nothing like that at all. They're flimsy, they're flashes, nothing to grab on to. It's the one part of my mind that I can't control at all. I can't block these images and I can't call them up; there is no particular trigger or time that they come. They used to come more often than they do now.

There is reality to them. I know that. I saw Maria and the kids there, dying on the dirt floor of that barn. I never saw them again.

I was told I was missing for eleven days, but that has no meaning. I fought back the only way I could, controlling my mind. I focused entirely on my breathing; everything else was outside that consciousness. I spread out my breaths as far as possible, trying to take only as many breaths as were necessary to stay alive. I extended each breath to make it as shallow as possible. It was more of a wisp than a breath. I was much closer to dead than alive. Sometimes people say they didn't care if they lived or they died; that wasn't me. I cared. I wanted to live. I wanted to live more at that point than ever before. Not because I was planning some vengeance, not because I was going to get even with them; even that level of thinking was beyond my capability at that point. It was simply that I didn't know how to do anything else except to fight for my life. That was my natural state. So I fought to survive. On some level I was sure that my team was out looking for me and was not going to give up until they found me alive or found my body. That was the code we all lived by; you never leave your buddy behind. That's why we had recovered those bodies from the bottom of Lake Managua. On some level of consciousness I knew that if I could just stay alive for one more minute, that might be enough. Then one minute after that. I never doubted they were coming.

I'll never know if my torturers believed I was dead when they took me down or wanted me to continue to suffer until I died. I know I slowed down my heartbeat to where it seemed like I had no pulse. I do have some memory of them sticking something up my nose to see if I was breathing, but I don't know if that really happened or not. If they did search for a pulse to determine if I was alive, they would not have been able to find it. I have no memory of them taking me down off that beam, transporting me somewhere, and dropping me in the mud of a hog pen, but that's where I ended up. Maybe they figured the pigs were going to eat me. My eyes were swollen shut and covered with crap, but I heard the pigs and I felt them pushing me. They didn't hurt me, though.

I don't know how I survived that long. If I had any water to drink during that period, I don't remember it. My best guess is that they forced it down my throat to keep me alive so they could continue to torture me. I know that my throat was burning raw, and when they found me all I could do was rasp, I couldn't really speak.

It was farmers who found me. They knew I was alive because I was still able to move a little and I could make some sounds. If I concentrated I could open and close my eyes. These people did not know who I was or what I was doing there, but they transported me to a local doctor. That's where the team found me, and they brought me to the hospital in Managua. I think pretty much everybody was amazed that I was alive. The doctors put me right into surgery. They had a lot of work to do to put me back together, everything from cleaning out my bullet wound, which had gotten infected, to pushing my shoulders back into their sockets. As soon as I was able to be moved, they got me out of the hospital and into the bunker in Somoza's personal compound, where his doctors took care of me.

I lay there and healed. I had nothing but time, which for me was the worst thing that could happen. My life had been endless action, always moving, always training, teaching, or fighting. Now there was nothing I could do but think about what had happened. My family was dead, and I needed to know who was behind it. There was no doubt in my mind what I was going to do. The emotion that drove me was vengeance. I started walking, then running; I could still barely stand up, but I started lifting again. Back at Fort Bragg with Mike and Chuck, I was bench pressing over 350 pounds; now I was lucky if I could pick up 10 pounds without my shoulders screaming at me. Each day I forced myself to do a little more than the day before. Pick up a few more pounds, do five more lifts, walk a few steps farther. All the martial arts I had been doing had put my body in tremendous condition, and that definitely helped me heal a little more quickly. As I regained each of my physical abilities I put it back to work. I began working out, doing whatever moves I could complete. Sometimes I thought about Mike, how he had used Hwa Rang Do to heal after he'd been wounded in the An Khe Pass. Mike couldn't walk unless he had his boot on, but he was kicking and fighting. I could do the same thing.

My body was healing, but not my mind. That was okay with me. I wasn't looking for peace or contentment. I knew that wasn't possible. Instead I put the word out that I wanted names.

The political situation was continuing to get worse. The Sandinistas had increased their attacks all over the country while Carter was putting more pressure on Somoza. There was a lot of political maneuvering going on, but I still was pretty certain that the Somoza government would survive.

It took months before I was even close to full strength. When I was ready I went to the American Embassy to find out if they intended to do anything about what happened. I always went to my government first, but they told me without actually telling me that with the Carter administration in power there was nothing much they could do to help me. I went directly to Somoza, and he told me, "What do you think I pay you for? Take care of the situation, that's why I pay you."

The intelligence people in the government gave me five names and told me these were the people involved. Five names. Five people who were Sandinista sympathizers and who were supposedly controlling the situation. I didn't know any of the names, and later when I found out what they looked like, I didn't recognize any of them. I had seen some of the people who held me captive, but I wasn't certain I would remember them or that my memory would be reliable. Whether this intelligence was accurate or not I didn't know, and at that time I didn't care. It's possible these were just people the government knew were working with the enemy and needed to be gone. None of that mattered to me.

The situation was not like in a normal country during peacetime. The military was in control of the cities instead of the police, so things could be done that otherwise would not have been possible. Legally it wasn't martial law, but there were a lot more military vehicles on the streets than police cars, and there was nobody checking to see who was carrying a weapon. Meanwhile, the word about what had happened to me had spread throughout the military community. I got contacted by friends from different parts of the world who volunteered to come help me settle the issue. There was a group in Panama, for example, who wanted to get in a car and drive up to organize a posse. As far as they were concerned it was *Magnificent Seven* time. I turned them all down. I hadn't ever been into vigilante-type thinking, that's not the way the military operates, but in this situation it became necessary. This was done to me, to my family, and if I was ever going to figure out how to live with it I needed to be the one who took retribution.

At that time almost anybody with any money or power in the city had some sort of personal protection. I didn't care about that; if I had to go through walls to get at them I would. That wasn't even a real barrier to me. The only thing that made my task slightly more difficult was the fact that it mattered to me that these people had to see me before they died. The Lakota Sioux used to show their strength by riding right up to their enemy in battle and slapping his horse on the rump, which was called "counting coup." They looked their enemy in the eye. I wanted these people to have at least an instant of terror. It wasn't enough, there was no such thing as enough, but I needed to be able to look them straight in the eye so they would understand that I was enjoying that moment.

There was no special order. I got actionable intel on each of them from the government, where they lived, where they worked, and what protection they had. Then I would watch them for at least one day, just me, by myself. When I figured out how I intended to do this, I recruited the help I needed. The first one went to the same restaurant every day, absolutely every day. He didn't even have a bodyguard. It was a popular place because the food was good and it wasn't expensive. It wasn't fancy, but all the tables were covered and there was a candle on each one. At night the lights were turned down low and the candles were lit, probably more to save the electricity than create an atmosphere. He liked to sit at a table near the side door, one of those secure metal doors with a heavy push bar, which led out to an alley. This was a long time before I saw the *Godfather II* movie that had a scene in which a bad cop got killed in a restaurant. When I finally watched that scene, I have to admit that it did remind me a little of this situation.

It was a nice spring night, so there were people out in the streets. I dressed in casual slacks and a loose-hanging blue sports shirt. I was in a vehicle that stopped in front of the place. I had a driver with me, a Nicaraguan sergeant major I had gotten out of jail. He'd been sitting there because he'd gotten into a fight with a lieutenant and killed him. I had trained him, and I trusted him with my life. Two soldiers sitting in an open jeep were parked at the end of the street, looking down into it. The restaurant, which was closer to the far end of the street, was crowded and noisy when I walked in. The place was a little darker than I expected, but I knew where he was sitting. My eyes adjusted pretty quick to the candlelight. I wasn't concerned about that—I knew he couldn't see me any better than I could see him, and in any event he definitely wasn't expecting me.

There were two men at his table with him, and he was sitting between them facing the door. I was guessing at least one of them was a bodyguard. Okay. I paused just briefly at the door. Nobody was paying much attention to me. I was carrying a Browning Hi Power. As I walked toward his table I didn't feel any excitement; if I felt anything at all it was that I was a little tired. I'd been living with my hatred for months now, and it wasn't as sharp as it had been. So for those few minutes I wasn't thinking about vengeance. I was on a mission. I was completely in control of my emotions.

Just as I got about 10 feet away from him a woman got up from another table and started walking in front of me, going to the ladies' room, I guessed. She wasn't in any hurry, and I couldn't make her move faster. I just fell in behind her. I stopped at his table. His head was down, and he looked up at me as if he were expecting the waiter.

It took him a few seconds to figure out what was going on. I didn't say a thing. Whether he knew who I was or not I'll never know, but he definitely understood I was there to kill him. He didn't have time to move. I lifted the pistol and shot him in the face. He was dead instantly, but I shot him again.

The two men sitting at the table didn't do anything to stop me or protect themselves. Probably they were too stunned to react. I looked at both of them, and they knew from the look on my face that this was personal, that I didn't have any beef with them. Still holding on to the gun, I turned around and walked out of the restaurant. People had ducked under their tables when I shot him, and a lot of glasses and bottles hit the floor and smashed, but there wasn't even much screaming. I'm sure there were other people in there with guns, and they probably pulled them, but in Nicaragua at that time nobody got involved in things that didn't concern them. There were a lot of crosscurrents running through those waters, and people just didn't want to get caught up in any of them. It was almost impossible to know who was going to be standing at the end, and nobody, absolutely nobody, was looking to make enemies. The best strategy for survival was to turn around and walk in the other direction.

I got back in the vehicle, and we left the area. The jeep at the end of the corner never moved.

There wasn't a word about it in the newspapers the next day. I would have been surprised if the other people involved in killing my family had figured out why the first person was killed. No question that he was involved in a lot of different things that might have upset people. When I killed the next one, though, they damn well began to make the connection.

The second guy I got right out on the street. This person had something to do with the oil business, and he had good security in both his home and his office. Like more and more people in Managua, he was living behind walls. I knew he had some connection to the Somoza government, but my guess was that he was working both sides. Just in case. The only times he let himself be exposed was in the morning when he went from his car to his office and then later when he went from his office back to his car. His security was good enough that he didn't show up or leave the building at the same time every day. I didn't care. If there was anyone watching the street to see if people were hanging around, I never saw them and they never saw me. When he left the building in the afternoon I was waiting. I walked right up to him. Right on the street. Right in front of whoever was walking there. There was one bodyguard, and he was holding open the car door and looking around. I guess he didn't have eyes in the back of his head, because he never saw me. With the heel of my boot I kicked him in the small of the back, sending him smashing into the door. His mouth hit the frame at the top, and his whole body bounced back and spun around. Instead of protecting his guy, he instinctively put his hand up to his mouth. Blood was pouring out of it. The target turned around and looked right at me. I hesitated but one second, just long enough for him to understand. Then I put two holes in his head. *Boomboom!* Right on the street, right in front of everyone. His head exploded. People started screaming and running. The bodyguard finally reacted, reaching under his jacket, grabbing for his gun, I guess. I had no reason to kill him. Instead I kicked him hard as I could with my steel-tipped boot in the groin. He folded straight over, then fell over forward in slow motion. I turned around and walked away. Fuck them both.

There wasn't any joy in any of this. I had nothing to celebrate and no one to share it with. I didn't feel good about it, I didn't feel bad, I didn't feel anything. This was a job that had to be done, and I was doing it. Every night I went back to my barracks room inside Somoza's bunker. I stayed by myself; I drank a little, ate a little, and went to sleep. Every night.

My third target was living in the city of León. The military had been watching him for me. He had a little cantina, a coffee bar on a central street. It wasn't much more than a few tables outside and a couple more inside. There was nothing about it that would draw any attention to it. Whatever he was doing for the Sandinistas, however he figured into what happened to me, this was a good place to be doing it from. He was a big guy, unusually big for a Nicaraguan, much taller than me and real muscular. He wore a tight shirt that showed off his build. You knew his type just by looking at him; he didn't take shit from anybody. I guess he figured he could take care of himself.

I didn't recognize him; if he was one of the men from the barn, I hadn't seen him there. That doesn't mean he wasn't there, just that I didn't see him.

His bar stayed open later than most of the other stores on the block. For a small place it got a lot of traffic, people coming and going at all times, sometimes pausing to have coffee and a cake, but other times just saying a few words, dropping something off or picking something up, then leaving. It looked to me like he probably was running drugs, which was a profitable side business for a lot of people. If I was right, if he was distributing drugs, then I knew there had to be some protection around somewhere, maybe police, maybe even military, but if it was there I never spotted it. A police car would roll down the street every hour, but it never slowed down. There were only two possibilities I could figure. Either I was wrong about him dealing drugs or he was so powerful that everybody in the city knew enough to stay away from him.

I wasn't from that city. Sometimes people sleep in the back of those cantinas, but not him. He closed up, pulling down a steel gate and locking it, then got in a Mercedes and drove somewhere. The Mercedes said a lot more about his business than his location. By the time he closed up, the street was very quiet. The information I was provided included a home address, but there was no reason for me to go there. He lived his life at that bar.

I waited until the third night. As he was locking up I strolled up to him. He wasn't paying any attention. When I got a few feet away I said to him, "Hey. Amigo." He stood up and turned to look at me. It was not a friendly look. He was the only one who didn't respond at all. He knew what was coming; he looked right at me and didn't move. It was like he'd been waiting his whole life for that moment. He knew that it was coming and had made his peace with it. Two shots. *Boomboom.*

The fourth person was a lawyer who worked in Managua. He was older than any of the others, and much more wary. He never walked on the streets; even if he had to go one or two blocks he would take a car. Sometimes a bodyguard traveled with him. There was no doubt in my mind that he knew by now what was going on. My people had staked him out and gave me good intel about his movements. Apparently this guy was also doing some good work for the government, but down there they respected the code of honor, so nobody tried to stop me. He had a mistress that he would visit during lunch, and they found out that when he was with her, he sometimes dressed in her clothes. It was suggested informally to me that maybe just circulating pictures of him dressed in a bra and panties would be enough to destroy his reputation, which to him was really important, but that wouldn't have been enough for me.

Setting this up was simple. In fact, they were all simple. This was a country under siege. Law and order were breaking down. There is no way I could have done these things if the situation had been different. I knew that I wasn't going to get arrested for what I was doing, I had the cooperation of the government. The hardest part probably should have been looking each of these people in the eyes and then pulling the trigger, but it wasn't. I was operating on hatred. This wasn't anything at all like it had been when I was out in the jungle; I didn't conduct any ceremony before or after to send them on their journey. As far as I was concerned these people could rot in hell.

I had two people from my unit working with me. We took two cabs. This attorney came out of his building before lunch, and I picked him up in my cab. He was alone, although I was prepared to deal with a bodyguard if necessary. Everything about him was successful. I could see his suit was expensive; he was balding, but the hair he had was neatly trimmed, and he smelled like fresh soap. I wondered why people like him had gotten involved with the Communists. I wondered what he had expected to get out of helping them. He told me the address, and I headed that way. It didn't matter to me which direction I was heading; he was going to end up in the same place. He was reading a newspaper. As we got closer I suddenly turned into a side street and pulled over. I turned around and pointed my weapon at him. At the same time he lifted his case to try to protect himself and half threw his newspaper at me to try to buy a few seconds. At that range it didn't matter where I hit him. *Boomboom.* One in the throat, the other in his head. I got out of the car, and the other cab picked me up. We were out of the area within minutes.

That was four. I had the identity of the fifth person, but before I could reach him I was told very specifically to leave him alone. He was not in business or government. Nobody gave me any explanation, they just said to leave him alone. There was nothing I could do; there was nobody to argue with. It was as frustrating as anything in my life. I know that he is still alive and since then has served in the Sandinista government.

I had options. I could have just gone ahead and done it; I could have returned to the States, or I could have continued the mission I had been hired to complete. I decided that I owed it to the people I had trained and worked with to stay with them. The situation in Nicaragua was changing almost every day. We were running out of ammunition. We were in desperate need, and there were three cargo ships of weapons and ammo coming from Israel. We were tracking their progress. If they got to Managua in time, we could still win; if not, there was not much we could do.

The Sandinistas had definitely won the propaganda war in America. One of the worst things that happened took place in June 1979 when American TV journalist Bill Stewart was stopped at what appeared to be a National Guard checkpoint, forced to lie down on his face, and shot dead. It was a cold-blooded murder of a reporter by men wearing Guard uniforms. The whole event was captured on film, which was shown on American television. If there was anyone in America still supporting Somoza, that probably ended right then. A few years later a version of this murder was shown in the Nick Nolte movie *Under Fire*.

That killing probably would have ended my support, too—except for the fact that it didn't seem to be what it looked like. There were a lot of journalists in Nicaragua then, and most of them were well known to the military. ABC reporter Bill Stewart was driving around in a very well marked two-toned Volkswagen bus, with the letters TV in white tape on the sides and back. There could be absolutely no mistaking this van for anything but what it was. These were American journalists covering the war for American television.

Admittedly, there were some people in the Nicaraguan government who were very unhappy with the way the war was being covered.

The American media was making the Sandinistas out to be noble freedom fighters trying to liberate an oppressed population, which as history has shown is not the way it was in reality. It sounded good, though, and as a result there were American organizations contributing millions of dollars to the Sandinista cause.

I don't know who murdered Bill Stewart. I do know that the film makes it look like he was killed in cold blood by the Guard at a checkpoint. Like with the assassination of Pedro Chamorro, the Somoza government was blamed, and like with that killing, there has never been a full investigation of what actually happened. In fact, Somoza's son, who was accused of planning Chamorro's killing, has always denied he had any involvement; he claimed he was willing to answer all questions and even take a lie detector test. The fact is that the Somoza government had absolutely nothing to gain by assassinating an American journalist. Stewart wasn't reporting anything that was much different or more dangerous than many other journalists were reporting. As far as I knew, the government hadn't stopped any American journalists from doing their job, and none of them had been threatened. It was the Sandinistas who had a tremendous amount to gain if this film was shown around the world. When it was shown in America, it reinforced the idea that the Somoza government was committing atrocities.

The checkpoint at which Bill Stewart was murdered was not under the control of the government. By that time most of the country outside the cities was being run by the Sandinistas. This checkpoint was in a disputed area. There was nothing we could do to fight this story, though. The three cargo ships from Israel got stopped by Carter's blockade. We ran out of ammunition. We literally ran out of ammunition. We had nothing left. Toward the end we were down to three bullets per man. So there was no way we could prevent the Sandinistas from setting up roadblocks. I still believe that if we had been able to get that ammunition, the situation would have ended very differently. A lot of things that took place would not have happened.

After Stewart's murder, my unit was asked to do an investigation. In that situation there isn't too much actual investigating you can do. I asked a lot of questions, and I didn't get the answers I needed. Either people didn't know the truth, they didn't want to tell it to me, or they were lying to me. It could have been any of those. As a result, we were never able to find the people who set up that checkpoint or the lieutenant who was in charge of it. This was a hectic time, and we couldn't do a thorough investigation, but we never were able to pinpoint those people. I am not saying I know this was a Sandinista plot to discredit the government. It could have been exactly what it looked like, but we were told to investigate it and never got any answers.

Whoever murdered Bill Stewart, the result certainly benefited the Sandinistas. Any last support for Somoza in the United States collapsed. By the beginning of July it was obvious the government couldn't lead the country anymore. I spoke with Somoza. He owned a lot of property in downtown Miami and planned to go there to live and organize a government in exile, but Carter wouldn't allow him to stay in the United States.

He left Miami and settled in Paraguay. Over the next few months I made several trips between Nicaragua and Paraguay bringing things to him. Most of the time I didn't know what I was carrying. People would make arrangements for me to pick up a van at a certain place and a certain time, and my job was to deliver it to him. I made some assumptions, but I decided I was probably better off not knowing. It didn't make any difference. I had a few complicated moments getting in and out of Nicaragua, but the situation was so disorganized that it was possible to bullshit my way over the border. A lot of people were on the move, and inside the revolution the Sandinista leaders had started fighting for power. There was a coup within the coup taking place as Daniel Ortega and Commander Zero fought for control, so pretty much everybody else hesitated to take any action that might eventually hurt them. Until it became clear who was going to end up in power, people were reluctant to stick out their necks. All I had to do was act like I knew what I was doing and mention a couple of names in the Sandinista government and I could come and go.

Somoza believed he was relatively safe in Paraguay. He told me something like "They got my country, they don't need me."

"You're wrong," I said. There were still a lot of people in Nicaragua who remained loyal to Somoza, and eventually those people could be dangerous to the revolution. If Somoza was dead there would be nobody for the opposition to rally around. I also reminded him that Castro wanted him dead because of his support for the Bay of Pigs. Maybe, he agreed, but he pointed out to me that the deposed Cuban dictator Fulgencio Batista had quietly lived out his life in Europe after being overthrown.

We discussed it several times. I kept warning him that he didn't have enough protection, that he was taking stupid chances, but he settled into his life in Paraguay. In September 1980 a seven-man Sandinista assassination team attacked his car with a rocket-propelled antitank missile and killed him. According to some people familiar with this type of operation, it had been planned with the assistance of Fidel Castro.

I was a long ways away from Paraguay and those people when it happened. I had fulfilled my obligations. When I left that place I wanted to leave behind what was in my head, but obviously that wasn't possible. I had been able to at least put it aside while I hunted down the people who did it and then fought the last battles in the war, but then I had to come back to nothing.

When I came back to the States I wasn't fit to be with people. I was filled up with anger and bitterness, especially toward my country. I had believed in my soul in the goodness of this country, and I had seen something else entirely. I couldn't understand how we could basically turn over our ally to the Communists, and there was nobody who could explain it to me. I couldn't understand why the consulate had turned me away when I needed to bring home Mike and Chuck and Bobby. These were people who had valued this country more than their own lives, yet they were abandoned. All the underpinnings I had were being pulled out from underneath; nothing was what it seemed to be, and I didn't have anything to replace it. I was lost.

When I came back I needed to be by myself. I went out to Vernal, Utah, to spend a little time with my grandmother. While I was there I ran into my half brother Wild Bill, who was doing construction work. Bill was the real crazy one in the family. He was a demolition expert who'd worked in the oil fields. He'd set nitroglycerin charges in a hole to allow the engineers to make a seismographic study of an area. Bill knew explosives, and even when I was young we would play with them. I can't admit specifically to some of the things we did, but I promise you there is at least one bridge in South Dakota that had a big motherfucking hole right in the middle of it.

Bill hired me on to work with him building houses and apartment complexes, and I tried to function properly. I got up in the morning and went to work and did my job and smiled in all the right places and was as polite as I was able to be. It was all phony, every minute of it. None of that was real; it had nothing to do with what was going on inside, where I was raging. Finally, after several months of existing like that, I couldn't do it anymore. I had to get out of there.

I bought a horse, a pack animal, and a dog, a 130-pound pitbull named Brutus, and walked up into the Tetons in Wyoming. I didn't want to see anybody or have to talk to anybody. I went into the woods by myself with the intention of cleansing my body and my soul. I only took the tools I needed to survive with me—a tarp-tent so I could make a lean-to, sleeping bag, warm clothes, a Hawken .50 cal black powder rifle, two knives, a pistol, my bow and arrows, matches, little stuff like that, and my medicine bag. To eat I took some jerky and some teas; there was plenty of game up in those hills, so I wasn't going to starve. I brought some medicine for my wounds.

Brutus and I spent our days up there panning for gold and hunting, but what I really was looking for was peace. I wanted to be able to gather my thoughts and my feelings and give them freedom rather than keeping them trapped inside me. Most nights I slept out in the open, although there were many nights I never slept. It was almost impossible for me to just relax, to become a whole person again. There were too many people I'd left behind in different places. I'd been running so fast to make sure my past couldn't catch up with me, but I stopped here and tried to deal with them all.

It would not be possible to accurately describe the beauty of those mountains. I'd hobble the horses and sit up on the mountainside or next to a stream for a day, sometimes longer, bathing in time.

I'd brought my meds with me, both my Native American medicine and the pharmacy kind, but there was nothing I could take for what was really affecting me. I was racing to catch up with myself, to find any kind of closure to what I had done, for what I had become. I knew that I couldn't live successfully as that person. That person didn't fit anywhere. I needed a different future.

I lit my prayer fires and spoke to the spirits in those mountains, sometimes asking for guidance, but more often just exposing the darkness inside me to them. When I needed food I hunted and I fished, and I ate what I killed. Maria was with me sometimes, but I knew those were memories I couldn't have. I've always lived in the present; I knew if I tried to carry the past around with me it would weigh me down. It was hard, though. It was so hard.

The days passed, the weeks passed. I found a little gold. The nights got freezing cold, and there were times I enjoyed the pain that caused. Physical pain was familiar. I knew how to deal with the pains in my arms and my legs, with the old wounds burning, with my fingers turning white from the cold. Those were the challenges I was accustomed to facing. I could put my mind to work on that. At those times I could draw on my experiences; I was hanging in a barn moving the pain around, I was lying on a stretcher in a helicopter falling out of the sky, I was in a firefight getting shot in the jaw and the arm. I could handle physical pain. The pain inside me was something different.

As I knew, the power of the mind can be used to do amazing things, but when it turns on you it becomes the strongest enemy imaginable. Where once the visitors in my mind had been the people of the fire, now they were flesh-and-blood people, the people that I had loved. They came into my mind and brought with them a feeling of complete helplessness. There was nothing I could do to make any difference.

It took me some time to understand that I couldn't fight it, that it wasn't something I could defeat. What I needed to do was embrace the pain and make it part of me. I was never going to be able to make it go away, I was never going to be able to change it, so I could either spend the rest of my life living in my past with this turmoil or I could accept it and go on forward, trusting time.

I went weeks without seeing another person except for one time I saw two people hiking, a great distance away. Brutus was all the company I needed—and he didn't have too much to say. I had never been too attached to the popular parts of normal life in America, the politics or entertainment or sports, so there wasn't anything that I felt I was missing. My days were filled with being in nature. I could spend an entire day rigging one fish trap or sitting motionless behind a rock waiting for game. This was one of the first times in my whole life when all I had was a little peace and a lot of quiet. When my mind tried to wander to someplace I'd been, I'd catch it and bring it back. It never got easier, ever, but gradually the bad points started getting spread out over a wider canvas, and after a while they began losing the sharpest part of their edge. I began to taste my food again.

Only a few people knew where I was; one of them was a Park Ranger. I don't know how long I would have stayed up there, but he came up and found me to deliver an important message. My father was dying.

I knew it was important for me to be with him before he died. I'd seen him only one time since the day I'd left his house. When I had been assigned to Blue Light, my grandmother had told me he was sick, so I flew out there and we sat on his front porch for two hours. He had remarried by that time, and he was trying in his own way to make amends to me, but I wasn't ready to listen to him. I needed an apology then, and he didn't know how to apologize. After two hours I told him I had to get back to the airport. I couldn't get out of there fast enough to get back to my real family, the Special Forces, that always welcomed me.

Brutus and I came out of the mountains and went back to Hutchinson, Kansas. I was a different person than I'd been the last time I was there. The experiences of my own life had allowed me to understand my father a lot better. He had been damaged by his own experiences in World War II, and it had affected his whole life, especially his relationship with his son. One of the few regrets I have in my life is that I told my father that his wife was cheating on him. I should not have done that. That was something I should have let him discover by himself. That might've changed a lot of the things that happened between us.

I intended to stay awhile. There didn't seem to be anyplace for me in the military, and my employment with that government agency hadn't ended so well. I had to jump-start my own life. I moved into the clubhouse of a deserted motel that an East Indian group had bought several years earlier. I believe they had intended to turn the motel into a meditation center, but that hadn't worked out for them, and they basically abandoned it. When I was growing up this had been a popular place for parties; they had a swimming pool with a little tiki bar. The owners had allowed it to deteriorate. The pool was empty, and weeds were growing through the concrete around it; the tiki bar was long gone. I made a deal with them that I would do some work fixing it up and pay a little rent in exchange for staying there.

This motel was about a mile from my father's house. I got a job welding heavy equipment at the JH Sears and Sons Construction Company in Hutchinson. I spent a lot of time repairing and cleaning up that swimming pool, and within a couple of months I got the pump working, repaired the cracks in the cement, pulled the weeds, and filled the pool with water. My father had always loved to swim, so as often as we could, we would walk the mile down from his house to the pool and spend the day together. I got to know my father for the first time. He was a good man whose life had taken some wrong turns. There were times when I asked him about my mother. That was just not a place he was willing to go. It hurt him too much to talk about her, he said, and for the first time I understood how that was possible. The only thing he would say was that he had loved her and she was a good woman. The medicine he was taking also affected him, and at times his memory got spotty. As much as I wanted to know more, I didn't push him on that.

I guess we made our own peace. Unfortunately, by the time I came to understand him it was much too late. He had always been a big man, 6'3" and maybe 240 pounds, but the disease was cutting him down. It did force me to look at my own life. Eventually I was able to become close to my own son because of what I learned from my father.

I stayed in Kansas for several months. Sears was a good place to work, and being there without pressure enabled me to regain my balance. One day, though, I got a phone call from one of the people I respected most in the world, Nick Rowe, who had been tasked by the army to set up a new school. SERE, it was called, Survival, Evasion, Resistance, and Escape. Being one of the very few people who had escaped from a North Vietnamese prison and survived, Nick was the absolute perfect person to do this. Nick told me right off this was going to be the toughest school in the army, and he wanted me to come back in and help him get it set up.

My response was no, I was done with the army.

Nick called me back and told me there was no problem getting me back in, and he needed me to teach sentry stalking and the silent kill as well as the mental techniques used to control your body and your emotions.

I still told him no, but I had started thinking about it. There was no place in the world where I was more comfortable than in the military. It was a culture I understood. I was far beyond the ticky-tacky bullshit, and the job Nick was offering me would allow me to teach what I knew the way I wanted to teach it, like Mike and Chuck and I had done for SF. So when I said no, it wasn't with the same conviction as the last time.

Nick called again, this time taking yes for granted and starting to talk to me about all the details. Nick's enthusiasm, confidence, and commitment were hard not to catch. He started talking about his dreams for this SERE school, telling me that they were going to leave us alone to do it right. It was a tremendous opportunity to save lives, he said, telling me that we owed it to people who were going to serve to give them the tools they needed.

Nick definitely could talk.

I had some cleaning up to do before I left Kansas. I spent a little more time with my father, and when I walked away both of us probably knew we would never see each other again. Less than three months later he was dead.

I flew to Fayetteville, North Carolina. Nick picked me up, boiling with plans, and took me over to Fort Bragg, where I raised my right hand and swore once again to defend the United States of America against all her enemies.

CHAPTER SEVEN

"Sao anh di tron?" he asked indifferently—Why did you try to escape? I didn't answer immediately. He continued, "Did you think you could successfully escape?" I sat up and faced him.

"Chung toi o day sap chet doi," I began, slowly, seriously—We were about to starve here—then went on, "Escape was our only chance of living because to stay here meant to die. You cannot expect a man to surrender his life without a struggle and the conditions in this camp forced us to attempt to gain our freedom." . . .

"Do you know that the people would have killed you if they had caught you?" he asked.

I thought for a moment and the reply was evident: "Would it not be better to die while attempting to regain one's freedom than to lie quietly and rot of disease and starvation? Would a soldier of the Liberation Army give up his life without fighting for it?" He sat quietly looking at me, and then stood and walked away, splashing through the calf-deep water to the guard hut.

Five Years to Freedom, *Colonel Nick Rowe*

I loved Nick Rowe. Loved the man till the day he was assassinated in the Philippines. I still love him today. I would have given my life for that man, but to do that I would have had to stand in a long line, because there were a lot of good men who felt that strongly about Nick Rowe. He served as an inspiration to so many people; he came into my life at the right time and smoothed off a lot of my rough edges. I believe that if Nick Rowe had lived, the world would be a very different place. There are not a lot of people you can say that about, but Nick was lined up to get his general's stars. Within a few years he would have become commander of Special Forces, a position he could have used to influence our military policies.

Nick and I bonded over our love for this country, our loyalty to its military, and the tragedies in our lives. Nick's family was from McAllen, Texas. When he was captured and listed as a POW, his girlfriend from down there enrolled in nursing school and became a nurse-officer in the army. The years of his captivity apparently were hard on her. In November 1967 she wrote a note that said she couldn't live like this any longer, and she couldn't live without him. She killed herself. Two months later Nick escaped. We never talked about that part of our lives, but we both knew it was there, and we both understood the pain.

Nick knew what it was like to be hunted and captured and to survive in torturous conditions. When the army asked him to set up the SERE Committee, he was determined to make certain the people he trained would be ready to deal with those conditions. In 1982 he asked me to become an instructor in sentry stalking, escape techniques, and resistance to interrogation. My official title for the course was chief instructor and Ranger liaison, but basically I was chief cook and bottle breaker.

I went back in as an E-5, which was way below the rank I had earned. Nick wanted to bring me in as an E-8, but he didn't have authorization to fill that slot. He told me he'd get me there as quick as possible. It didn't make any difference to me—the mission was what mattered. That and the opportunity to work with him in creating a school that would save lives. The SERE course was one of the six training departments at the U.S. Army John F. Kennedy Special Warfare Center and School at Fort Bragg and Camp Mackall.

To qualify for this position I first had to go through a two-week Instructor Training Course, which teaches the professional standards demanded of the military instructors. It was a good course that basically included how to plan, prepare, and present the course material—putting a class together, writing a lesson plan, adapting teaching methods, and standing up on the platform to lecture, which covered everything from projecting your voice to controlling your mannerisms. The last thing you have to do to graduate is conduct a class for your instructors to demonstrate that you have mastered the concepts. The class I was going to teach was how to take out a sentry.

A key element of everything I had taught was the value of surprise. When I came back, everybody wanted to see what I was going to do. They'd heard about me blowing the building off its foundation, so they wanted to see what I intended to do for an encore. Admittedly, there were some people who thought I was crazy and wanted to be there to see my next act. So I had a lot of guests in my classroom. For the aggressor, catching your enemy unprepared or unready to defend himself often makes the difference between the success and the failure of the mission. For the defender, being prepared for any eventuality is a necessity. It is the element of surprise that allows a smaller force to defeat a larger force, or even makes it possible for a single warrior to inflict substantial damage upon the enemy. I had seen that in combat over and over. If there was one thing I wanted people to take away from my course that was it, but I had to make that point in my class.

I arranged it on the schedule so that I would be the first person after lunch to present my demonstration class. So while everybody else was having a nice lunch I was in the classroom, hiding a friend of mine in the ceiling. We pushed up the ceiling tiles; he crawled in there and lay on a beam.

The only three people who knew about my lesson plan were me, my assistant instructor, and the person in the ceiling. I didn't tell anybody else, including Nick, the sergeant major, and the person who was going to serve as my demonstrator. After lunch the commanders and instructors from the Instructor Training Corps came into the classroom and sat down.

I began my lecture. As I did, I had my sentry, my demonstrator, who was carrying his weapon, moving around the room. It was a distraction, which was exactly what I intended. I talked about preparation, mental projection, and finally the element of surprise. As I did I moved my sentry to the place I wanted him to be. When I said, "Even when the sentry is on his guard the element of surprise can be devastating. You can come out of nowhere," the person I had planted in the ceiling suddenly dropped down, grabbed the sentry's shoulder, moved his knife across his throat, and spun him down to the floor. Then he ran out the door and he was gone. The whole attack probably took less than fifteen seconds. When he had dropped down there was kind of a gasp in the room, like one big breath, but then it was silent, except for the sentry grunting. After he was gone, there was some stirring around as people adjusted to what they had just seen, but nobody said a word. There was just a blank look on their faces. I think some of them were scared shitless.

I had definitely made my point. I continued teaching my class. When I reached the end, I talked about teaching the mental techniques necessary to accomplish the mission. As I did I reached under the podium and took out my ice pick and a 5-gallon bucket of water.

I stuck the ice pick through my neck, picked up the water bucket with it and spun that bucket around, then put it down. I pulled out the ice pick and without hesitating flipped it across the room right into a target, the outline of a man, I'd hung on the wall. That was the end of my class.

Afterward people asked Colonel Rowe if that was what he intended to teach in the SERE course. "You're damn right," he told them. "If I had the knowledge that O'Neal is teaching, I wouldn't have been there for five years."

That was one of the biggest compliments I'd had in my career.

Nick brought together some of the most knowledgeable individuals to create this school. The staff included veterans of Vietnam, Special Forces people, and experts in weapons and fighting techniques. The course was three weeks long. We taught them techniques of escape and evasion, resistance to interrogation, and how to survive and avoid detection. That included making field-expedient weapons and clothing, trapping game, fishing, procuring food and water, which plants were edible and which were poisonous, celestial navigation—everything a man alone and desperate to avoid being caught would need to know.

Nick and I got real close. He had a great impact on me. "You know, Gary," he told me once, "you have amazing capabilities, but if you ever became a POW you wouldn't last ten minutes. You're such a hard-ass they'd just shoot you. Every chance you got you'd fucking head-butt the son of a bitch or bite him and do everything possible to take him out. They'd know they were never going to get any information out of you, so they wouldn't waste their time and their food on you. They'd just take you out and kill you."

My belief had always been that I would never give up my weapon and I would never cooperate with the enemy. If the enemy wanted my weapon he would have to kill me, and like I'd done in Nicaragua,

I would never voluntarily give up any information. By the Geneva Convention all that I was required to give them was my name, rank, and serial number, and that was all I would ever tell them.

Nick taught me different. We would discuss his experiences as a captive, and he told me what he had learned there, explaining, "There's a time and a place to be a hard-ass, but there's also a time to be soft. You have to know when to give them just enough to keep you alive."

The goal, he taught me, was to live to fight another day.

We had some good times together, Nick Rowe and I. One time I was in the hand-to-hand pit and he came out to get some feedback. We were standing there talking, and a few feet away the camp mascot, a dog named Ranger, was lying on his side licking his balls. Nick looked at him and said, "Damn, I wish I could do that."

So I told him, "Well, don't be shy. Just go on over there and ask him! He won't mind."

There has never been another school like SERE. Originally it was set up to teach survival techniques to those people most likely to find themselves needing them—Special Forces, air crews, and other people working in enemy territory, or anyone involved with special ops of any type. Eventually it was expanded to include Department of Defense and State Department employees and their families who were assigned to unfriendly countries and were at risk of being kidnapped. A lot of people like to describe parts of their military training as torture, but this was the only place where it was actually true. This wasn't one of those bullshit picture book courses, this was hardcore. Both Nick and I knew what it was like to be brutalized by your captor, to not know from second to second if you were going to survive, and we wanted to create an experience that would be as close to that as possible. Nick was one of the best-connected and most respected men in the military, and nobody fucked with him; they didn't ask a lot of questions about what he was doing. Just like with me,

I suspect they figured that for their own careers they would be better off not knowing all of the details.

We were also fortunate that at that time the commandant of Camp Mackall was Colonel Bob Howard. Bob Howard was just as hardcore as Nick, and they respected each other. Both of them were true leaders of men, frontline leaders, not TV leaders like some of the command today. Bob Howard is the only person I have ever known about who was recommended for the Congressional Medal of Honor three different times, finally receiving it for saving several lives during a rescue mission in Cambodia in late December 1968. Most people believed Colonel Howard was the most decorated soldier in the army since World War II.

I'd met him in Vietnam. At Camp Mackall he was running Special Forces training, and at times, in addition to the SERE course, he would ask me to teach hand-to-hand or patrolling and recon tactics. I'd be out there working with the troops at 4:30 A.M. and then go back to work at the SERE Committee. For me, working for both Nick Rowe and Bob Howard was the greatest situation possible. This was the elite of the United States Army; they did not get any tougher or smarter. If either one of those people wanted me to do something, I made it happen. The only thing I told them was don't ask questions. They were smart enough to accept that.

One time I was with Bob on a 12-mile rucksack march. We were humping really good when Bob went down with some type of heart problem. We didn't know if it was a heart attack, a stroke, or something less serious. We wanted to medevac him out, but he wouldn't let us. I think his exact response was "Fuck off." Instead he took a nitroglycerin tablet, stuck an IV needle in his arm, tied the IV on top of his rucksack, and continued marching. He refused to say another word about it.

Team 22 and 26 link up for extraction in Vietnam. *(Gary O'Neal Personal Collection)*

Gary's last training mission. *(Gary O'Neal Personal Collection)*

Training Ecuador Army Heavy Weapons Company 4.2 motors. *(Gary O'Neal Personal Collection)*

Overseeing training. *(Gary O'Neal Personal Collection)*

Me and my son, Shawn; I was being deployed. *(Gary O'Neal Personal Collection)*

Weapons training 2nd Battalion, Honduran Special Forces at El Cahon, Honduras, Central America. *(Gary O'Neal Personal Collection)*

Weapons training 2nd Battalion, Honduran Special Forces at El Cahon, Honduras, Central America. *(Gary O'Neal Personal Collection)*

Mental discipline training 2nd Battalion, Honduran Special Forces at El Cahon, Honduras, Central America. *(Gary O'Neal Personal Collection)*

Mental discipline training 2nd Battalion, Honduran Special Forces at El Cahon, Honduras, Central America. *(Gary O'Neal Personal Collection)*

Fight/sparing training 2nd Battalion, Honduran Special Forces at El Cahon, Honduras, Central America. *(Gary O'Neal Personal Collection)*

Mental training at USAJFK-SWC SERE School. *(Gary O'Neal Personal Collection)*

Mental training at USA-JFKSWC SERE School. *(Gary O'Neal Personal Collection)*

Team 22 C/75th Rangers after a firefight. *(Gary O'Neal Personal Collection)*

Taking a break, Pleiku, Vietnam. *(Gary O'Neal Personal Collection)*

Mental training USAJFK-SWC SERE School. *(Gary O'Neal Personal Collection)*

Myself, my son, Shawn, and the World Champion USAPT RW team. *(Gary O'Neal Personal Collection)*

Mental training with the 82nd Airborne Division. *(Gary O'Neal Personal Collection)*

Combat HALO tandem jump. *(Gary O'Neal Personal Collection)*

Mental training USAJFK-SWC SERE School. *(Gary O'Neal Personal Collection)*

Training the Venezuelan Special Forces. *(Gary O'Neal Personal Collection)*

Nick could get away with doing things that nobody else in the military could accomplish, primarily because he had backup like Bob Howard. None of us were sticklers for rank. One time Nick told me he needed to spend forty-five minutes with a young student and was not to be disturbed. As far as I was concerned, if Nick did not want to be disturbed, he was not going to be disturbed. I was sitting outside his office when a two-star general came in and demanded to see the colonel immediately. I explained to him politely that it wasn't going to happen. He got pissed and tried to push me into letting him in. I stood at attention like he told me but added, "But sir, you are not going through that door."

"I gave you a direct order," he said.

"Sir, you are not my commander. My commander told me he does not want to be disturbed for forty-five minutes, and by God that is what is going to happen. If you'd like to come back in an hour you'll go right in." He glared at me. Generals are not used to being told "no" by E-5s, but when Nick Rowe was around, the rules changed, and everybody knew it. He had earned such respcct that nobody was going to dare pull rank on him. You did not screw with Nick Rowe. Period. The general finally grumbled something, turned around, and walked out.

Basically, the SERE course as we established it was the Wild, Wild West. We didn't play by the rules. In every other military course, students knew that whatever it looked like they actually had nothing to be concerned about; their safety was paramount. They could go along with the program because they knew that nothing bad was really going to happen to them.

They didn't know that in SERE. They thought we were wild-ass crazies, slightly deranged and maybe even a little sadistic, which was what we intended them to think. We liked to refer to it as highly controlled chaos, but the students saw the chaos and not the control. For the course to be effective, they had to believe that they were physically in danger. Naturally, I encouraged that brand of thinking. One time, I set up a demonstration so quietly that even Nick Rowe and Bob Howard didn't know about it. A friend of mine named Paul Ford was teaching night fighting to the Phase I SF students. It was basically an introduction to hand-to-hand. I dressed up as a student, not an instructor, and I took a little plastic bag, filled it with my own blood, and taped it to my palm where no one could see it.

This class took place in the sawdust pit just before dawn, about 4:30 A.M., when the light wasn't real good and everybody was exhausted. We timed it so everybody could sort of see what was going on but wouldn't be able to identify anybody. Colonel Rowe and Colonel Howard were observing from the side. Paul was doing a demonstration of bayonet fighting and asked his class, "Any of you guys think you can take this knife away from me?" He was flipping it pretty easy. Then he challenged, "None of you losers got any guts. Let's see you come on up here."

With that I pushed my way right through the class. I had my hat pulled down low over my face, and we were all wearing camo. I kept moving. I went right up to Paul holding my own knife, an intentionally very dull blade, and when he thrust at me, I sidestepped him and chopped him and picked him up into the air. As I did, we cut that bag of blood and it just exploded all over everybody. I flipped it off and sort of dropped Paul, who lay on the ground quivering. There was blood all over the place. I raced out of that pit.

We had set up the whole thing so a Medevac would show up in a few minutes. The medics raced in and put Paul on the stretcher, put him on an IV, and took off. Man, that was chaos. The students didn't know what to do. A student had killed an instructor.

Meanwhile, I went over to the SERE building and got rid of my bloody clothes, then went running over to the pit to see what was going on. I was there for about five minutes when Paul walked back in, most of the blood cleaned up, and announced, "That concludes my demonstration of a surprise attack on a sentry." I swear, Colonel Howard was so happy Paul was alive he wanted to kill us both.

Of course, there were also many things we did that are still classified and can't be discussed.

Those things definitely saved lives. That class was 29½ hours straight; as far as I know, that was the longest class taught at one time in SF history. I taught them how to use the total environment, stealth movement, light discipline, understanding lines of drift, and everything else I had learned in my career. My students loved this course. Sometimes they didn't even want to take a break for water.

For the final exercise they had to use everything they'd been taught in an escape and evasion scenario. They had to escape from a compound surrounded by a 10-foot-high chain-link fence guarded on all sides by armed sentries. The sentries were trainees who had just started SF School dressed in enemy uniforms.

After escaping, my people had to get past three additional sentries without being discovered, then approach the fourth sentry and take him out. By take him out I mean "kill" him. They were armed with hard rubber knives, which they were to use as they snuck up on this sentry and slit his throat. Most of the time we ran this program, that fourth sentry was Colonel Rowe. He loved role-playing. One night a pretty confident captain had completed the course—except for taking out Nick. Just as he was making his approach, Nick felt his presence and turned around. He looked right at him. In response, this captain immediately snapped to attention and saluted. Colonel Rowe didn't hesitate, he looked at this man and knocked him out. Pow! Out. Fucking cold. Nick never cursed, but he could make his anger known. As this officer came to, Nick was standing over him screaming, "How could you salute me? I'm your enemy. You flunked this course."

If the students failed at any part of the task, if they were spotted or apprehended, they had to go back to the compound and start all over again, which they did not want to do because then they would have to deal with the wrath of me on their ass.

There was a lot happening that the students didn't know. I always had one of my AIs, assistant instructors, go in with the group like he was a student. When they were planning their escape he'd point out to them, "Look at those cameras out there in the compound. Look at those guards walking around. How we gonna get past them? The answer is we can't. So if we can't go overland, then we've got to go underground. Now how the hell are we going to do that?"

Inevitably someone would suggest digging a tunnel. I never could understand it—digging a fucking tunnel in one night—but someone who obviously had been watching too many war films would suggest it.

My AI would explain that it would take too long to dig a tunnel and then direct them to look at what tools they had to work with, which was always the key. Use what you have available. The AI pointed out that there was running water in the compound, so there had to be a drainage system. That water had to come from somewhere and it had to go somewhere. Eventually the students would find the drainage system and determine which pipes went in the direction they wanted to go.

Using the stealth tactics I had taught them, covered by environmental noises that I provided, like battlefield sounds or helicopters, they would make their way through the compound, staying in the shadows, until they reached the entrance to the drainage system. The pipes were 2½-foot concrete pipes, which was plenty wide enough for a man. They would crawl through them and get out of the compound.

When they came out of the tunnel I was waiting there for them, but they never saw me. I was camouflaged, just like they were. I would trail those students through the entire exercise. We had the new Panasonic night-vision video cameras in the buildings and trees; we filmed them going into the drainage system, coming out of the system, and walking along the trail. After they had completed the course we would go over the tapes, and then I would describe in detail exactly what they had done. They couldn't believe we had been observing them every step.

While they were in this POW camp they were subject to interrogation. That's a nice way of describing what happened to them in captivity. I can't describe much of what happened there, but it is fair to say they got shook out of their safety zone.

The basis of most of what I taught was the mental aspects that it takes to resist interrogation and to escape from captivity and evade detection—specifically, how to control your body, your mind, and your emotions, especially your fear, as well as how to project an image to your enemy that he will accept. When these students got to Colonel Rowe, he wasn't pretending he didn't hear these people; he wanted to catch them. If they got to him, they had done their job. I had been studying and learning these mental techniques my whole life, and they encompassed all of my own experiences as well as those other people had told me about. In Vietnam, for example, SF people had cover stories that they stuck to if they were captured; Nick probably saved his life by denying he was SF, insisting for five years that he was an army engineer. I got word several years later that one individual who had gone through my resistance to interrogation training had been snatched up in Colombia. They had put a bag over his head and waterboarded him with a mixture of jalapeño juice, pepper juice, and water. That was particularly brutal. It's basically acidic gas. It got in his eyes and up his nose and in his throat and burned him so bad he could barely breathe, but while this was being done to him he remembered what I'd taught him; he projected himself to a different place, slowed his breathing, and withdrew into himself, which enabled him to survive being tortured.

Nick would often talk about mental projection, explaining how it helped him get through his captivity. He once told our mutual friend Colonel Dave Kutchinski, who he had known most of his life and had even babysat for when Dave was a kid, that after he came home his father asked him how he managed to survive. Nick told him, "Astral projection."

As Dave told me, Nick's father thought that was all hocus-pocus, he didn't believe any of it—until Nick told him, "On such-and-such a day you went out fishing at the Falcon Reservoir. You forgot to bring gasoline for the boat, so you had to go back to the station to get gasoline, but when you got there you realized you hadn't brought the gas tank with you, so you had to go back to the boat."

Nick's father's jaw hit the ground. "You were there?" he asked.

"Yeah, I was there," Nick told him. "That's how I got through it. I would just leave."

None of us talked about mental projection too much in public, because we knew it was a controversial subject. We knew that most people thought it was all bullshit, and we weren't interested in convincing them, but all of us had a strong belief that the mind had powers that hadn't been fully explored, powers that could be harnessed and used. Physically, for example, there is no way you should be able to have a jeep drive over your chest without it causing any damage, but with the right mental focus we learned how to do that. You shouldn't be able to stick an ice pick through your neck without it bleeding badly, but we all learned how to do that. There was more than that. I also saw Nick Rowe shatter glass by projecting his thoughts. I absolutely saw that, and I know what I was able to do in combat to sentries.

The fact is that in my life I have had some paranormal experiences for which I can offer no rational explanation. As a warrior, my bottom line has always been the bottom line—you live or you die—but I do know that there is more to this world than we know right now. For example, one night when I was in Nicaragua I was coming back to my office, which was in a military compound, from a three-day training mission. My office was on the top floor of a small building. It was like a big studio apartment, maybe 30 by 40 feet, and I had a bed in there. This was shortly before I got involved with Maria. I liked working at night, I liked being in the dark, which allowed me to stretch out all my senses, not just depend on my vision. When you turn on the lights at night, all of your other senses are depleted. For that reason, when I walk into a room at night I don't naturally turn on the lights unless I have to. In this case I took a couple of steps and stumbled over a body lying on the floor. I knew what a body felt like, and there was no doubt in my mind I had just kicked a body.

There were no shades on the windows, just shutters, which were opened at an angle to allow ambient moonlight from outside into the room. I looked down and saw myself lying motionless on the floor in a puddle of blood, with a chunk of shrapnel in my left shoulder.

When I turned on the light the body was gone. There was nothing there. I had stumbled over air. I felt a presence in that room. I sat down at my desk and got everything ready for the next day's training, but I could never shake the feeling that something was happening. I didn't sleep well that night.

On the street the next day I was approached by an elderly peasant woman I did not know. I don't believe I'd ever met her before. Latin American people are often more spiritual than Americans;

maybe because they have fewer possessions, they remain more strongly connected to the mysteries of life. This woman told me she knew all about me. She told me about an unsettling conversation I'd had with my grandmother back in Utah, a conversation only the two of us and the Creator knew about. When she told me that, I knew she had the gift. Then she told me why she had approached me. She knew I was going to die.

She had come to warn me. I had ended my experience the night before by turning on the lights, but she had seen the whole thing. I died, she told me, not from my initial wounds, but rather because I had not gotten medical attention in time. I'd bled to death. Then she told me the time frame in which this was going to happen, which was during the following week. I listened to her, but I can't really say that I totally believed her. There had been other times while I was there that I had been warned about things that never happened, things that might be prevented for just a few dollars.

The following week I was scheduled to go visit the border with El Salvador to familiarize myself with the situation there. I was so busy training troops in Managua that I considered canceling that trip to complete the training cycle, but finally I decided I needed to go.

While I was gone, a bomb went off near my office. When I got back and looked around, the first thing I noticed was that the shutters on one side were all torn up. It looked like somebody had broken in while I was gone. When I sat down at my desk, I discovered a big chunk of jagged metal, a shell fragment, stuck into my desk. I sat there looking at it for a moment. Then I took a length of string and ran it from the broken shutters to that piece of metal. If I had been sitting at my desk it would have gone right through my left shoulder.

Mike Echanis, Chuck Sanders, and I used to work on our mental projections when we were at Fort Bragg. There was a story people told about Mike Echanis that supposedly took place during our course there. At that time the SF operated what was known as "the Goat Lab," which was where we learned emergency medicine. Goats would be shot or stabbed, and we had to figure out how to stop their bleeding. It was pretty simple. If your goat died, you went in front of the board to defend your actions. If you followed procedures and the goat still died, you were good to go, but if you screwed up anything, you were gone.

According to SF First Sergeant Glenn Wheaton—the character George Clooney played in the movie *The Men Who Stare at Goats* was based on him—one day Echanis had brought a goat with him down into the hand-to-hand combat pit. At the end of a class Mike asked his students, "Where is your mind?"

I was not there when this happened, although I was told this story by people I believe. Apparently Mike grabbed the goat by its horns and tied it to a stake in the pit. According to Wheaton, who witnessed this, "Michael focused on the goat pretty intensely. It started to bray like a donkey or horse. It dropped down to its forelegs; blood began to drip from its nose. About twenty to thirty seconds later red suds began to froth from the goat's mouth. The goat lost its equilibrium and passed away in a fit.

"Michael never had to touch the goat, other than dragging him and sinking the anchor in the sand. A demonstration we required he repeat." Wheaton goes on to add that in other tests Mike was able to use projection to burst balloons filled with ink. I never saw anything like that. Our commander at that time, Colonel Juan Montes, who we later worked with in Nicaragua, always said, "You have to control your mental power to reach your highest combat capability, and you have to train for that also.

"Mike had that power and I respected him for it. I saw him fight ten men at the same time. This was part of a demonstration for President Somoza and his son. He had a line of ten people, and by focusing his mind on one person he could push him and the other men behind him would fall like dominos. Then he challenged three of Somoza's strongest and best fighters at the same time, one of them being almost 250 pounds and 7' tall, and they had to pull Mike off him because he could have killed him. Physically, there was no way one man should have been able to defeat three men, but I attest to that, I saw it.

"But Mike could hypnotize people. He hypnotized me. I was watching him training people in a gym and he literally put me to sleep. He asked my permission and I said, 'When I wake up am I going to be the same guy?' Before he answered I was asleep."

At the same time Mike, CW, Chuck, and I were teaching our class at Fort Bragg, another research group was running a program that became known as Project Jedi. It mostly involved physical tests, like running with heart monitors, to determine if we were capable of controlling our heartbeat, lowering our blood pressure, regulating body temperature, and even focusing our hearing to eliminate distracting noises. I'd been doing these things practically my whole life, so none of it was difficult for me. As with a lot of military testing, we never got the results, but that didn't matter. We didn't need confirmation of what we already knew to be true.

Later, while I was assigned to SERE, Nick sent me to Duke University to participate in a study that was being conducted about paranormal abilities, specifically whether people were able to project their thoughts and control pain. They put me inside a small glass-enclosed chamber, which I called a bell jar. Outside this chamber they had sensors monitoring every sound in the room; if a breeze blew or if a mosquito flew by, it would register that sound on a graph. Inside that chamber they wired me up completely so they could measure my EKG, EEG, blood pressure, body temperature, brain activity—and they also monitored all sounds. There was a target in front of me, just a wire with a small red bulb at the end of it, and I was supposed to project energy into that red sensor.

I sat in that booth staring at that red bulb, projecting energy at it. Outside I could see people frantically writing stuff down. A lot of this stuff was classified, so I never did get the results.

They also tested my ability to control my heartbeat and my blood pressure. They would pick a number, and my job would be to either lower or raise my heartbeat to that number, which truthfully was not difficult for me. That was something I had been able to do through my breathing for a long time. It was the same technique yogis used. I didn't need to see written results to know I could control my breath and slow my heartbeat to a few beats a minute. There were some bodies in Nicaragua because I had learned that lesson.

While I loved working with Nick, it wasn't easy putting my life back together. My running partners in Nicaragua, Mike, Chuck, and Bobby, were dead. Maria and the kids . . . I'd let out my emotions for them, and the results were devastating. So I put the cork back in. At night, rather than hang around, I took a job working at a bar just outside Fort Bragg. My job was to check IDs, help the female bartenders, and control unruly patrons. Maintaining order turned out to be a burdensome task.

Being a bouncer turned out to be a fine outlet for my aggression. There were always some people who found it necessary to challenge me. This club actually had two bars, one in the restaurant and one on the dance floor. I worked there with a big Samoan, big enough to have played just a little pro football. One night five PFCs from the Engineer Corps decided to reach over and take the tip jar off the bar. These were big cocky guys. When the bartender came around the bar to get his money back, they decided it was amusing to hit him with a beer bottle. They broke his nose and his jaw and started beating on him.

One of the female bartenders started screaming. I went back there and started pulling these guys off the bartender. When this started my objective was trying to keep the peace. We were all wearing clean white shirts, and I did not want to get my shirt dirty.

I pulled them off and tossed them back into the room. Then one of them picked up a longneck Budweiser and split my head open. He ripped a strip of skin off my forehead, and blood started flowing into my eyes. That was when my instinct kicked in and I went into combat mode. I didn't think, I reacted. I started killing that fucker; I had him by the throat and I was beating him with the bar stool. Broke his nose and smashed his teeth, broke one of his arms. I was back in the realm. I was pounding on him. A few people tried to pull me off him, but that wasn't going to happen. This was my enemy and he needed to be beaten into submission. There were some strong riptides just below my surface, and when someone got caught up in one the result could be brutal. I was simply doing what I had spent my life training to do. Even the big Samoan couldn't stop me. It was the manager who finally got my attention; I heard him screaming my name, and I looked up and saw his sparkling white sweater. It was that white sweater that brought me back to the moment. I wasn't in the jungle, I was on the floor of a bar in Fayetteville, North Carolina. I stopped and stood up, almost slipping down in all the blood covering the floor. I didn't realize at the time how much of that blood was mine.

The police arrived soon after. They took us all outside. The fresh air, the lights, the whole environment helped me calm down. When I did, I started throwing up, puking all over the cops' shoes. The witnesses told the police that these people had been beating on the bartender and then me, and that I'd acted in self-defense, but the cops still had to take a complete report. As we were standing there they brought out one of the Engineers. This one guy looked at me and gave me the finger.

I grabbed the fucker, picked him up over my shoulder, and slammed him down on the hood of the police car. *Whoomp!* The cop was stunned. Instead of beating on me, he wanted to know how I had moved so fast.

I actually was hurt pretty bad. I had to go to a plastic surgeon several times. Eventually the case went to court. I had no recollection of what happened in that bar after I got hit in the head, but several witnesses testified that I had done nothing wrong. I protected the bartender, and then myself. The decision was that the Engineers had to pay all our medical bills.

The provost marshal didn't have to get involved, because this was a civilian matter, so it didn't have any effect on my career. This was the worst fight I had on this job, but it certainly wasn't the only one. In fact, during the years I worked at this job I had several assault charges filed against me. Okay, eighty-four assault charges.

Eighty-four—it was part of the job. The population of Fayetteville was essentially thousands of confident young fighting men with money in their pockets, a drink in front of them, and not enough women to go around. There were definitely going to be some problems. It seemed like every time I threw someone out of a club he would file charges against me. He would claim I beat him up or hit him. That was true only if he had resisted. Nobody who wasn't bothering other people got tossed out of the club; we wanted their business. Once a person became unruly, though, I had to do my job. The police knew me—with eighty-four charges filed against me, we were on a first-name basis—and they never arrested me, not one time. They would tell me, "Gary, when you finish your shift go downtown and see the magistrate and fill out the paperwork." I filled out a lot of paperwork.

I spent almost three years working with Nick at the SERE Committee. After the course was established Colonel Rowe was promoted and took command of battalion headquarters. He discovered that the HALO Committee was critically short of qualified instructors. He called me up and asked me to come over to the HALO Committee to run their R&D shop, which included finding, developing, and testing new equipment and delivery systems, adapting tandem jumping to military missions, and helping develop the school's SOP to reflect applicable combat tactics. Basically, he wanted me to come in and look at the HALO program and figure out how to integrate the new technology that was coming online into its procedures. That included everything from brand-new GPS systems to breathing apparatus for HALO/SCUBA operations. I always considered myself a professional tinkerer. My grandfather and my father had taught me not to be afraid of tools. Once you figure out how to avoid being killed by electricity, research and development is pretty simple; you just keep plugging at it until you get it to work. Beginning in Vietnam, I had always been modifying my equipment to make it lighter and more deadly. I streamlined or redesigned just about every weapon I ever used. So I was never intimidated by technology. If I didn't understand something, I took it apart and played with it until I figured it out. The biggest advantage of not having much of a formal education is that you're not limited by knowledge. You don't know how much you don't know, so you take nothing for granted. You start at the beginning. There still is no better system for inventing than trial, error, and stubbornness.

Colonel Rowe knew this was the perfect assignment for me. I have never once turned down a chance to jump out of an airplane in my life. There was no feeling I enjoyed more than floating unencumbered in space. For those seconds sailing through the air, I didn't have time to think about the burdens I was carrying, I was free. My focus was on the wind and the weather and the adjustments I had to make to reach my objective. It was high-flying instantaneous calculations; each jump was a test of your capabilities. As far as I was concerned, jumping is the best thing you can do with your clothes on. Nick was offering me permission to make almost any type of jump I wanted, with whatever equipment I wanted to use, to accomplish things that had never been done before. I certainly wasn't going to turn down that opportunity.

The primary advantage of HALO is that it allows troops to infiltrate an area without being observed. We knew how to do that, but one of the challenges we had to deal with at that time was how to deliver matériel and equipment to those men. We developed a system of remote control servomotors that allowed HALO and HAHO jumpers to deliver bundles weighing as much as 1,200 pounds to their target. Basically, the steering lines of the parachute we developed came down into small servomotors. To turn to the left, for example, all we had to do was press a button that would pull down the proper steering line. It was a remote control steering system, and when it worked it was a beautiful thing. Of course, it didn't always work.

Eventually we were able to use this system to guide a bundle weighing more than 1,000 pounds to a specific landing point as far as 50 to 100 kilometers from the place it left the airplane—followed immediately by the team that was going to utilize it. It was the ideal system to get weapons, ammunition, and later even motorized vehicles on the ground completely undetected.

Some of our experiments got a little bit hinky. We wanted to use this technology to deliver four-wheeled vehicles to troops on the ground. Mobility is always a factor in a mission, and the more you can increase it the better chance of success you have. We were trying to perfect a system that would allow troops to sit inside a vehicle, which was basically a souped-up dune buggy equipped with roll bars and a weapons system, drive it out the open back end of an aircraft, ride it down while guiding it to a predetermined LZ, and when it landed pull a quick release to get rid of the canopy and drive off before the enemy even knows you are there. Sitting in that vehicle as we floated down, controlling the canopy with a remote, was a lot of fun, without doubt the greatest roller-coaster ride ever invented.

It also was a very complicated and dangerous process. We did a lot of the testing, and we had some malfunctions. On one jump from about 14,000 feet, the main parachute had a tension knot in it that caused it to spin wildly as we went down. I had no control over this vehicle, so I dived out and free-fell for a while, then popped my canopy and followed what was left of that vehicle to the ground.

We tested just about every type of parachute and eventually helped bring square canopies on the HALO Committee. It was at about that time in 1983 that the legendary Ted Strong had just invented the tandem rig, which was revolutionary. It allowed two people to jump safely on one canopy. Ted Strong was one of the true pioneers of skydiving, and we had become good friends. We'd done a lot of jumps together. His company, Strong Enterprises, was down in Orlando, and whenever I had some new thought I'd call him up. "Hey, man, I got this idea, what do you think about it? Can we do it?"

He'd ponder on it a little bit, then respond, "Sure we can. We'll build the rigs down here. Come on down when you can and we'll do test jumps on it." Ted and I happened to have been born on the same day of the year, although he was a decade older than me, so we thought alike. Truthfully, neither one of us minded going above and beyond to accomplish our goals. We worked together to turn theories into facts. Ted Strong was definitely my type of individual.

Soon after Ted developed his first tandem rigs, I wanted to bring them into the military through the HALO Committee. Together we worked up and tested several different military applications. The obvious one was taking an individual who was mission essential but had never jumped before, strapping him on, and getting him on the ground to infiltrate without being discovered.

We also realized that a tandem rig could be extremely useful for jumping into a small LZ in an enemy-occupied area. The passenger would ride shotgun, like on the old-time stagecoaches, taking out the sentry and blasting the enemy, allowing the tandem master to concentrate on landing on the top of a building or even inside a prison camp.

We also designed a strategy for using the passenger to focus on steering the bundles. The passenger could operate the servomotors to direct the equipment to a designated LZ. They could land the bundle on a target about the size of a normal backyard, and the team of eight or twelve people would follow it right in. Ted Strong and I developed the tactics and wrote the papers for the HALO Committee.

At right about that same time, Nick Rowe was over at the Golden Knights speaking to them about the SERE Committee, and my name came up. They were looking for a comp team leader and told Nick they wanted me. We were finishing up our work at the HALO Committee, so Nick volunteered me to return to the Knights as the competition team leader.

More than competing, the Golden Knights were doing demonstration jumps all over the world. We were a very effective army public relations tool. In late December we were scheduled to go down to Orlando to jump into the Citrus Bowl. We had just been given a brand-new aircraft for our demonstrations, and the government spent something like $3 million painting it our black and gold colors. It was pristine, and this was scheduled to be the inaugural jump from that plane. I was definitely looking forward to it, because the military coordinator of that jump was a man I had been wanting to meet for a lifetime, Joe Kittinger.

Colonel Joe Kittinger was the ultimate high-altitude parachute jumper. He was the pioneer, and I'd been hearing about him since the day I made my first jump. At that time, nobody else had ever done what he did—and he did it three times. In 1959 he jumped from

76,000 feet, lost consciousness when his equipment malfunctioned, and survived only because his chute opened automatically. After another jump from that height a month later, in 1960 he jumped nearly 20 miles, 102,800 feet, from a gondola beneath a helium balloon. He free-fell 84,000 feet for more than four minutes, traveling more than 600 miles per hour. Until 2012, it remained the highest jump in history. During his third tour of duty in Vietnam his F-4 Phantom was shot down on his 483rd mission, and he spent eleven months as a guest in the Hanoi Hilton. So I really did want to meet the man.

We landed at the Orlando Executive Airport. An old World War II DC-3 owned by the singer Ricky Nelson, who was scheduled to perform at the game, came in right behind us. His pilots ramped up their engines before shutting them down and blew all kinds of debris, sand and dirt and grit, over our newly painted airplane. Oh man, I was pissed. I went and banged on the door of that plane until it got pushed open, and Ricky Nelson was standing there. I told him, "If you ever want to sing again, you don't ever do anything like that again. 'Cause if you do, I'm gonna rip your fucking lips off." Then I turned around and walked away. A few minutes later Ricky Nelson and his pilot came over to accept responsibility and apologize. He turned out to be a good person, and we got together several times that week.

Then I met Kittinger. We definitely shared a love of jumping out of aircraft. I don't really remember how we arrived at this point, but I do remember offering to bet him that I could land within a few feet of anyplace he wanted me to land. Backyards, rooftops, highways, it didn't matter. I told him, you name it, I'll do it.

He asked me what I drank. "Wild Turkey," I told him.

"Okay, then, I'm gonna be sitting at a picnic table at Church Street Station tonight. That's where I want you to be."

I promised I would meet him there. There was only one problem: There wasn't one thing legal about the type of jump I had just bet I could make. I went to my team, including the pilots and our first sergeant, and I told them I'd just met the greatest parachute jumper in history. "You people want to make a jump, let's jump tonight. Our first demo jump out of this brand-new aircraft should be for him. Let's do it right into downtown. We'll shake this place up." We couldn't get FAA permission to make a demo jump, but as I explained that was actually the least illegal and least dangerous thing about this jump. We didn't have the proper equipment for a night jump, we had to stay below the approach to the Orlando Airport, and we were jumping right into the center of the city. I was proposing breaking every fucking rule that there is in parachuting, in aeronautics, and in the FAA's rulebook.

Everybody wanted to go for it. We agreed that if anybody bounced we would drag him off and put his body someplace else.

Church Street Station was an old railroad station that had been converted into an entertainment complex. As I'd informed my team, we had no landing lights, no drop zone, no lights on our canopies, and no permission to do anything. Normally we were supposed to open up our parachutes at 2,000 feet—we were below that when we left the airplane. Way below. We opened up at about 1,200 feet. There were a lot of people in the area, and I suspect they were mildly surprised to look up and see it was raining parachutes. Our LZ was the large parking lot, but as I was coming down I spotted Joe sitting at a picnic table. It was a little hard to get to, but I steered through power lines and landed right on top of the picnic table. Soon as I got settled I sat down and took the top off the bottle of Wild Turkey, and me and Joe commenced drinking that bottle. With more to follow.

I spent two years at the Golden Knights, during which time our relative work (formation building) team won two world championships. Then in 1987 the government initiated counterinsurgency operations and Operation Snowcap, which was a joint action between the DEA and Special Forces, to combat narco-terrorism in South America. These were real-world missions, which allowed me to get back into the mix. Jumping for me was recreation, but when I had the opportunity I always chose to be in a combat environment. So I went back to 7th Special Forces Group, and began working in South America.

I was back in the jungle fighting guerrillas. I'd been down there briefly a couple of years earlier to train counterinsurgency troops in El Salvador, but this was an SF deployment.

At that same time, Colonel Rowe left the SERE Committee to become head of the Joint U.S. Military Advisory Group, which was training counterinsurgency units of the Philippine Army. The Philippine government was fighting the Communist New People's Army. As far as I was concerned these New People were the same old people I'd been fighting my whole life. I had seen that movie before, and unless we made some changes I knew it ended badly. The Philippine government requested American military assistance, and Nick went down there to work with the CIA in training their army. As soon as he got settled he wanted me to come down.

Nick put in my papers and got my orders to go the Philippines, and suddenly they were changed. They were bounced right back at me. I put them in again, and again they came back at me. It was really sort of a strange thing. This was the type of request that usually got rapid approval, especially when someone like Nick got involved. In fact, we put in that request five different times, and each time it was approved and then it was changed. I never got an explanation, and nobody could figure out what was going on, but clearly there was some reason for keeping Nick and me apart. Finally Nick told me that he would have a better chance to get me if I was a warrant officer. So I put in my request for that school.

A warrant officer is a rank between being an enlisted man and an officer. It's above a sergeant major but it is not a commissioned officer.

Basically, it's a workingman's rank. A warrant officer has advisory skills that are valuable to the command. The school lasts almost a year, and previously I had never seen the need for it. When Nick told me it was necessary, though, it was necessary.

While I was waiting for my class at the school to get started, General James Guest, the 7th SFGA commander, asked me to be the technical adviser for a series of Be All You Can Be recruiting commercials. They were being shot by the greatest skydiving photographer, Norman Kent. We were shooting at Fort Bragg, and General Guest instructed me to make certain that everything they filmed was technically and tactically correct. I did all the air work. For example, I did a HALO jump carrying a full pack and weapons, landing on the girder of a building under construction, and then the camera came in for a close-up of . . . this handsome young Latino! Apparently some honcho who looked like me was not going to encourage young people to enlist in the army. So I would do the entire stunt, and after I landed the director shouted "Cut," and this handsome kid wearing the same equipment as me would step into my place and smile for his close-up.

The director was a nice young man who clearly was intending to be an artist. He was going to make his reputation with this commercial. There was one battlefield scene in which he had several Bradleys supported by aircraft sweeping across a terrain that clearly was supposed to be a desert. He did about twenty-nine takes of that same scene, every one of them looking almost exactly like the one before it. It was about 110° on that field with no wind, and troops were out there marching in that sun without any breaks. It was obvious he didn't have a clue about what he was doing.

I felt it was necessary to remind him that people needed a break. For one shot a helicopter came directly at the camera. I got up in that copter and told the pilot to take me right over that director's head. We came in on him and the blades started kicking up dirt and dust, and at about 20 feet I jumped out and landed in the soft sand no more than 3 feet from him. He was absolutely pale, and I said to him, "Okay, enough is enough. You don't want to keep those people out there in this heat any longer, do you?" That young man suddenly saw the wisdom of my suggestion.

It was right about this time, in early 1989, that Nick told Dave Kutchinski and me that his intelligence sources had warned him that the Communists were planning a series of political assassinations in the Philippines and that he was near the top of their most wanted list. They wanted to take out a high-profile target in a city, especially an American, to prove they were strong enough to reach anyone, anywhere. The Communists had a real hatred for Nick, who had escaped their captivity to become one of the military's most successful and dedicated anti-Communist warriors. If there was anybody in the world capable of taking care of himself, it was Nick Rowe; we knew that, but we wanted to get over there to provide whatever assistance he needed. Fuck orders, we decided, we were going to take space-available seats on a military flight and get there. Dave had the contacts there to get us the weapons we would need, and we figured once we were in the Philippines, we would deal with the consequences.

Before we could make that trip, Dave was transferred from Fort Bragg to Tampa to run a program he had designed that had suddenly been approved, and I was warned quietly to stay put. On the morning of April 21, 1989, Nick was attacked by a team of assassins on his way to work in Quezon City. He was in an armored vehicle that had to slow down to go through a traffic circle a few blocks away from his office when a stolen white car pulled up alongside and the killers opened up on him with M-16s and .45 caliber pistols. Nick had a bulletproof attaché case with him, and as soon as he saw those weapons sticking out of the car he dropped down to the floor and put that case over his head. They fired twenty-one shots. Twenty of them bounced off Nick's car, but one round supposedly went underneath the molding of the rear glass, ricocheted off the roof, then bounced down and hit him in the back of the head, killing him instantly. It was a one-in-ten-million shot. His chauffeur was wounded, but recovered.

Less than a half hour after it happened, Skip Coughlin called me and gave me a direct order not to leave my quarters. They knew what I would do, and they wanted to stop me. A few minutes later there were two guards standing outside my door. I wasn't permitted to leave; essentially I was placed under house arrest. It was bullshit, but there was nothing I could do about it.

Dave found out about the same time. He got a phone call from someone who said through his tears, "They got him, my God, they got him."

"Who?" Dave asked.

"Nick. They got Nick. He's dead."

It seemed obvious to us that Nick had been betrayed. Among the strict rules Nick followed was never take the same route twice, never establish a pattern, because your enemy will take advantage of that. That was hardwired into him. So how did the assassination team know his route? The magic bullet that found the one weak spot in the armor, bounced around the vehicle, and struck him in the back of the head was either the luckiest shot in the world or something entirely different. There has never been any evidence that anything happened except as officially reported, but personally I have always had questions about that killing. The way it supposedly happened just didn't make any sense to me. It was badly planned and badly executed—but they hit their target.

Nick was dead. More roses at Arlington. I did not like having guards at my front door. At that time I was furious about it, but maybe it was a good thing. The army prevented Dave and me and a lot of other dangerous people who loved Nick from going to the Philippines. I don't know what we would have done once we got there, but we would have made our presence known.

There was a big ceremony for Nick, and everybody called him a hero. KILLED BY TERRORISTS, it says on his tombstone. When you lead a military life, especially when there is fighting taking place, you get used to people you care about dying, but this was tough, very tough, on a lot of people who loved that man.

I didn't know what to do, where to turn. One more time, I felt like my whole foundation had been yanked out from under me. Throughout my career, from Pappy Wells to Nick Rowe, there had been people watching over me. While I knew a lot of good people who were serving this country, my plans had been to move forward with Nick. I was committed to Warrant Officer School, but General Guest knew I was going through a rough time and asked me what he could do to help me. I told him I'd like to have a couple of months off just to find my bearings. No problem, he said, take three months. Which is how I ended up going bowling with Mick Jagger.

My life definitely has taken some interesting turns. Mick Jagger was making a movie in Atlanta called *Freejack*. In the most important scene in that movie a Formula 2 race car gets airborne, crashes into an overhead bridge, and explodes in a burst of flame. They needed somebody to create that special effect. Some of the people I'd met while doing the Be All You Can Be commercials recommended me. Blowing up a race car was a fine way of clearing the darkness from my mind.

What made this stunt difficult was that there was a million-dollar Nissan sign on the overhead bridge, which we were not allowed to damage. So we had to make it look like the car crashed into it without actually touching it. I designed the special effect. Instead of hitting the bridge, we had to hit an 18-inch beam in front of it. If we missed that beam and went above it, we would destroy the sign; if we went below it, we blew the effect. It was an interesting engineering problem. Basically, we put the car on a forklift and braced it so it could only move forward, and we fired it into the sign like an air mortar. It was considerably more complicated than that, but it worked. That car exploded into the bridge in a big burst of flame without even singeing the sign.

As long as I was on the set I also played several small roles, most of them bad guys. I got to put on a mask and be a tough guy. It's fun being tough in a movie. Before they finished shooting, I had to report to Fort Rucker, Alabama, to begin my course. Solving that movie problem took me out of my comfort zone and put me into another world. It gave my mind a purpose beyond wondering why an impossible shot had killed Nick Rowe.

After completing the first phase of the course, I happened to be passing through Atlanta when they had the wrap party, the party for the whole crew after they finished shooting the movie. Mick Jagger leased a whole bowling alley. Turned out Mick liked to bowl. During the party I got to sit down and talk with Emilio Estevez, who also starred in the film. Jagger was a little bitty guy, but very intense. What I remember most about the party was that for some reason they served Iraqi food. I figured I would be going to that part of the world pretty soon, so I didn't eat the food. I was getting ready for what was to become Desert Shield. As it turned out, I never got into it in the desert. Instead I went back to the jungles.

CHAPTER EIGHT

The most famous American investigative reporter of the time, Jack Anderson, once wrote, "The Colombian-based cartel, which does $18 billion worth of business every year in the United States, is a greater menace to America than the Soviet Union."

Eighteen billion dollars? Maybe, but perhaps more. It is impossible to know. I know that Pablo was earning so much cash that each year we would simply write off approximately 10 percent of our money because the rats would eat it or it would be damaged beyond use by water and dampness.

Roberto Escobar, The Accountant's Story

In 1982 President Ronald Reagan declared war on illegal drugs. The problem was that the American people didn't believe it was a real war. It most definitely was—there were some real bullets flying downrange. A war is fought by soldiers, in this case Special Forces. We were sent throughout South America and Central America to train the national armies to fight the narco-terrorists and also Communist guerrilla movements. These were called FID missions, foreign internal defense missions. Our assignment was to train the Rangers or Special Forces of Honduras, Guatemala, Venezuela, Ecuador, Costa Rica, Colombia, Peru, Argentina, Panama, El Salvador, just about every country south of our border.

Seventh Group was always at the head of these missions, and my team was often the one that was designated. I had a reputation of being easy to work with and hard to kill. Also, because of our experience winning hearts and minds, my team emphasized working with the local populace, which made people want us in their country. We trained infantry units, counterinsurgency units, counterterrorism units, and special ops. We did the whole spectrum of SF training, SCUBA to shooting to HALO. We taught them how to secure their border and how to kick in a door in the city, how to control a large crowd or take out a single sentry, how to set up an ambush and work with the indigenous peoples. I was definitely a hands-on trainer, as well as sometimes foot-on and fist-on. Every morning I gave my students PT. I ran the crap out of them, but I ran every step with them. I never asked my people to do anything I couldn't do, wouldn't do, or hadn't done. Then when we got back to where we started, I'd fight with them. Any of them who wanted to fight me, I took them on. Hand-to-hand was basically "show me what you got." I put pads and gloves on everybody, and we would go three three-minute rounds or however long it took me to knock them out. It was a tremendous motivational technique. *Here's your chance to beat up the bastard who's making your life miserable.* They were lining up to take that opportunity. I told them, "This ain't the only chance you'll be getting. If you can't do it today, come on back tomorrow." When I trained troops they stayed trained.

My Spanish was as good as it needed to be. I always figured out a way to make my intentions known. I might have mispronounced some words or used the wrong words at times, but I had a translator and I had a way of communicating. A smile and a fist can go a long way.

I spent considerable time going in and out of Venezuela, and one of my students there was a young lieutenant named Hugo Chávez. Like some of the other people I worked with, he thought that because he was well connected in his country, he didn't have to work hard to get through the course. For example, he didn't want to run those hard miles before sunrise. It was something like "I do not have to do that, I am an officer."

I quietly told him, "Well, I'm an NCO, and I'm going to kick your fucking officer ass if you do not get up there and start running."

There was no question that he was going to graduate from the course no matter what he did, but I wasn't going to make it easy for him. When he made his first jump he was terrified. That wasn't unusual; there were a lot of people who felt that same way, and just like we did with Lieutenant Chávez, we helped them exit the airplane. In his case, though, I should have cut his static line.

It wasn't just the officers who hadn't learned how to follow orders. One time in Honduras I was sitting with a general watching a training exercise. Officers were training conscripts who did not want to be there and were making that unhappiness known by refusing to follow orders. There was one soldier in particular who was refusing to do anything at all. They were telling him to low-crawl, get up, and shoot, and he was telling them to screw off. An officer was hitting him with a switch, screaming at him, but there was nothing that was going to motivate that soldier. I told the general, "Sir, I can make him move. I promise you, he'll do anything I tell him to do, and the rest of them will follow him. Is it okay if I intervene?" When he gave me permission, I warned him, "Don't be shocked at what I do."

I walked over there and told that soldier in Spanish, "You need to do what he orders you to do. How come you're not obeying your officer? Let me tell you something, son. You don't learn it here, you're going to die in combat. Now, truthfully, I don't give a flying fuck if you die, but I do care about the people around you who are gonna die because of your stupidity."

Turned out he just didn't give a damn. "I do not want to be in the army," he told me. "Let them send me to the stockade, and then they'll send me home."

"Tell you what, Private," I said. "I'm gonna be nice about this. I'm gonna give you a choice. How about this—either you move or you die. That's your choice."

"Ah, gringo," he said, and it didn't seem like he meant it as a compliment. Clearly he did not believe me.

So I pulled out my .45 and put one shot right between his legs. He looked down at the puff of dirt rising and then looked up at me with a startled expression. Suddenly he wasn't so sure of himself. Then I stared him right in the eyes and put the next round about 4 inches from his ear. He immediately put up his hands and backed off, meaning that he appreciated my argument. "Good," I said. I put the gun back in its holster and walked over and sat down next to the general.

Trust me, that private got right to work, low-crawling like a bastard. The general considered the confrontation for a few seconds and then agreed, "That is one way of training soldiers."

Like in any army, there were some good troops and some slackers. Some of the people I worked with and trained down there are the equal of any soldiers I know. We were in an odd situation. Officially, it was only training. The rules of engagement put out by our secretary of state and reaffirmed by the different ambassadors to these countries were that we were there to train these people but we were not, repeat in a loud voice, we were not to lead them into combat. Our government did not want it known that we were in the mix down there in those countries. If an American had gotten killed it could have created an international incident.

There is one thing we said in the army when I was pretending to be my cousin in Vietnam and we were still saying two decades later: Shit happens. What we did generally was camouflage our objective. It was surprising how often we just happened to be doing a training mission in the same area where the drug cartels were operating. There is no better training for combat than combat. Period. I always kept my team back, but a lot of times the local command wanted me to help with tactics and to lead by example, which I did. I was always instructed not to get killed. The generals knew that if anything did happen to me it did not happen there. It happened wherever my body happened to be found. That way everybody was covered.

I also knew that if something did happen to me and I had the misfortune to live, I would be court-martialed.

No matter where we were, we always seemed to find creative solutions. In Honduras, for example, we were training the Honduran 2nd Special Forces battalion when the leader of the largest drug cartel in the country got busted. That became a complicated situation because the cartels were supporting public services like cheap buses that the government couldn't provide, and they stopped running when he was arrested. Like in many of those countries, the drug cartels employed thousands of workers who depended on that income to survive. They didn't care who used the drugs, especially if they were Americans; all they knew was that they were losing their jobs. As a result the people rioted in the capital city of Tegucigalpa. They attacked the American Embassy and tried to burn it down.

I was ordered to take 2nd Battalion into San Pedro Sula, Honduras's second-largest city, which was an industrial and farming area and the place where the country's biggest cartels were located. Our assignment was to be ready to knock down any riots and protect the city. Once we got there I was told that when we were not out on patrol, my people were not permitted to leave the compound under any circumstances. It was a sensitive situation because some of those troops sympathized with the cartels, and the government wanted them off the streets. My problem was how to make sure they stayed in our compound.

After considering the situation it occurred to me that no one had actually identified a specific compound, so I decided to make up my own. We had the president's doctor traveling with us—I had trained him in martial arts, and he had become a black belt—and he had the power to cordon off any area I picked. I picked several blocks in the city known as "Two Lemp Alley," after the Honduran currency, the lempira. Two lemps was about equal to one U.S. dollar, which was the cost of a prostitute. Two Lemp Alley was the city's red-light district. So what we did was corridor off the entire red-light district, which became our legal compound. We ran everybody out of there except for the bartenders, the hotel staff, and the hookers. Then I ordered my troops not to leave the compound.

We were there for several days and I didn't get a single complaint.

I paid for most of the food myself, but the management in the area was glad to have us there protecting their interests and supplied some of the other activities. It also was a good teaching opportunity. I would take small patrols out into the city, where we practiced taking control of an environment. We were teaching urban warfare, riot control, and supression of resistance. They learned how to corridor off and blockade a street, clear it, impose security, establish a curfew, and patrol it. As each patrol returned to our compound, I gave them R&R, rest and relaxation, and took out another team. The team that had just come in had access to food, drink, and pretty ladies. These people performed for me, I suspect, mostly because they wanted to get back to the compound as quickly as possible. We maintained control of that city without a single shot being fired. The 2nd Battalion had a reputation in that country, and nobody wanted to mess with them. It was good training and better R&R.

Whatever our mission was, I always tried to find a way of making it a little bit different. For example, I was teaching HALO at Tamara Air Base in Honduras, and one afternoon we were flying back from a jump into San Pedro in a well-worn Chinook. The pilot was a crusty old reservist who'd flown missions for Air America, the CIA's air support, so I figured after what he'd been through he had to have a reasonable sense of reality. I wanted to have some fun with him. At about 12,000 feet I crawled out of the roof hatch between the two rotor blades, crawled forward, and slid down on the windshield. I lay against the windshield spread-eagled like a splattered bug. Then I flipped him off, did a back loop, and skydived down to the field.

That pilot didn't think it was as amusing as everybody else on that aircraft. He thought I'd put his flight in jeopardy. When he got on the ground he reported me. I never did see the official report, but I could imagine it read "Pretended to be a bug splattered on the windshield at 12,000 feet."

The general didn't seem to mind too much. By this time I think they knew they weren't going to be able to train me. He just told me something like "Stay away from that pilot and don't do anything like that again."

For almost five years I never knew where I was going, how long I was going to be there, or what I would be doing. When I was back in North Carolina I kept my bags packed at all times. The phone would ring, sometimes in the middle of the night, and somebody would say the code. That meant I was to grab my bag and be ready to travel. They told me nothing else, but usually there was someplace that had been in the news, and I figured that would be my destination. While officially these assignments were all considered training missions, each of them had different problems that needed to be addressed.

Every mission began in Panama, because we had to go through Southern Command to train up, get acclimatized, and debrief before reporting to our duty station. The 7th Group was there, so we also trained Panamanian troops. I met the leader of that country, General Manuel Noriega, a few times. The first time was when we did a demo jump for him; we all sat down and drank some beer afterward. The man liked beer. We never had a problem with him; of course, we didn't know he was allowing his country to be used to transport tons of cocaine. In 1989 the United States invaded Panama to arrest him. That was a tough time for me, I wanted to be on the ground with my team, but instead I was assigned to General Guest's staff to assist in planning the invasion. We had to get two more battalions down there to protect our strategic assets, from airfields to ammunition dumps. It was a strange feeling; we were going to war against the troops we'd been training. Eventually the invasion involved almost 30,000 troops and 300 aircraft. There was some fighting and we took some casualties, 23 KIA and 325 wounded. Noriega managed to avoid capture for several days, but eventually the U.S. Marshals Service was able to arrest him.

My team requisitioned the thick mahogany door to his office and his desk chair, which we installed in our team room at Fort Bragg.

Some hellacious fighting took place against the cartels, especially in El Salvador, but mostly I stayed out of it. From time to time there would be some incoming, but these were mostly hit-and-run attacks. I was in excellent condition, though, and I was still perfecting my American Warrior Free Fighting System. In the cities we worked in, there were bad areas; these weren't the slums so much as areas controlled by drug gangs. Different groups had different streets, and if a stranger happened to come into their territory they didn't have any hesitation about mugging him and, if he resisted, killing him. In some of these countries, there definitely was an abundance of bodies. There were places where you could hire someone to kill a person for you for five dollars or even as little as two dollars. I was in one of these places with a good friend, and we went into a little restaurant. We didn't have any fear—we had our weapons if we needed them. If anybody wanted to try to fuck with us, adios amigo. When we were off duty, as we were at this time, we dressed in civilian clothes, trying to look as much like the natives as possible. We weren't interested in advertising that we were American military advisers, as in some countries that was not a popular occupation. So we basically pretended that we were tourists.

We were standing outside the little restaurant, eating meat on a stick and some rice, when I saw these three men standing across the street showing considerable interest in us. I will never know if we got compromised or just happened to be in a bad place at a bad time, but I got the feeling that this was not going to go easy. We finished our meal and started to walk down the street. It was in the middle of the day, and there were people on the street, life taking place, when they attacked us.

I was keeping an eye on the people across the street when we walked by an alley. Before I could make a move they were on top of us and pulled us into that alley. I have no idea how many of them there were, but more than enough to make it impossible for me to get to my gun or knife. We didn't know if they had weapons. I had to assume they did, but I didn't wait to find out. I attacked.

Instantly, I was back in combat. All my American Warrior Free Fighting practice got unleashed. React. React. React. No thought involved. I grabbed the one guy closest to me, a small guy but real strong, and spun him around. Using his body weight I put my arm around his head and twisted, and I pulled his head right off his body.

That was not my intent. It just happened. I just grabbed him, put him in that technique, threw his body, and his head snapped and ripped. Taking somebody's head off is not as difficult as people imagine. You just need enough torque and anger. Then out of the corner of my eye I saw somebody else coming toward me, so I flipped the head and hit him right in the chest. Nobody's real comfortable having a head thrown at him. He scrambled away from it, terrified. I grabbed a third guy behind him by the arm and flipped him over my shoulder, using his twisted arm like a fulcrum. He'd come flying about halfway over when his arm snapped in half like a chicken wing.

That was enough for the rest of them. Those fuckers took off running. We moved out of that area real quick, leaving two bodies lying there, one of them still breathing. The last thing I wanted to do was cause an international incident. There were benefits to working in this particular country, and that included the fact that nobody ever saw anything, and apparently the police didn't feel it was necessary to investigate too aggressively.

Twisting off a head is much tougher mentally than physically, but it didn't bother me. Beyond the surprise that it could be done so simply, I put it in some type of compartment. I'm not saying I slept without a care that night—once adrenaline starts flowing, sleep is not going to happen—but I was completely unaffected emotionally by the obvious brutality. To me, this was entirely justified. It was self-defense, and my being was based on the belief that when you are attacked you will become an animal. The animal I most admire on earth is the wolverine, known and admired for its bravery, ferocity, and strength, which is much greater than its size. The wolverine never backs down, never hesitates, and never quits; it is the nastiest creature on this earth. When I am threatened I become the wolverine. I explode with that intensity. What happens, happens. There is no second place in combat.

That is who I am, and it has always been what I teach. We each of us have amazing abilities beyond what our conscious mind tells us. When the spark is lit, we need to have ready access to those abilities.

We also did a lot of good in those countries, beyond teaching their armies how to fight the cartels and the insurgents. No matter where we went, for example, we brought medical assistance. I would go up into the hills with the medics, and we would inoculate hundreds of kids. We gave them the basic shots children get in the United States, including polio. We'd go out into the rural areas and the jungle to treat the indigs. When you look in the anxious eyes of a child you are not the wolverine, you're the American soldier doing good in the world because you have been taught that is the way to live. There wasn't one time I looked at a kid and didn't see someplace in my heart five bodies in a blown-up hooch in Vietnam or remember my own kids fading in and out of my consciousness as I hung in that Nicaraguan barn. No amount of doing good was ever going to settle those debts.

Still, we always set out to help if we could. One time in Colombia, for example, a meeting went too long and I missed a convoy into a city, so I hopped on a local bus. I did that type of thing as often as possible. There was a pregnant lady on that bus, and all of a sudden she went into labor. SF trains you for a lot of medical emergencies, but delivering babies is not one of them. I had all my stuff with me, and fortunately, it does not take a lot of expert knowledge to stand there and watch the wonder of birth on a bus. What I did do was cut the umbilical cord and tie it off and make her tolerably comfortable.

Whenever it was possible I would go up into the hills or into the jungles to spend time with the natives, the Indians. As always, I was drawn to them and wanted to learn as much as possible. Whatever I was searching for to complete myself, I just felt that I might find it among those people. Mostly I was welcomed, and I would offer what little assistance I could. One time, though, in Peru, there was a village dealing with a rogue leopard. It was coming into the village and dragging off children. This leopard had gotten the taste of human blood and had come back for more. When I got there they were organizing a hunt, and they asked me to join them.

I went into the jungle with several young men from that village. They were carrying bows and arrows; I had my Colt 1911 .45. We tracked down that cat, and I shot it. It wasn't a difficult hunt or shot, but it changed the life in that village. We took the leopard back and gave it to the chief. What they did was take the eyetooth out of that cat and fill it with gold. They put it on a gold chain and gave it to me. I don't have many souvenirs from my career, but this is something I wear proudly. It is one of the few pieces of jewelry I own that has meaning to me.

I spent as much time as possible in those villages. At its core, every culture faces the same problems—how do you feed and protect your people so your civilization can survive? I was always interested in learning the methods they used to find food, to treat their illnesses, to fight their enemies, to teach their children. These were people who understood their environment much better than I ever would, and I knew I could learn from them. I didn't speak any of their languages, although I picked up a few words of languages like Miskito, but I still managed to ask my questions. I learned how they made their weapons, things like crossbows and arrows, spears, knives, clubs, and blowguns. I had been teaching survival in the jungle, but during this time I got my graduate degree. The natives of the different countries taught me about edible plants and poison plants, about the different herbs and teas you could make, the lessons of maybe a thousand years living in that environment. Once they trusted me, man, they just opened up their armory and medicine cabinet to me.

I knew about curare, for example, but they taught me how to extract it and how to use it and how to treat someone exposed to it. They would put curare on their darts, for example, when they shot monkeys for food. Curare is not a poison that kills instantly, but rather a numbing agent that shuts down your respiratory system so you suffocate. The advantage of it was that you didn't have to hit a vital organ to shut down your target. All you had to do was clip your target, draw a little blood, and that curare would get in its system and eventually become lethal. To survive, as silly as it sounds, you had to keep breathing. As long as you could pump oxygen into your lungs you'd stay alive, so the trick was to keep oxygen on the victim until the curare wears off.

Much of the information I learned became part of the courses I taught. In addition to my regular classes I also taught some that were extremely specialized. You can't get much more specialized than one-on-one with selected people who were going by themselves into hostile territory and were going to be living in harm's way for prolonged periods. This was classified instruction, and it was different than the lessons I taught in my regular classes.

It wasn't just the techniques of survival and warfare that I wanted to know about when I went into those villages, it was also their spirits. I wanted to know where they looked for meaning, which gods they prayed to, how they caused it to rain, and if they honored their enemies. I wanted to know how they welcomed their babies and saluted their ancestors. I sat through their ceremonies and, at least a few times, I smoked their pipes and drank their potions.

Like the Native Americans, these peoples had been living this way of life for hundreds of years. They had their own system of myths and legends. Sometimes there were people there who spoke enough English to communicate with me, and I would ask them about the creatures of their folklore who lived among them and where life went to when the body died. It was simple for them to show me the things of their lives, how to cook a monkey stew, which insects to eat, and how to make a blowgun, but it was just about impossible for them to communicate their culture, their way of thinking. What I did notice, though, was how much these people had in common with the Native Americans. All the peoples who lived close to the land, whether they were in the Dakotas or on a mountain in El Salvador, had an appreciation of it that maybe has gotten lost. They respected what nature gave them, and used it; this was universal among all those peoples. I wished I had a lot more time than I did to spend in these villages. I left a lot of important knowledge there.

I was in and out of those countries for almost a decade. I have no idea how many people we trained, but I watched proudly the progress that many of those countries made in fighting their own drug wars and attempts to destabilize their governments. At the end of every class I taught, which lasted an intense three or four months, we would have a team picture taken, and at that time there was one little thing I liked to do. For my students this was a very solemn moment. I only taught the elite of each country's military that we were turning into Special Forces, the 1 percent of the 1 percent. For most of these people, being awarded their beret was the proudest moment of their life.

We would all line up, the officers, NCOs, cadre, and my students. Everybody was so serious. So just as the picture was about to be taken, I'd grab the ass of the person standing right next to me and squeeze. That man would yelp and start laughing, everybody would turn around to see what was going on, and they would laugh—and I would be the only person in the picture staring right ahead looking serious. I had that same type of happy picture taken throughout Latin America.

By the early 1990s I had been at it a long time; the world had changed. With the breakup of the Soviet Union the worldwide threat of Communism had been greatly diminished, and the primary support for guerrilla movements had disappeared. We faced different types of threats in different parts of the world that required a different type of warfare. When the war in Iraq started, I went over there as part of General Guest's security team. A lot of people I had trained were involved in the planning and fighting, but that was not my war. I never got near the fighting. Instead, I would get messages from my former students telling me proudly what they were doing, and their words sounded just like those things we'd said during Vietnam. These were my kids, all of them; this was the next generation being tested, but it was also a test of our legacy. After Vietnam we had rebuilt a tattered army, and this really was the first time that army was going into combat. It did occur to me that in many ways I'd become Pappy Wells, the veteran who had been there, wherever you were.

I had never considered retiring from the military. I had no answer for that question, "what do you want to do next?" I was doing exactly what I wanted to be doing; next was not yet part of that equation. Part of the problem was that I already was all that I could be, I was a warrior, but it was beginning to look like the wars were passing me by. The army had evolved. When General Wayne Downing, who commanded special operations, wanted me to return to the HALO Committee as a training officer to create a new POI, program of instruction, I accepted it immediately. The cliché is that when a four-star general tells you he wants you to jump, you jump. In this situation, that's exactly what he wanted me to do.

I was the HALO officer for 7th Group, which meant I was jumpmaster. General Downing—his full name was Wayne A. Downing and he was short and squat, so people close to him called him "the Wad"—just lived to jump. He was awesome, a hell of a Ranger. This one afternoon we were jumping from about 25,000 feet, and he was strap-hanging with us. Now, most units in the army have what is called a challenge coin. That's a coin imprinted with the unit symbol. Special Forces started it. The rule is that if you're in a bar and somebody puts down his challenge coin, everybody in the place has a certain amount of time to produce their coin. If everybody does, then the person who made the challenge has to buy the round for the whole bar. Otherwise anyone who doesn't have their coin has to spring for it. Before we jumped out at 25,000 feet I put my challenge coin in my mouth under my oxygen mask. At about 14,000 feet I pulled off my mask and flew right up to him. When he saw the coin in my mouth his eyes got real big, but he couldn't answer my challenge.

When we got down on the ground he locked my heels and told me, "Get over here, young Ranger. I need somebody over at HALO Committee, and that's where you're going."

He knew I didn't want to go back over to the training side, I wanted to stay operational. So I told him, "No, sir. I got a good team right here. I don't want to go there."

"You're going."

I stuck my claws in because I was having a good time in 7th Group. "Sir, I don't want to."

"Young Ranger, I outrank you. I'm a four-star general and you're a warrant officer. If you don't do what I tell you, I'm going to send you back to Ranger School."

"Fuck you, you four-star fuck," I told him. Which was the Ranger way of saying "yes, sir."

That's how I ended up back at HALO Committee. After I was back there for a little while, the company commander was transferring to his next assignment, so they decided to make me acting company commander, HALO Committee, B Company. I guess if I had taken the time to think about all the company commanders I'd given headaches to, I would have had to laugh. I was proud of my record, but I did a lot of things my own way.

I was scheduled to take command on the morning of November 27, 1993. I happened to be in the office at 4:30 A.M. getting ready to go to the drop zone. As I walked down the hallway I ran into my mentor from as far back as Vietnam, Frank Norbury. He had retired from the military after Vietnam as a sergeant major, but had come back to work at HALO as a civilian employee. He was discouraged; maybe the politics of the military had gotten to him the way it sometimes got to all of us. He put his arm around my shoulder and told me, "Gary, I put in my papers. I'm retiring in January. My advice to you is get out and go to school. You've paid your dues. People like us, we can't make a difference anymore in the military. There's a different type of person coming in these days."

We talked about it a little more, and then he looked at his watch and told me that if he didn't hustle up he was going to miss his jump. Nobody ever wanted to miss a jump.

A couple of hours later he jumped out of an airplane and was killed. Just like me, Sergeant Major Norbury had made thousands and thousands of jumps. He'd been banged and bruised and broken bones. This time he just ran into some bad luck. The HALO Committee had been having difficulty getting support, so we were using a Forest Service plane. The pilots had never flown HALO jumpers before. According to the reports that I heard, they had too many flaps for the speed they were flying, so they had to correct. That meant the aircraft was flying at an angle when he stepped out. The back of his head hit the horizontal stabilizer and it killed him. They got him medevaced to the hospital, but there wasn't anything that could be done for him. I had to go over to drop zone Luzon to pick up his body. We saluted him and put him in the ground.

A few months later I decided that Frank Norbury had been right, it was time to get out. I put in my papers. Among the many honors I received when people found out about it was a ceremony in Venezuela.

In appreciation of the work I'd done there, that government gave me a celebration that was right for a king. They put a C-130 at my disposal, and we spent a long weekend, HALO jumping, partying, tactical SCUBA diving, and more partying. Even though there was a strong anti-American sentiment and it was obvious I was an American, I was treated extremely well. They awarded me their two highest military awards, one of them being the Venezuelan Order of Merit.

Back then the army had a program to prepare people for retirement called Project Transition. Basically it gave you the time and support to test-drive your future. I had some ideas, some offers, particularly one from Joe Lombardi at Special Effects Unlimited; I'd met him on *Freejack*. I was real interested in getting involved in that business. It was a good fit for me. There wasn't anything I couldn't fabricate, and I knew as much about working with explosives as anybody in that business. Coincidentally, it turned out that the so-called action actor Steven Seagal was preparing to do one of his *Under Siege* pictures and was supposed to come down to Fort Bragg and watch while we put on a mock demo for him. About the only person who took Steven Seagal seriously was Steven Seagal. Supposedly he was some type of martial arts expert, but nobody I knew had ever seen him do anything except talk about himself. What I didn't like was that I'd seen photographs of him on the street wearing a green beret. That did not set well with me. The green beret is a hard-won award, not a fashion statement, and he hadn't earned it. I didn't mind him wearing it as costume when he was filming on set, but it bothered me greatly that he was trading on the sacrifices people had made to give that beret its meaning. You do not wear that beret with a long ponytail, walking down the streets in New York trying desperately to look tough.

At that time a man named Bobby Vasquez, who had been with me in Vietnam, was doing security for Seagal. I got the word out to Bobby that there were some people, besides me, who did not like the way Seagal was exploiting the green beret, and if he got caught wearing it on the street he was going to get his ass kicked.

I helped make up the schedule for his visit to Fort Bragg. Among the things I put on that schedule was an opportunity to experience the air tunnel. The air tunnel is a large room with giant air blowers that allow you to float; it's a great place to practice skydiving maneuvers. Once you are in there you are trapped until the wind speed is turned down below 20 mph. We used to go in there and do hand-to-hand combat while floating. We referred to that as "air fooing." My intention was to get him in there and bounce him off the walls a little bit, then remind him about paying proper respect to those people who had earned the right to wear the green beret.

Unfortunately, he never got there. When he was down in Florida at Eglin Air Force Base, they gave him something to drink and then took him for a bumpy ride. I'm told he got so sick that he just stayed in his hotel room and never got up to Fort Bragg. I was disappointed, but it saved him the embarrassment of getting in the wind tunnel with me.

I did hear a rumor later on that Seagal was on a set in Hollywood when a martial artist friend of mine walked up to him and choked him until he passed out. When Seagal got conscious this person supposedly told him, "People do have long arms, you know."

I did get to do some other movie work while I was slowly being processed out. Blowing shit up? That was an area of my expertise. North Carolina had become a popular place to film, so there was plenty of work there. I turned an old Volkswagen into a helicopter for Bruce Willis's *Die Hard 3,* for example. I built skids, blades, everything you needed onto this piece of junk, and then we blew it up in the parking lot of a truck stop in Baltimore. We loaded that bug up with sparks, igniters, and various types of ordnance and operated it remote control like a scale model. After we got done, I promise you, that Volkswagen would never fly again. I burned up Samuel L. Jackson's BMW in *Amos*

& Andrew, which was supposed to be a comedy. I even did some acting in a movie called *Sophie and the Moonhanger,* in which my role was to beat up somebody. I guess that would be called Method acting.

This was a movie set in the 1950s. I played a member of the Ku Klux Klan. In my scene I came driving up to a store in a 1953 Chevy, kicked the door in, grabbed the black shopkeeper and flipped him, then kicked his ass and left. We did a filmed rehearsal to get the cameras set. I went in and did my role, flipped him, clipped him, and left. That was it, the director said, the actor playing the shopkeeper was too terrified to do it again. He said he saw the look in my eyes and it was so intense he wasn't sure I remembered I was supposed to be acting. They just took that scene, put it in the box, and went to the next scene.

I could do whatever was necessary. On a film called *Virus* I did some underwater demolition and safety work. At the end of each day, though, I went back to my place and wondered if I really wanted to spend the rest of my life doing this.

If I used words like "psychologically," I would write that I was not psychologically ready to retire, but I was worn out. I was tired. I'd been carrying my baggage for a long time. Most of me did not want to retire, but I began to have difficulty doing tasks I'd never even broken a sweat doing before. With all the wounds I'd suffered—tiny pieces of shrapnel still pop out of my skin from time to time—I should have put in for a disability. I should have taken the medical and got out, but I was too hard on myself to do that. When I submitted my papers I had to fill out a complete military history and take a battery of physical tests.

They looked at me inside and out, which is when they discovered I had post-traumatic stress disorder, PTSD. I had sort of taken that for granted. After where I'd been and what I'd been involved with, I would have had to be crazy not to be stressed. I'd just done a very good job holding it down.

When I let it loose it ran wild in my head. I look at these kids coming back from the Middle East and I wonder how they are going to deal with those demons. My demons attacked me.

Anybody who has served in combat and seen real war has met them. They're there; hidden, buried, ignored, locked away. This isn't something warriors talk about much, and they never complain about it, even when they're alone with people who have also been to those places. A lot of people, soldiers like my father, have fought them silently and ultimately unsuccessfully their whole life. The barriers my father put up to keep them away robbed him of his ability to lead a life with all the human emotions. When I was with my friends we'd tell our bragging funny stories, we'd wonder about the people we served with, and we'd piss on the enemy—but I never remember a single cold-sober talk about the pains we all carried. I can't even admit that I knew they were buried there just waiting for an opportunity to surface and take control, because I didn't know that, and I had absolutely no idea that they could be so potent.

The army doctors had put me on a cabinetful of medications to deal with my physical problems, especially some painkillers, including Vioxx and Ultram. I was doing exactly what they told me to do, but sometimes I felt my life was like water going down a drain. That water spins around the drain in smaller and smaller circles, and it speeds up and it goes faster and faster until there's just a little bit left and it's racing and then it disappears. It's gone. That was what was happening inside me.

It was frightening. I had always been able to mentally control my pains, to impose physical discipline on myself. I had always found ways to deal with my experiences. These medicines clouded my ability to control my mind, and as soon as that gate was opened up, all the emotions I had corralled inside stampeded.

My body was failing fast. Because of the medications, I began having problems with my heart and my blood pressure, so they had to put me on other medications to dull the effects of the first pills. I was diagnosed with Hepatitis A-through-Z. Name something, I had it wrong with me, and they gave me something that was supposed to cure it. I was on so much damn medication my body was bouncing. I had spent my life maintaining control except when I was in a combat situation. It was like the dam burst. For the first time in my life, I really was out of control.

I had strong, terrible nightmares in which my past, my fears, and some fantasies got mixed up and came at me in a jumble. Whatever happened, I was in a bad place and knew I couldn't stay there. For the only time in my life, I really didn't care if I lived or died. I was physically and mentally tired. I was in the worst mental and physical shape of my life. I was getting in trouble because I just didn't care about anything. I was getting in fights over nothing, over absolutely nothing. I was angry at the world, but I took it out on people I cared about. My attitude was *Fuck you, man, you got a problem with me, go ahead and shoot me. I don't give a shit. You're doing me a favor.*

At one time, for example, I was doing some work with Dave Kutchinski and we got into it. He went out to his car and came back with a .45. He put it in my hand, then put the barrel right up against his chest. He told me, "Gary, if you believe I would ever hurt you, I want you to pull the trigger right now." I looked him in the eyes and handed him the gun. There was still something left inside me.

Everything I tried to do seemed to go wrong. If there was such a thing as karmic payback, the enemies of my country were having their day. I didn't know what to do, I listened to my doctors, I listened to my friends, I listened to everybody. Finally I did what I knew I had to do.

I checked myself into the VA. I got my own room, and I slowly started rebuilding my life. Nobody bothered me. I didn't have to worry about food, I didn't have to worry about my people, I didn't have to worry about being somewhere. I was where I needed to be at that time.

I started getting terrible headaches, just excruciating pains in my head, migraines that were beyond anything I'd experienced. For a time I needed to be in the dark. If just a prick of light came in and touched my hair, it felt like I was being stabbed in the head with ice picks. Just touch my hair! I was certain I was dying, and at times I welcomed that.

Those nightmares came on stronger. They focused on malfunctions and combat; they focused on terrible deaths. What I learned, eventually, was that my mind could no longer tell the difference between reality and my dreams. When I dreamed about action my body started producing adrenaline, just as it would have in real life. I didn't have a red light on my mind; everything was full speed ahead. Apparently my body was releasing unholy amounts of adrenaline. That adrenaline was ripping through my heart, lungs, eyes, and brain. I would wake up dizzy, my head pounding, and I'd start vomiting.

I was frustrated because I didn't have the tools to deal with any of this. When I tried to fight back with my spiritual side, which had always been so strong, it just got knocked down. The headaches got worse, if that was possible. At times it felt like my body was ripping itself apart from the inside. I had spent my lifetime building up my mental capabilities, my will and self-discipline and mind control, till they were unbelievably strong, so when all of those techniques were turned in on me I had no defense against it. There are some diseases called autoimmune diseases in which your body physically attacks itself; this was a mental process in which my mind was using all of its tools to attack.

They gave me a female psychiatrist, and it was impossible for me to speak honestly with her. The stories I needed to get out I was not capable of telling to a woman. I was brought up trying to protect women, not to subject them to my horrors, so that attempt failed. Finally she handed me over to a young kid who had only recently gotten out of school. He had all the knowledge from his books, but very little real-life experience. He could not conceivably have understood what I was going through, but he was smart enough to help me get it out, all of it. So we began helping each other; I was back training him while he was guiding me on this path. We would meet every day, for a couple of hours, and for the first time I was able to talk about my experiences. It was as painful as hell, but it was like punching a hole in those nightmares, which got less and less threatening to me.

I began regaining control of my self-discipline, and as I did I was able to start working out again. I started getting back into shape. It wasn't easy. There had been a lot of damage done, both mentally and physically, and I was trying to heal a lot of wounds in a short period of time. I had to push myself, but I could feel my health easing back into my body. The doctors reduced my medicines, which also helped a great deal. Every day was just a little bit better and, for the first time in a long time, I began to see tomorrow.

I started doing simple creative things to occupy my mind. I started doing those little paint-by-numbers landscapes. I worked on big jigsaw puzzles; I remember one of them was a scene of all the classic World War II planes flying together, and another was animals. I started focusing on what I wanted to do with the rest of my life.

The VA gave me my disability, which gave me a financial foundation, and the doctors had helped me learn how to deal with my past. What they couldn't do was give me a future. That one I had to figure out for myself. As a kid I had been a wanderer, and at the end of my search I'd found the military. The army had given me structure. It had provided the outline for my life and allowed me to fill it in using whichever colors I picked, but it was the army that taught me what I needed to know and sent me where it wanted me to use it. It was the army that fed me, equipped me, provided my housing, and paid me my salary. My life had belonged to the army.

Now they were shaking my hand, wishing me well, and telling me the rest of the time was up to me. Thank you for your service, have a nice life. I was taking with me a lot of memories, a lot of friendships, some skills, and a big hole in the center of my soul that needed filling.

One thing hadn't changed, there was nothing anchoring me to any place. For someone who had lived his life by following orders for more than twenty-five years, having to find my own place to live made me more anxious than jumping out of an airplane at 22,000 feet. I knew by then that there was something inside me that I had managed to beat down and deal with, but I couldn't be certain that it wasn't going to show back up in another form.

I had taken some college equivalency courses through the years. Looking at my life, the thing that I loved more than anything was aviation. I'd loved to fly and jump out of airplanes since I'd learned how to do it in Vietnam. I loved fixed-wing aircraft and helicopters. If it lifted off the ground it intrigued me, so I decided to enroll at Embry-Riddle Aeronautical University in Daytona Beach, Florida, to get my pilot's license and study aviation mechanics. Officially the course I enrolled in was called American Aviation and Technology, and it covered everything about aircraft from nose to tail, including component design, fire suppression, and all kinds of support and repair.

A few years later Dave Kutchinski and I would get a patent for a system that replaced halon with water and compressed nitrogen to put out an onboard fire. We figured out how to get the nitrogen off the turbine engine to create a thick fog, which took out the oxygen feeding the flames, extinguishing the fire. To run our tests, the two of us completely rewired an entire DC-10 cargo area in one week. Nobody had ever done that on a DC-10 before us. Halon is a dangerous substance; it displaces all the oxygen in your lungs, and in addition to a fire it will kill anything in the cargo area in a few seconds. The aviation industry has been looking for an alternative. We filed for our patent, prepared the airplane, and did the tests. When we did our personal tests, the system functioned just like we expected. When we were taking the FAA tests, we passed every part until the third day, which was actually the easiest test, putting out a flash fire. We punched in the wrong code and the system never turned on. The FAA doesn't give you a second chance.

I moved down to Florida and enrolled at Embry-Riddle. The routine of my life was being taken care of; I intended to find work in aviation, but the rest of me was uneasy. I was still searching, I just didn't know what it was I was looking for. One weekend I attended a powwow, which is basically a Native American market, a place where Indians could sell or trade their handiwork. There also was some singing, dancing, and drumming to attract an audience. While I was there I met several Lakota people who told me about the tribal sun dance being held in the Hoosier National Forest in south central Indiana.

The sun dance is a religious ceremony that has been passed down through many generations of Native Americans. Basically it consists of a series of rituals done over several days as a sacrifice to the Great Spirit or the Creator. While different versions of it are done by different tribes, an important part of some of those ceremonies is making a direct physical connection with the Tree of Life. To do that male sun dancers are pierced through their nipples and attached to the Tree of Life for several days; and they spend all that time dancing and praying.

It is a great honor to be allowed to participate in a sun dance. In fact, presently a lot of tribes don't even allow nonnative people to observe it. When I went on up to Indiana I had no idea if the elders would allow me to participate. All I knew was that I was being called there by something inside me and I had to go. I didn't believe that somehow I was going to magically find the answers to calm my soul there, but I knew it was a good place to start the healing process.

I met the elders of the Lakota Sioux and gave them tobacco as an offering and told them my story. I told them I had no official documents that proved I was one of them, but there was no doubt about it in my heart. They asked me if I was prepared for the ceremony. Did I bring my skirt, my pegs, my ropes; did I have my sage and my medicines? I shook my head. "I didn't bring any of it," I told them. "I am right here. I am coming to you bare naked. The only thing I bring with me is my spirit and my physical being."

I went back to my campsite and lit my fire, and another runner arrived with more questions. I waited; what was going to be was going to be. There was nothing for me to do. Eventually one of the chiefs there, my old friend, my adopted brother, Looks for Buffalo, came to me and presented me with a canupa, a sacred pipe. Then another man showed up and handed me pegs, then a woman arrived and gave me some sage, a second woman gave me a skirt, which was a long garment that went down to my ankles, and piece by piece they prepared me for the ceremony.

I went into the sweat lodge, the inipi, with the leaders that night. I took my canupa, and we lit the fire and started singing and praying, and I felt a tremendous relief flowing out of me. I felt like I was home. The purpose of the sweat lodge is like going to church. It is the womb of Mother Earth. Once inside, you drink certain medicines and begin praying with the elders. Also, you smoke the canupa, the sacred pipe, and drink water, because water is the source of all life. When the fire softens, the fire keeper brings in the sacred stones, the grandfathers, to be added to the fire. Each stone has a prayer. Once the stones are in place the flap is closed and it is completely dark inside the inipi. When the sacred stones have heated up, water is fed to them, which brings the steam that allows people to sweat out the impurities in their minds and bodies. The sweat lodge cleanses you, as all the troubles inside come flowing out of you.

At the end of the night they gave me my choice. I could spend the days dancing in the arbor and then camp out at night without taking any food or water; in the morning I would go sweat to purify myself and then go back to the arbor. Or I could choose to be pierced and attached to the Tree of Life for four days and nights without sleep, food, or water. "I am a warrior," I told them. "I have always been a warrior." I had come much too far to sleep in a tent at night. I wasn't looking for comfort.

On the first day, it was explained to me, when they call the people they are going to stake out I was to come forward. Then they would see who I really was.

This was in early July. The sun was so hot it was shimmering off the ground. My sun dance began in the sweat. I didn't eat breakfast or anything. We just went in there and witnessed and cleansed. When we came out we went into the arbor and danced. I didn't know all the dances, so I just followed the best I could. The Lakota people had heard that a wasitu, a half-breed, had been given permission to sun dance, and they turned out to see if a half-white could handle it. After noon, when the sun was at its height, they laid me down on a buffalo robe and stuck the bone spikes through my chest and attached the ropes to the Tree of Life.

There were four of us pierced, and we were set in position around the tree. You didn't have to be pierced to dance, and even if you were pierced you could stop at any time. I was at the west gate, which is the spiritual gate. At the beginning of the ceremony, prayer ties—Indian tobacco wrapped in cloth—were wrapped around the tree. The sacred bundles were placed in the tree, and our ropes were tied below them.

My rope was the top rope, closest to the bundle. I stretched the rope out as far as it would go and began dancing. The heat, the dancing, the drums, the total lack of food and water, all of it over time came together to bring me into a new reality, a new place in my head where I had never been. It stretched all my perceptions, and I kept going. There was no time to think about what I was doing in any type of conscious way, I just kept going. I danced myself into a hypnotic state. Eventually I was beyond thinking about what I didn't have or what I felt or what I needed. I just kept dancing and praying, dancing and praying. At night the other three men would sit and lean their backs against the tree while I stood there, keeping my rope tight. I refused to sit down for the whole four days and three nights.

The third day is the healing day, and that morning the sick people came to the tree to allow us to dance around them. The third night the grandmothers came out; the grandmothers are the only people permitted to touch the sun dancers and give them whatever medicine they might need. This one grandmother I had never met came out and put some medicine under my tongue, and then she put a thimbleful of liquid in my mouth and cautioned me not to swallow it, but instead let it evaporate. I never found out what it was, but I felt it in every part of my body. In some ways it reminded me of the natural potions I'd tried in the villages of Vietnam and Nicaragua, El Salvador, Colombia, all of them, but somehow it was more pure. Whatever it was, that night my body was cleansed, completely cleaned. It seemed like all the toxins were gone. As I danced through the fourth day, I couldn't even feel my feet touching the ground.

At the end of the fourth day there is a special way of separating yourself from the Tree of Life while leaving a piece of you there forever. This is probably the most sacred part of the ceremony, and other people may describe it, but not me. I respect it too much. At the end in one great burst you release all your prayers and all your troubled thoughts that you have been containing for the four days.

Then it's done. With the LRRPs there were missions on which I stayed awake three or four days, and there was so much adrenaline surging through my body that even when we got back I couldn't get right to sleep. This time I laid there exhausted.

It was a good feeling, though. Something had changed, even if I couldn't describe it. I was different than I had been days earlier. That night the dancers sat with the chiefs as we ate. I had folded up all the items that had been loaned to me for the dance. I presented them to the chief, and he folded his arms and looked at me. "I'm bringing back everything that was loaned to me for the dance," I said.

"We can't accept it," he said. I asked him why and he stopped me. "Don't question us. You earned it. The canupa belongs to the people, but now you are its keeper. That's a right you have earned. Carry the canupa, and when something happens to you it will come back to the people."

That night I was accepted back into the people. No one ever asked me about my ancestors; whatever was, was. As far as they were concerned, I was adopted. The fact that I had accomplished a sun dance in the original native way attracted a lot of attention, and in response I made a pledge to sun dance for four years.

When I left that place I hadn't won my personal war, but at least I reached some type of armistice.

CHAPTER NINE

> Grandfather, bless our elders. They are the grass roots of our nation. They have earned the four sacred feathers that you have set forth for them: the plume of the tribe, the hawk feather, the eagle feather and now, the owl feather. Grandfather, bless our elders so that, as they journey home, we may take their place. We are next in line and we look up to them for their knowledge and wisdom. But one day that is going to stop and then we will have nobody to look up to. When they look around and look the way we come, they will see our children, and their children, and their children, and our grandchildren, and their grandchildren.
>
> *A Prayer for the Elders*, Learning Journey on the Red Road, *Floyd Looks for Buffalo Hand*

After everyplace that I had been, after all the battles I'd fought, it was a beat-up old Chevy that almost got me killed.

Adjusting to civilian life is one of the most difficult transitions any career military will ever face. The rules of the world are different, and it means breaking familiar behavior patterns and thought patterns. All of a sudden I was responsible for doing all those things that had been done for me as a member of the United States Army. In addition, I had to make every one of my own choices, from what time to get up in the morning till what time I got up the next morning. For people like me, who are most comfortable belonging to an organization, it meant finding another place where I fit. Being honest, there aren't a lot of places like that. That's what led me eventually to the native people.

At the university my life was running in neutral. I was making progress toward my degree, preparing to ease into the next part of my life, whatever that might be, and I was successful at keeping the worst memories at bay. It was a calm time, which I needed and welcomed. That changed in about an instant. One afternoon I was on my motorcycle going to the VA. I was on a four-lane road going pretty good when I heard sirens and started moving to the side. I was behind a semi and was screened out. The police were chasing some bad guy in a rusty old Camaro. I don't know if he ever saw me, but he hit my bike from the rear and turned me into a human pinball. The bike flipped way up in the air; I went flying. As I came down *bam!* I got clobbered square in my left leg by an oncoming car, which tossed me again. I got hit again by the police car, *bam!* Then I went flying into a parking lot and bounced off a parked car, *bam!* Then I slid along the ground in that parking lot.

It all happened like I was in slow motion, but really it was *bam-bam-bam!* Next thing I knew I was lying on the concrete in a growing pool of my own blood. Everything around me was stopped. I heard some woman screaming. What was left of my bike was scattered all over the street; it looked like a bomb had gone off, like it had exploded. I had been wearing my favorite pair of Tony Lama boots. The boot had been knocked off my left foot and was lying in the road. I looked down at my feet and I couldn't see my left foot. I didn't know that my leg had been broken and my foot and my calf were inside the pant leg; all I could see was a bone sticking out of the bottom of my jeans, and I assumed that my severed foot was still inside my boot. What was surprising was that I didn't feel much pain. I felt like I was completely conscious and, more than in pain, I was really angry. I was screaming at people to go get that boot with my foot in it so they could reattach it to my leg, but nobody was paying any attention to me.

When the ambulance came they tied me down on a stretcher and lifted me into the back. An attendant started to cut off my right boot, and I told him to leave it alone and go get my other boot. Those boots were $1,600, my retirement present to myself. He didn't pay any attention, just cut it off. I pleaded with him to get the other boot, and finally he asked me why. "Because my fucking foot is in that boot. Bring it here and we'll take it to the doctor and we'll sew it back on and I'll be good to go."

I started raising holy hell, screaming at them to get my boot. Instead, they gave me a shot to calm me down, but it didn't take. I wanted that boot. I needed that boot. I did not want an artificial foot. I didn't lose my foot in combat, I'd be damned if I was going to lose it in traffic—but the ambulance took off for the hospital leaving my boot lying there.

I was rushed into the emergency room. There were doctors and nurses all around me, and I kept telling them that somebody had to go get my boot. They looked at my identification and saw that I was retired military. "I was Special Forces," I told them. "I was a medic. I want my boot and my foot that is in that boot because you are going to sew on that son of a bitch or we're gonna be fighting about it, and then if you don't I'll do it myself. I want my foot."

For whatever reasons, the doctor didn't tell me that I hadn't lost my foot. Maybe he figured I wouldn't believe him anyway. Or maybe he did and in my mind I didn't believe him. This guy was a hell of a medic, though. He did his best to calm me down, and he called in Dr. Aontéa, a young orthopedic surgeon. Soon as he got there I had the same discussion with him, go get my boot and sew my foot back on. Eventually they stabilized me and put me in a room. By then the word had spread a little, and people were coming to see if I was still alive. They told the doctors some stories about me.

The doctor asked me, "How's the pain level?"

I sat up and told him, "Fuck the pain, I want my foot."

"Wait a minute," he said, then he took scissors and cut my left pant leg all the way up. Son of a bitch, there was my foot. It looked brutal, bent over. Soon as I saw it I took a deep breath and lay back down. "I think we can fix it," he said, "but I have to warn you, you might lose your leg."

I shook my head. This man just did not know me. "I ain't losing my leg, Doc. I'm telling you that right now, it ain't coming off. So just go ahead and do what you need to do." Then they wheeled me into surgery.

Both of my legs were broken, my hips were broken, and I had a dislocated shoulder; old wounds were open and old breaks were re-broken. I was like Humpty fucking Dumpty. Most of the injuries were easily fixed, but they had to insert titanium rods in my legs from my ankles to my hips. Maybe I wasn't the $6 million man, but I sure was the $500,000 man.

Even after the surgery they were worried I was going to lose my left leg. They couldn't find a pulse in that leg. It had swelled way up. They used a scope and a stethoscope trying everything to find some evidence that blood was getting into my foot. Finally the doctor shook his head and told me, "Look, if we can't find the pulse we might have to amputate that leg."

I asked him, "You got an ob-gyn unit here, right? Go get their portable ultrasound machine." How did I know about that? "Doc, I worked as a medic. When I did my training I worked in ER."

They went and got that unit, and me and that doc worked together to try to find a pulse. The ultrasound picked up a faint pulse in my big toe. He followed it up my whole leg. It wasn't much, but it was enough for me to keep my leg. That's the way he worked; find the pulse and follow it back up. "Maybe when the swelling goes down the pulse'll get louder," he said hopefully. That's exactly what happened.

Eventually they gave me what I called my Frankenstein boot, which was like a big metal cast that kept the bones straight. I could take it off to clean my foot and leg. Using a walker with wheels I was able to move around. I pushed myself as hard as possible. I didn't know any other way. I was always best when I had a challenge to meet or better. In some ways this was good for me; it allowed me to completely refocus my attention on walking again.

About a month later I was out of the hospital and going into a drugstore to get my meds. When I walked through the automatic door, the back of my walker clipped it, causing it to close and knock me down flat on my face. As I fell, that walker folded up on me. I was so angry I picked it up and flung it across the place; it bounced off the counter and knocked all the stuff off of it. I shouldn't have done it, but it was my frustration venting. Fortunately, nobody except me got hurt.

Everybody came running over to help. One person went and got my walker and brought it over. "You go ahead and keep it," I told him. I was done with that. Instead I went out and got myself two extendable canes that could be operated by pushing a button—and a brand-new motorcycle.

I got back my mobility. I could move around pretty good with those canes, and it wasn't any problem for me to ride that motorcycle.

I went to stay with a good friend whose wife was a nurse. I started working out, using my martial arts moves to get back my flexibility. Those days when it was tough I thought about Mike Echanis, who had retained his ability in Hwa Rang Do even after he lost the use of his foot. Mike could do it; I could do it. I kept going forward, that was the only direction I knew. I thought I was doing okay, too, until that night the alarm went off.

It has always been my practice to keep my handgun nearby when I go to sleep, usually on my nightstand. What I didn't realize was that when my friend's wife made my bed, she moved my pistol from the nightstand to under my pillow. I was asleep one night when the house alarm went off. I reached for my pistol. It wasn't there. I heard footsteps coming toward my room. When I couldn't find my gun I grabbed the nearest weapon, which was my samurai sword. I stood next to the door and raised the sword above my head, ready to hack and whack.

The door opened and my friend's wife walked in. I caught myself. She turned and looked at me, standing there stark naked except for one Frankenstein boot, a sword held over my head. "Hi, Gary," she said. "What are you doing?"

There wasn't too much a naked man with a samurai sword could say in response.

Slowly my body was healing, but I needed to prove that to myself. I was scheduled to go to another sun dance. I spoke with my doctor, who was a little reluctant. I told him, "I can't get any more disabled than I am already, you know. So it isn't going to make any difference." When the doctor told me that some of his patients ride their disabilities, I told him, "You know I want to heal. I got things to do and I ain't got time to mess around." As long as I was able to change my own dressing and tubes he permitted me to go. Truthfully, I would have gone anyway.

Before I left he offered me a job as his assistant. He wanted me to stay in Florida and work with him. It was a great compliment, but I knew that wasn't what I wanted to do with my life.

When I got to Pine Ridge the elders saw my legs all broke up and didn't want me to dance. They were afraid my legs would swell up and I would do permanent damage. They wanted to put me in a wheelchair and let me sit in the arbor. I needed their permission because sun dancers aren't supposed to have any metal or materials; they are supposed to be naked except for the ritual clothing. Finally they agreed to let me dance, and some of the young people made me a set of wooden crutches out of chokecherry. I was pierced and roped to the tree.

Like before, I stayed on my feet the whole time. My dancing wasn't pretty, but I stood tall as a warrior. I was wearing braces on my legs, which were basically being held together by pins, but somehow I managed to get through it. The only concession they made for me was that every day the grandmothers would come out and give me all my meds, some medicine tea to wash them down, and two pieces of buffalo meat. I chewed one piece and swallowed it, then let the second piece sit in my mouth so I could savor its juices. When I was done, after the fourth day, both of my legs swelled up like balloons and I could barely walk, but I'd completed my task.

After it was done I had some conversations with the elders about me staying in Pine Ridge. It was far away from the regular world, and that had a great appeal to me. I could be mostly alone. It was clear that I would be welcomed there. As a gesture of welcome, Looks for Buffalo, Floyd Hand, asked me if I wanted to do a vision quest. I was honored.

In a vision quest you go up the mountain and stake out a small piece of land, and for four days and nights you are not permitted to leave that area. During that time you are given the gift of knowing yourself. As far back as my childhood I had done my personal versions of a vision quest; I'd gone down to the cottonwood trees by myself, struck a fire, and stayed there for the whole day visiting with my elders. This was the first opportunity I'd ever had to participate in a traditional vision quest. I was taken to Bear Butte, which is a few miles off the reservation and one of the most sacred sites in North America. Like a sun dance, I began my vision quest with a sweat. When I was cleansed, they put me at the west gate, on the farthest side of the mountain. I walked up there with two people helping me carry those few things I would need. As I struggled up to the mountain I saw that the trees were covered with colorful prayer cloths and other offerings to the spirits that people had left behind.

They put me on a little bluff that overlooked the great prairie. It was an honored place, where great chiefs like Sitting Bull, Crazy Horse, Black Elk, Red Cloud, Fools Crow, and others had done their vision quests for thousands of years. When we reached that point they put four stakes in the ground, forming an area no larger than 4 feet square, then put my prayer ties on them. I had to stay inside that perimeter for four days and four nights. I had my little altar, prayer ties, sage, chokecherry, and my canupa.

At the same time I was on the mountain, the medicine chief was in the sweat lodge doing his own ceremonies, tied to me by the Creator. Around him other people were singing and chanting, and playing the drums. All of that supposedly enabled him to see my visions.

A lot happened to me as I sat up there on the mountain. I asked the elders to guide me onto the right path and give me the understanding to know when I get off that path. I saw the sun rise and move across the day until it set; I saw the stars fill the night sky and the clouds drift into shapes that told me stories. I heard the busy discussions of nature, and the more I listened the better I was able to understand the bonds between the wind and the trees and the birds and the spirits of life. The eagles soared, and my own spirit left me and went to play with them in the blue-white skies, and only when those eagles returned to their nests did my spirit come home to me, exhausted but exhilarated.

I prayed and sang and fasted, and I smoked my canupa. Up there time was not a concept; there was no difference between four days and forever. I sang, I said my prayers, and I asked the Creator to guide me. I might have stayed up there forever and been happy. The prayer ties waved like butterfly wings in the breezes. The visions came from everywhere and eventually left me alone. I was visited by the spirits of the elders who had sat there on that same cliff before me, and they joined hands with me. They told me stories and prayed with me. They reassured me that everything was going to be all right, that soon I would get my strength back, that I knew who I was and that I didn't need to be searching anymore, because I had come home. I was free.

Later the medicine chief told me that he had seen my visions, and that they belonged to no one else and I was never to tell anyone else about them. They were visions of the past, the present, and my future. They were my story as it had been and as it could be.

When I came down I left my prayer ties, my offerings, and much of my anger on Bear Butte. What happened on that mountain freed me from my deepest pain. From that time on, anytime the nightmares come back, instead of fighting them and trying to keep them away, I have welcomed them because I realized they were just the films of my experiences. I understood they could not hurt me spiritually and mentally anymore, unless I permitted them to. The events of my life were done, and nothing I could do could change them—but I learned that I could take away their power just by choosing to, and if I did that they could never be a danger to me again. They came back friendly, and unwound in front of me, but instead of nightmares it was like watching Westerns on TV. Once I took away their potency, I was able to hold on to my memories mostly without pain. Mostly.

I also was given my proper name among the native peoples; it translates to mean Iron Wings.

In 1999 I went back down to Florida to finish my aviation courses, but by then I knew I didn't want to stay there. I had found something that was good for me on the Pine Ridge reservation. I spoke with the chiefs, and they told me to come back home. There was an old cabin that had belonged to "Uncle Pete," who had just passed away, and I moved in and it was there I lived.

I was happy. It was a simple life. That cabin was completely off the grid; my nearest neighbor was about two miles away, and it was about an hour-and-a-half drive to Rapid City. I didn't have any phones or electricity; I had a wind generator and a windmill for pumping water. Water got pumped to a cistern, and then gravity brought it down to the cabin. While I would often see people, basically I was out of modern civilization. I was in my element, living with the animals. There were animals everywhere; coyotes and wolves and antelope, buffalo, deer, and horses, especially the horses. I never even had to put bridles on them. I'd ride them bareback.

The days got filled. Looking back, if I was to describe what I was doing for those years, I'd say, living. I filled the hours easily, doing the chores, camping, hunting, being alone with all those spirits. The spirits were all around me. I would wake up in the morning and smell their sage and sweetgrass, although there was nobody around me burning it. I would feel them with me, and I would hear them. Sometimes I just sat and listened to the music of nature, the way it must have been a century or more ago, when none of it was drowned out by the sounds of progress and commerce.

As soon as I'd got settled there, I went to the Veterans Hospital in Sturgis, South Dakota. When they told me the name of my rehabilitation doctor I smiled. I knew the name; he'd been with 10th Special Forces Group at Fort Devens, Massachusetts. When we finally linked up I told him, "You were with 10th Group, right?" He had been, he said. So I pulled 10th Group's challenge coin out of my pocket and asked, "Got one of these?"

He smiled and shook his head. "I wish I did."

I bounced it across his desk practically into his hand. "You do now, but you owe me for it."

"What? A beer or something?"

"Nothing that easy," I said. "I want my legs back, I want my health back, and I want to know what's going on with my system."

"Is that all?" We both laughed. He began working on me, and I found out pretty quickly that he definitely knew what he was doing. He put me on a program in which my nerves were stimulated electronically. It was sort of like futuristic acupuncture. I'd lie on a table and he'd hook me up with needles and electrodes to a computerlike device that shocked my nerves into responding, and slowly those nerves started growing back. At the same time I also was going to a chiropractor in Rapid City who was readjusting my back and my neck and my legs, an acupuncturist who was working on my old injuries, and the native medicine people who were treating me with sweats and the traditional medicines, and it was all coming back to me; I was walking without a cane, without even a limp. I was like the sleek, new-model O'Neal.

One beautiful twilight I was riding my motorcycle back from Sturgis. The sun was just disappearing behind the Black Hills, and as it does that there are some moments when the glare off the road and the grass makes it difficult to see. At just that moment I hit an antelope and my bike went down. I slid across the road onto the grass and underneath a barbed wire fence. I was wearing protective clothing so

I wasn't hurt too bad, but the front end of my bike got messed up good. Fortunately, some people were out working in the pasture and saw the accident. They put my bike in the back of their pickup and drove me home. I felt fine, except I noticed there was some rectal blood. I wanted to make certain I didn't have any internal injuries, so I went to the VA.

They did a colonoscopy and discovered four tumors, one of them ready to turn stage 1 malignant. They cut them right out, along with two feet of my intestines, and I healed up. They haven't caused me any more problems.

I was content there, and I probably could have stayed in that cabin, but when we invaded Iraq in 2003 I had this overwhelming feeling that I was missing something important. It was the same itch I'd had many times before, only this time there was no way I could scratch it. I'd tried; believe me, I'd tried. In early September 2001 I had been visiting some friends and cleaning up some paperwork at the aviation school in Florida. On the morning of September 11 I was on the road, driving home. I listened to the reports of the attack on the World Trade Center and Washington, D.C., and then I stopped and watched those buildings fall. More than anything imaginable I wanted to be back in uniform that day. I wanted to fight back. There was not one doubt in my mind where we were going from that day forward, and I knew I should be part of it. I had the knowledge and the experience to keep young people alive, and I desperately needed to share it. I wanted to get back in uniform. I called a considerable number of people, some of them with real pull. They all gave me the same answer: *Are you out of your mind? You're 100 percent disabled. There is no way we can take you back.*

Two years later the army was at war and I had no part in it. I took great pride in the work done in Iraq by Special Forces, and people I had trained were right at the center of it, but I felt like a little kid standing outside on Christmas morning looking through a window at a family opening its presents. As much as I wanted to be part of it, there was nothing I could do.

At least that's what I believed. Then in late 2003 I got a message from Command Sergeant Major Dave Clark, who was retired but was working in operations for the Special Warfare Training Group. Dave Clark and I had been through the wars together; he was one of my mentors. He asked if I wanted to come back in uniform as a warrant officer. I wished I could, I told him, but there was no way I could pass any physical tests. He didn't even blink. "Okay, well, then, come back as a civilian employee. I got a slot for you. I want you to go out to Camp Mackall and train 'em up. Somebody's got to put some fire in them. I want you to do that."

When Dave Clark asks a favor you do not say no, you say, when you do want me there? They gave me a GS-11 slot and sent me to Robin Sage to put troops through the final segment of their Special Forces training. I didn't have much to pack; I paid my respects to the elders and told them that there would come a time when I would return, but I couldn't tell them when that would be. Then I aimed my vehicle at Fort Bragg and stepped on the accelerator.

I was going back. Not exactly in uniform, but close enough for me.

Robin Sage was named after the nearby town of Robbins and the legendary Colonel Jerry Sage, who spent three years in Stalag Luft III as a German prisoner of war during World War II and was one of the original members of the OSS, the forerunner of the CIA. The character Steve McQueen played in *The Great Escape* was supposedly patterned after him. While imprisoned Colonel Sage became known as "the Cooler King" because he was repeatedly sent to the "cooler," the isolation box, for trying to escape. Finally he helped organize the digging of three secret tunnels. When the prisoners began their great escape, instead of going right out he snuck into the camp commander's house, stole his alarm clock, and left him a note. Then he escaped.

I was assigned to teach unconventional warfare, which I did, unconventionally. This was similar to what I had done before, but this time I had a greater appreciation of our mission. UW is the meat, potatoes, and cake and icing of the Green Berets; the ability to operate effectively in enemy territory is what makes Special Forces unique. During this final phase of Special Forces training about fifteen counties in central North Carolina become a fictional country called Pineland, and the candidates have to support guerrilla forces operating in the area. The towns and the farms and the people who live there become part of our training scenario. We taught our people how to turn raggedy-assed guerrillas into a deadly fighting force. We taught everything from living off the farmland to taking over a building. As many as four hundred civilians in that area participated as role-players.

I used a lot of props. I had people send me enemy uniforms from Iraq and Afghanistan, which our aggressor force wore. One of the training props I used was an entire freight train. In the scenario I created, this was a supply train carrying munitions that had to be stopped. The problem was that the troops on board were holding hostages. I wanted my people to set up an ambush that would stop the train without killing the hostages. I used local police as the enemy, and they carried their weapons loaded with blank adapters. Just for fun I tied the local mayor to the front of the train.

That train came barreling down the tracks with the mayor squealing. I warned my people, "Don't you kill the mayor, now. You be careful."

My students stopped the train by "blowing" the railroad tracks both in front and behind it, so it couldn't go anywhere. Then they attempted to board it. The first time they tried it, they blew the train up and got all the hostages "killed," the worst possible outcome, but eventually they figured it out.

We graduated about eight classes a year. I tried to attend every graduation. Like young Americans have done for longer than two centuries, they were going off to war, off to fight for their country, to fight for "we the people." If they successfully completed Robin Sage, they were ready to represent this country. By the time we handed these people their green berets, they were the equal of any fighting person in the world. The only thing they were missing was experience, and I had no doubt that they would have their opportunities.

Sometimes when I looked at them standing there all proud, it was hard not to think about my own past, when I stole an identity to enlist. Just like these people, I had absolutely no concept of what I was getting into at that time. Nobody who hasn't been there could know that, but whatever the army offered, it seemed like a lot better than I had where I was. What I'd found in the army was my true identity.

I looked at the faces of these young men and women, and in my heart I welcomed them into a very exclusive fraternity of warriors. I remembered all of the people I'd known who'd worn that beret, the places they'd been, the lives they'd changed, the bodies we had left behind. Through the years a lot of them hadn't come home from their missions, and I wished every one of these kids could have known some of the people I knew, even for a day, to appreciate the men who had come before them and given that beret its meaning, to truly understand the fraternity they were joining. There hasn't been one day in my life, or in the lives of the people I've served with, that hasn't been defined by that beret.

North Carolina was a healthy place for me to be. I was back in my environment. I had settled in and began building my new life there. My son was still living there, which was pretty much all the family I had or believed I needed. About the only thing that was missing from my life was a good lady to be with, but for the obvious reasons that was a difficult role to fill. There had been women in my life after Nicaragua. When I was beginning to think about retiring, for example, I had almost settled in Ecuador. I wanted to buy some land there and live quietly. It is a beautiful country, the people are good, and the weather is perfect. It's a nice place to just be, and I had made some good friends there. However, to buy land there you have to be either Ecuadorian or married to an Ecuadorian. So I had met this real pretty, real smart young Ecuadorian woman, and if I was serious about staying there marrying her seemed like the sensible thing to do. Her dad had some farmland, and I was planning to go into business with my friend Edgar Narvaez to build the skydiving industry there.

For several reasons I was not permitted to retire down there, as it turned out, which meant I had to come up to Fort Bragg. She came with me, and it just wasn't the right place for her. There were some things we could not get together on, and she returned to her country. So I had been without a lady for several years, and I suppose I could have spent the rest of my life like that. Instead I got lucky, real real lucky.

When I got back to Fort Bragg, a friend of mine insisted on putting me onto an online dating site. It didn't seem dangerous to me. I liked technology and I liked women; putting them together seemed like a real good idea. He wrote up my profile, which included everything from SCUBA diving to Harley riding, shooting to skydiving. It was definitely active oriented. One of the women who saw this profile was named Jo McEwan. She was former military who had been married to a Special Forces veteran and was teaching English at Fayetteville Technical Community College. She definitely knew all the drills, and she was smart enough to wonder if everything in my profile was true. She had a lot of friends who had served, and one afternoon she showed my picture and profile to Kenny McMullen, a combat veteran she trusted. "Does this sound real to you?" she asked.

Kenny stared at my picture for a little while and told her, "Jo, I know this guy."

"So?" she asked. "A good guy or a bad guy? Do I need to avoid him?"

The answer to that question probably depends on which side of the border you're standing on when you're answering it. "Yeah, he's okay" was the response. "Maybe he's a little rough around the edges, but he's what he says he is."

That's when Jo responded to my profile. We communicated for a while, first through e-mails, then on the phone, although she didn't tell me too much about her background. Truthfully, I didn't tell her too much about my background either. Finally we agreed to meet for lunch. When I walked into the restaurant she was sitting in a corner. I introduced myself to her and sat down. After taking one look at me she said, "You're retired military."

"I am," I said. "I'm retired Special Forces."

She said, "Oh? My husband is retired Special Forces."

Sirens, bells, whistles, everything started going off in my head. Not only was this woman married, she was married to one of my comrades. There was no way I was going to get involved in this situation. We started talking, and I asked her husband's name. Turned out that I had known him for a long time. We had worked together, and we'd had many a late-night beer. "You mean Scotty?" I asked.

"Yes," she said.

I started to get pretty upset. "Well then, what are you doing here with me?" I asked her, and I started to get up.

She heard the irritation in my voice, "Calm down, Gary," she told me. "Just calm down. Just sit there for a minute." I started to say something, and she interrupted me. "I guess you don't know that Scotty passed away two years ago. I'm a widow."

I sat down again. I had been out on the reservation when it happened, and I hadn't heard anything about it. Scotty McEwan was a warrior, a man I respected. and if this was his woman I was pleased to be sitting there with her. Besides that, on her own she was pretty and smart, with a fine sense of humor and just enough sass about her to make me pay attention. Clearly she understood what it took to be with one of us. I got interested right away.

On our first real date we went to a reunion of the Son Tay Raiders. While she hadn't met the people who were there, she knew them all by reputation. She had spent her life as part of our larger community, so she understood me right away much better than other women I had spent many months with. From the very beginning she allowed me my silences, never trying one time to mold me into something different than I was. It's definitely true that on occasion a warrior can be difficult to be with. We do hear the sound of distant trumpets a bit louder than most people, and we are compelled to respond to them. So it's almost impossible for us to be with someone looking for a regular life. Jo had passed those hurdles a long time before I met her.

We started seeing each other regularly. Our dates weren't typical. One time I took her skydiving. She'd never jumped before, so this was a tandem jump although we weren't hooked together. Whatever she was thinking, she didn't hesitate to jump out of that airplane. That seemed to me to be a pretty big statement about her feelings about me. On the way down I circled around her a couple of times, then I moved in real close and kissed her.

One time we even went to visit her husband, John "Scotty" McEwan. He was a hell of a warrior. He served on a lot of classified missions, including going into Iran as part of Operation Eagle Claw to try to rescue those hostages in 1980. He's up there in Arlington, with the rest of them. We both put roses on his grave.

We just fit so easily into each other's worlds. The only demand she ever made was that she be treated with the same respect she gave to everybody else. You didn't give her that, she would make you aware of it. Eventually we became partners in the best meaning of that word.

In addition to my teaching at Robin Sage, I also put some structure into the American Warrior Free Fighting System, which was the culmination of all the martial arts and weapons training I'd ever done. I turned it into a course, and I've begun teaching it to civilians who want to learn how to defend and protect themselves and their loved ones. I teach that version of it over a long weekend, which enables students to learn the basic knowledge they need. The great majority of assaults take place within an arm's length, even assaults with weapons. As a member of my cadre, Paul Pawela, the director of law enforcement training at the American Police Hall of Fame, says, "Our research on gun to gun, gun to knife, and gun to violent assault at close distances reveals that defenders get beat for one main reason: They have never pointed a gun at another human being, let alone pulled the trigger on a target at close range." That will no longer be a problem to students who go through this course, that is absolutely guaranteed.

For those people willing to truly dedicate themselves, American Warrior Free Fighting is the toughest and the most effective martial arts technique in the world. I've done them all—I'm a sixth-degree black belt in American Karate-do, and I've got my black belts in several other disciplines—and none of them, zero, incorporate the range of physical and mental techniques required to become an American Warrior black belt. The teaching includes all the weapons commonly used, as well as field craft, tradecraft, and electronic warfare in a variety of environments. Maybe more than anything else, though, American Warrior Free Fighting is not a competitive sport. There are no tournaments, no way for an opponent to submit or quit, and we don't award trophies. The techniques that we teach are designed to kill an aggressor.

To earn a black belt, students have to pass a series of tests to show me that they can shoot with different weapons from a long gun to a pistol, fight with a knife or any available tool, and fight hand-to-hand. When they have passed those hurdles they have to show me they are mentally prepared. To begin with they have to do the needles, lift a weighted bucket with a needle stuck through their neck. Then they have to lie down on the ground while I drive a car onto their belly. *Do not try this at home!* While the full weight of that vehicle is resting there, they have to answer several questions that are the equivalent of name, rank, and serial number. We do that because if you have the strength to be able to resist that pain and still concentrate enough to answer questions, you have achieved the proper mental state. If you can do that, I know that if you were on a field or in an alley and somebody kicked you in the stomach or butt-stroked you from behind, you would still be able to deliver pain back to your attacker.

After an individual has done all that, there is one further test. This is where my team shows up at their house at night as intruders. This is the test of what to do in the worst possible emergency situation, when your family is in jeopardy. It's human nature for a person to worry about your family, but if you do that you are probably going to end up greatly increasing the chance that everybody is going to get hurt. Just like in combat, any thought you put between recognition and action is going to amp up the danger. A hesitation of a tenth of a second can make all the difference in survival. Focusing on attacking aggressors in a systematic way when there are numerous distractions taking place all around you is the ultimate test of the warrior. We never do this without the student's wife cooperating and knowing everything that is going on. Family members are instructed where to go for safety. In that sense it's just like a fire drill. Otherwise, basically a team goes into the house, and to earn that black belt the student has to clear them out. Inevitably, that means shooting them with marking rounds, basically little BBs.

Students who are not married have to clear wherever they are living. We have had a few women go through the course, and they have to accomplish the same result: Clear the house of intruders. Doing this test can be really intense. Our object is to make the student forget that this is a controlled situation and respond as if every bit of it was really happening. If a person doesn't believe their loved ones are actually in danger they'll hold back. Just like in life, there is no reward for holding back in American Warrior Free Fighting. Hold back, you lose.

From 2004 when I came back in through 2007 I was officially a master instructor trainer in unconventional warfare at Robin Sage. At the end of 2007 I retired officially, if not finally. I still teach the techniques of unconventional warfare to our military people, averaging about two weeks every other month. The exact nature of the course is classified, but basically it's survival and intelligence-gathering techniques. In addition to my work promoting American Warrior training, I also own and operate the Old Warrior fabrication shop in Raeford, North Carolina. It's a machine shop in which my son and I and several other people do everything from traditional smithing to building off-road vehicles, motorcycles, and hot rods. Basically, if it needs making or fixing, we can handle it.

The remains of the helicopter that saved my life, number 235 from the 189th Attack Helicopter Company, is sitting out front of that shop. Right now it isn't more than a rusting memento. There are a lot of patched holes in the fuselage, and when I put my hand on them I can almost hear that staccato *clip-clip-clip* sound of bullets ripping through metal. My intention is to fix it up enough that I'd be able to crank it up and appear in parades and air shows. Like all of us who served there, it's now a piece of history, and it needs to be preserved.

It took me a long time to understand that, and to embrace what we tried to do for our country and for the people fighting next to us. At times my entire military career just seemed like one continuous battle, like if I didn't stop, I'd never have to think about those things I did not want in my head. As long as I kept going I wouldn't have to look back. It's only in the last few years that I've been able to deal with them successfully. It saddens me greatly to know that so many other people, from all the battles of my lifetime, brought home those same thunderclouds and have been wrestling with them for years. I am glad my country is finally dealing with this issue, this PTSD, which probably didn't even have a real name until a decade ago. I was so fortunate to find the help that I needed, because tough as I can be, this was not something I could fight alone. I got that help though professional people, through the elders and the traditions of the native people, and finally through my friends and Jo.

We live on a beautiful lake, and out in the backyard I have a small inipi. I go in there regularly for a sweat, which is the way I release my tensions. I don't know that I'll ever really be at peace. I'm not sure I was made by the Creator for that, but I have found a degree of contentment, of satisfaction. I understand and I've accepted the fact that the trail I have followed, the path of the warrior, is never an easy way, but it isn't supposed to be. The challenges come at the warrior from all directions, they can take many different shapes, but in any form they can be dangerous.

I have been honored. In 2010 I was inducted into the Ranger Hall of Fame. What made that especially nice was that the description of my career on my plaque was written primarily by Jo. In addition to that I am a member of an organization called Thor Omega. This was founded on July 4, 1976, by operators for operators. It consists of no more than sixty invited members who have served long and well, and our purpose is to do as much as possible to help veterans find their place when they come home. For instance, the legendary soldier Audie Murphy, the most decorated GI in World War II, came home and found himself sleeping on the floor of a local YMCA, with no job and no place to live. When Audie Murphy titled his autobiography *To Hell and Back,* everybody assumed the "Back" was the easy part. As I learned, it can be its own hell, and what I now try to do, through my memberships in many organizations, is help other people by telling my own story.

On the proper occasions I wear my medals now, with great pride as well as to celebrate and honor those people no longer here to wear the awards that they earned.

I had never spent a lot of time talking about the past, much preferring to live in the present while preparing for the future. In December 2009, I found out that Congressional Medal of Honor recipient Colonel Bob Howard was in the hospital suffering from cancer and he wasn't coming out. I called the hospital and left a message for him that Gary O'Neal was offering prayers for him. I didn't expect to get a response, not at that time, but his son called and told me that his dad wanted to speak with me. I waited for that call.

Colonel Howard's voice was weak and raspy but instantly recognizable. "Young Ranger," he started, "do not say a word. Just listen to what I have to say to you. You have been trained by some of the best warriors this country has ever produced. You have a lot of knowledge, and you took that training to another level. You need to get that out to young soldiers and to Charlie Mike—continue the mission."

I wanted to say something to him, to thank him for the contributions he made to our country. I said, "But sir—"

He interrupted me. "What did I tell you? This is all I have to say: Continue the mission." Then he hung up on me.

I know how fortunate I have been. I have lived my own life. I've survived the bumps. I've seen many terrible things along the way, but on my journey I have also seen beauty in so many dazzling forms. I've seen the sunrise after the darkest nights while lying completely still in a rice paddy, I've seen a baby born on a dirty South American bus, and I've seen countless examples of kindness and courage that are impossible to accurately describe.

Finally I put down the phone, knowing I would never speak to Colonel Howard again, and vowed silently to myself that in the name of them all, all the warriors, I will follow orders and continue the mission.